THE ELEMENT DICTIONARY OF PERSONAL DEVELOPMENT

Michael Waters BA, MA, PhD, FCollP is an education consultant with one of the UK's main providers of management and curriculum services to schools. He specializes in the provision of training and consultancy in many areas of personal development.

THE ELEMENT DICTIONARY OF

PERSONAL DEVELOPMENT

An A-Z of the Most Widely Used
Terms, Themes and Concepts

Dr Michael Waters

E L E M E N T
Shaftesbury, Dorset ● Rockport, Massachusetts
Brisbane, Queensland

First published in Great Britain in 1996 by
Element Books Limited
Shaftesbury, Dorset SP7 8BP

Published in the USA in 1996 by
Element Books, Inc.
PO Box 830, Rockport, MA 01966

Published in Australia in 1996 by
Element Books Limited
for Jacaranda Wiley Limited
33 Park Road, Milton, Brisbane 4064

Cover design by Max Fairbrother
Page design by Roger Lightfoot
Typeset by ABM Typographics Ltd, Hull
Printed and bound in Great Britain
by J W Arrowsmith Ltd, Bristol

British Library Cataloguing in Publication
data available

Library of Congress Cataloging in Publication
data available

ISBN 1-85230-834-6

Acknowledgements

I am indebted to the many personal development writers and speakers who have contributed to my own development and whose selfless sharings have made this book possible. Thanks to Julia McCutchen, Editorial Director of Element Books, for her enthusiastic support of the project, to the many friends, colleagues and family members who have made the right kinds of noises about it, and to Dr Barry Stanley, a good friend and one of the world's positive thinkers. I am especially grateful to Jennifer Ayers for having given up so much of her own time to poring patiently over my scribbles. If the book is my baby, then she is its midwife.

Introduction

The term 'personal development' has a number of meanings. Firstly, of course, it is a process we undergo as we live our lives, as we learn from our accumulated experiences. Secondly, personal development (PD) is an all-embracing term applied to a category of resources, from books and tapes to lectures and courses, which are designed to aid and promote this development. At this level, PD can be seen as being whatever booksellers, publishers and provider organizations decide to make available under the heading 'Personal Development'.

In addition, however, PD has the potential to become an area of study in its own right and as such presents us with a number of concepts and themes which are central to its understanding. These are highlighted and discussed in this dictionary in relation to both personal development *and* PD.

The wide diversity of subjects discussed underlines the multi-disciplinary nature of PD. An abbreviated list of these might include: various branches of psychology (cognitive, development, humanistic, sports, etc); psychotherapy and other therapies; healing practices and helping processes (eg, counselling); management theory, including human resources development and training; education and learning theory; the brain-based sciences; the human potential movement, including the literature and technology of success and excellence, as well as 'New Age' interests in spiritual development. I've sought in this book to identify some of the contributions made by these and other perspectives to the burgeoning world of PD, and to draw attention to the many differences of interest and emphasis.

For me, there is nothing more important than personal development and nothing more absorbing than PD. Taking seriously the subject of PD doesn't mean turning it into something scholarly or academically 'respectable'. It means enjoying the personal benefits that come from having a better understanding of the main concepts in PD and the approaches to it. One of these benefits is likely to be a clearer view of where we stand personally in relation to these many differing approaches. Another is access to the 'lessons' and practical pointers that may be gathered from a variety of writers.

Whilst I have covered a wide range of subjects there has naturally been a degree of selection. I have omitted some major terms and concepts, such as 'learning' and 'training', for which substantial bodies of literature already exist. Likewise, I have not been able to include separate entries on all the major psychotherapies but many entries refer to therapies, psychological and otherwise.

Most of the entries are discussed in more depth than the term 'dictionary' tends to imply so as to place each in the broader context of personal development and also to comment on current developments in thinking.

In some instances, I have considered separately terms which are semantically very close or which would normally 'go together' (eg choices/decision-making/responsibility). Entries are cross-referenced to each other by highlighting key terms in bold type and also by listing entries of direct relevance.

Apart from PD, I have used a few other shorthand terms. I generally use 'PD programs' to encompass not only audio/video cassette programs on personal development, but also books, other materials and courses. I've used the term 'PD tutor' to refer to just about anyone who offers PD programs. It's a catch-all term for authors, speakers, success gurus, therapists, trainers and anyone else who might be considered an 'expert' or service provider in the world of PD.

ABC Theory

A theory of how we get into (and out of) irrational and negative ways of thinking about ourselves and events.

'A' stands for an activating event of some kind, 'C' for the consequences to which it seems to give rise, and 'B' for the beliefs which 'A' in reality triggers. 'A' might be a situation in which we see our partner laughing at a TV programme. This leads us to feel annoyed ('C') because we assume that she finds the TV programme more entertaining than our company ('B'). The heart of ABC Theory, then, is that it is not an event which triggers a particular (often maladjustive) emotional response, but rather thoughts we have about the event. If these are based on irrational beliefs then the thoughts they give rise to will be faulty and self-defeating, leading to feelings of anger, rejection, depression, anxiety, or whatever.

Our faulty ABC patterns can be tackled in various ways, but all involve greater **self-awareness**. One way is to isolate, and then avoid, the events that activate the relevant 'B' and 'C' elements (not being around when our partner watches certain TV programmes, for examples). Avoidance, however, is not a real solution. The main site for action is the belief system. This is done by identifying the relevant cognitive distortions so that they can be challenged.

The ABC model was named and propounded by Albert Ellis (1962, 1975, 1987) who developed rational-emotive therapy to help people whose irrational beliefs lead to high levels of emotional distress. A feature of this is a great deal of negative **self-talk**, sometimes called 'automatic thoughts' because it arises spontaneously.

ABC Theory is clearly very relevant to cognitive and emotional development, to the process of developing a more positive self-image and to some of the things which work against this, including self-defeating **beliefs** and negative **self-talk**. It is also highly pertinent to personal development as it relates to interpersonal relationships. Many relationships suffer from the distorted thinking of one or more of the partners (see McKay *et al*, 1994) Finally, ABC Theory is part of one of the more prominent themes in current PD: the power of thinking, including its determining effects on feeling and, ultimately, behaviour.
(See   **Attributional   Theory;   Cognitive   Distortions; Musturbation.**)

Accelerated Learning

A set of learning technologies and methods designed to make learning rapid, easy and efficient.

The techniques of Accelerated Learning (AL) owe much to state-of-the-art research in neurophysiology and related fields, though some of the general principles have been known since classical times. These include an emphasis upon strong visual imagery and associations, **mind maps**, the use of peripheral texts assimilated by peripheral vision, an emphasis upon the personal involvement of the learner and the use of all kinds of mnemonic techniques. Rhythm and some kinds of music (eg Baroque) also play an important role in facilitating learning.

Advocates of AL point out that traditional approaches to teaching and learning have not been in tune with how the brain actually or most efficiently works. Academic teaching, with its emphasis on language, numeracy, logic and analysis, engages predominantly the left side of the brain. But it is the right side of the brain which deals with images, patterns and music, helps us see the 'big picture' of whatever we are learning and gives relatively easy access to the subconscious. AL makes sure that the whole brain is engaged in learning. AL is also holistic, involving the mind and body working in harmony.

Traditional approaches have also emphasized the hard, conscious effort of learning. The assumption of AL approaches is that we learn best when in a relaxed but receptive state of mind, ie when the brain waves are alpha rather than beta. In AL, much attention is paid to the physical context of learning. Advocates call for a return to more 'childlike' learning environments in which fun, play and spontaneity are valued.

Accounts of AL in practice can be fascinating and often subvert received notions about how we learn and develop. One of many cited by Colin Rose (1985) is of a lesson where the students are learning Spanish. As the teacher asks a question, he throws a ball to the student. In catching the ball, the student is distracted into giving the right answer, which seems to pop up naturally from the subconscious.

AL also calls into question the incline of difficulty principle which underpins most formal courses – that is, the belief that the simple material should be presented first and the rest of the course should become progressively more difficult. From an AL perspective, it is better not to make concessions at the start (which means artificially limiting the words used in the case of language teaching, for example) and at the same time not to expect the student to learn everything presented to him. If the student is relaxed but alert, he will doubtless learn a lot anyway. Telling students that the work is going to get increasingly tough also sets up expectations that learning will be a joyless, uphill struggle – which, by the power of self-fulfilling prophecy, it then becomes.

AL ideas are found in other areas of personal development as disparate as **meditation**, play therapy and **neuro-linguistic programming** (NLP). The major contribution of the latter has been the idea that learning can be accelerated by **modelling** the techniques of excellent performers. Analysing the system you are dealing with is unnecessary, at least to begin with. As O'Connor and Seymour (1993) put it: 'Accelerated learning is learning to do something and only later learning how you are doing it.' The powerful techniques of NLP applied to the acceleration of learnings can be found in books such as *Mega Teaching and Learning* (Van Nagel *et al*, 1985).

One of the imperatives behind AL is the quest for learning technologies appropriate to an age in which knowledge is growing rapidly and appearing in ever more varied forms. The old ways are too slow and inefficient. This has, perhaps, interesting implications for other areas of personal development.

Accentuate the Positive

A prescription that captures the essence of **positive thinking** 'theory'.

The expression itself is simple, almost banal, but the ideas it represents are pervasive in PD literature and programs. The theory, in its simple form, runs like this. Any situation is likely to be a mix of positive and negative elements. More accurately, in any situation it is likely that we can perceive positive things, such as successes and strengths, and/or negative things, such as weaknesses and anything we don't want. What we perceive is at least partly a matter of **choice**. We can choose not only between noticing the positive or the negative, but also between less and more positive responses – between 'I'm fine' and 'I'm fantastic', for instance. The first tool of accentuation is **focus**. We can make something more significant, more likely to occur, simply by attending to it, and encouragement and reinforcement can amplify the effects. And when we focus upon the positives, the negatives are starved of attention and are likely to be weakened as a result (see **Atrophy**). If we were to 'complete' the prescription or turn it into a truth statement, then it might be: 'Accentuate the positive and your mind will work to make it a reality'.

Acting 'As If'

An approach to producing a result that we seek by presupposing that it has been or will be realized.

Acting 'as if' can be a self-development technique. Instead of saying to ourselves, 'I don't know how to hit a golf ball' or 'I don't know how to be confident with people I've never met before', we act as if we know how to do these things. We are actually at the stage of conscious incompetence, but we lay claim (to ourselves) that we are at the stage of conscious or even unconscious competence. According to many contemporary PD tutors, this approach can help us to acquire **competence** more rapidly, efficiently and effectively than acknowledging our incompetence.

We can explain the success of the acting 'as if' principle in a number of ways, but essentially it has to do with focusing and mobilizing many personal resources at once. 'Acting' means that we overcome inertia and passivity; we become a doer not an onlooker – which is so important when trying to bring change about. The 'as if' implies empowering **beliefs**, a conviction that the result is a possibility, if not a reality, for us. In all probability, we have a **vision** or a mental **model** of ourselves performing the relevant skill successfully. As Anthony Robbins (1992) comments, 'people can succeed if they imagine something vividly enough just as easily as if they had the actual experiences.' That model may itself be informed by our images and memories of real-life models – of the golfers we've seen using a golf club, for example. So that even if we are learning also by trial and error, or by 'trial and succeed' as Rusk and Read (1986) more aptly put it, there is still a reference point. If the 'as if' behaviour is rein-forced internally, by positive affirmations ('Swinging a golf club is easy for me') and visualization, then we are also getting the subconscious and creative mind to collude with the fiction that we know exactly what we are doing.

We can use the acting 'as if' technique to develop not only a skill but also a role (eg when a student teacher acts as if he were an experienced teacher) or to be the kind of person we want to be. However, acting 'as if' is not only a technique for facilitating and accelerating the learning/development process. It can also be an extremely effective approach to interpersonal communi-cation situations. By acting as if someone else had a positive intention towards us, we can 'encourage' them to express that intention by 'showing' them a preferred possibility for their own behaviour. For example, if in a difficult situation we act as if we expect others to be co-operative rather than hostile, then the likelihood is that they will be. In this sense, acting 'as if' is one form of **personal power**.

Action

Hill and Stone (1961) once observed that 'The secret of getting things done is to act.' This might seem obvious, if not tautolog-ical, but it's a lesson many of us never seem to learn: that there is no development without action and, invariably, we are the ones who must take that action. The need to act in order to

achieve has been a constant theme in self-improvement literature for half a century. The current generation of books and
tutors tends to be better on techniques and theories (earlier
generations were higher on anecdote and exhortation!) but the
message remains the same. Effective individuals, like effective
organizations, have a 'bias for action'. The 'extraordinarily
successful person' differs from the 'average person' in 'their
ability to get themselves to take action' (Robbins, 1988).

It is a truism of personal development psychology that you
cannot get someone to do something they don't want to do. PD
tutors know of another truism: that you cannot get most people
to do what they *do* want to do. At least, you can't get them to
take the action that might produce the results they want. The
frustration of this can be sensed in the brusque imperatives ('DO
IT NOW!' 'Just do it!') which pepper self-help literature.

Action precedes development, but within the rational model
of development implicit or explicit in some self-improvement
books, action *succeeds* other things. These other things include
cognitive processes like thinking and planning which have to
take place to ensure that action, when it comes, is the 'right'
action. As Egan (1994) neatly puts it: 'Internal action prepares
the way for external action.'

To be productive, action must be aligned to purpose, so the
first step in the rational development model is deciding where
you want to get to (goal-setting) and why (clarifying **values**
and **mission**). This is best followed by a **self-audit** to determine
the present situation. Going through this sequence ought in theory to ensure that action is not misdirected. So, for example, if
you decide you want to develop a more muscular body, you
should first be clear about why and how this goal relates to your
values and other development priorities, then you should set
precise **goals** with timescales related to your mental image of
your new physical self. This should be done in relation also to
the body you currently have. Only then should you decide upon
the action you need to take, and take it.

The problem with this rational approach is that often it doesn't
work! Sometimes we don't take the pre-action stages seriously enough. Sometimes we don't 'follow through' to the
implementation stage – in other words, we don't act. There are
two possible responses to this. One is to use a different model of

development. The main alternative to the rational, linear model is what we can call the 'Do Something' or the 'Ready, Fire, Aim' model. This model rests on the assumption that our main problem is overcoming inertia in order to be able to take the first step. Thus doing something, almost anything, is better than doing nothing. Its consequences are likely to be less dire. If the action is not the 'right' action, then we can note this and change our behaviour accordingly. At least a start will have been made. A similar strategy has been recommended for overcoming writer's block. Write anything, even if it's nonsense; you can edit it or write sense later on (see Elbow, 1973).

The second response is to prepare more thoroughly for the action stage. This is the concern of much self-improvement literature. The emphasis is partly upon enhancing our capacity or readiness for action, and here the topics include motivation, **leverage**, achieving 'definiteness of purpose' and **commitment**. It also includes building up our psychic resources generally through higher self-confidence and **self-esteem**. Ideally, there would be a shift from (at best) a willingness to try, towards a position of complete determination – a 'do whatever it takes' commitment to action.

There is also a huge amount of self-improvement material which addresses the factors which prevent or hinder action. They include: 'excusitis'; procrastination; overcoming fear (of change, of not being able to control the consequences of action); a preoccupation with long-term gain; belief systems not conducive to action; and **self-awareness** to see how we feel about the proposed action. (If it feels wrong, then it probably is.)

A related area of attention might be called 'perception management'. Sometimes we don't act because of the magnitude of the task before us which overwhelms or frightens us. It is comparable to the often 'enormous gap between getting an idea and putting it into action ... that frightens off the majority of people and condemns them to inaction' (Poissant, 1989). One solution is a 'Think big, start small' approach. Start with a vision of where you are going, but break the process of getting there into small, specific steps which seem achievable and are not off-putting.

Another area of interest is quality action. Tom Gilbert (1978) noted that competence is a matter of accomplishment, and not behaviour alone. Quality action yields results with efficiency. What distinguishes 'excellent' from merely 'competent' action? How is 'smart' effort different from 'hard' effort? This is partly the province of **NLP**. More generally, quality action is about identifying excellent models of the actions in question; ensuring that the action is appropriate to the task; and noting the small number of actions that are most productive of results (ie, an application of the Pareto principle that 80 per cent of the results come from 20 per cent of the causes).

Attention is also given to the benefits of action – action as cause and consequence. We may fail to act out of fear. But as Schwartz (1959) observed many years ago, 'Action cures fear'. Action can also distract from an unhealthy degree of self-concern – a preoccupation with our own failure to develop, for example. As many therapists have noted, we can sometimes heal ourselves more effectively by helping someone else, ie, by switching from excessive internal action to other-directed external action. The psychic and bodily effects of the specific behaviour which make up our actions are also receiving a huge amount of attention through **NLP** and a variety of mind-body studies.

Finally, it is worth noting the irony that exposure to self-improvement messages can actually make us *less* likely to take action for self-improvement. Reading **self-help** books or listening to self-help tapes can be a very enjoyable substitute for 'real' action. We can become motivational junkies, hooked on imbibing the calls for action but inclined, at best, to engage only in the pseudo-actions of completing exercises and rehearsing the principles in our heads. O'Connor and Prior (1995) point out that this can be the 'disempowering' effect of motivational training on salespeople, 'encouraging them to rely on outside motivation and distancing them from their own values and goals'.
(See **Action Plan; Alignment; Excellence.**)

Action Hobbies

Leisure pursuit activities that involve significant action and physical effort. In theory, any hobby or leisure time activity can afford **opportunities** for personal development, but there is much support nowadays for the view that action hobbies such

as sports, mountain climbing, cycling and hang-gliding are particularly rich in growth opportunities. Action hobbies almost always provide **challenges**. They also afford thrills and excitement for those of us who may experience little of either in our working lives. They can enhance our **well-being** by, for example, improving our concentration and reducing our stress levels. According to research, they can also enhance job prospects. A survey commissioned by Volvo Cars UK in 1995 revealed that nearly 50 per cent of the UK bosses surveyed said that they favoured sporty candidates, whom they assumed would be energetic, confident and achievement-oriented.
(See **Outdoor Development.**)

Action Plan

An 'ensuring' device. An action plan ensures or makes more likely the achievement of an objective or goal. The objective might be something very specific, such as a resolution (to get fit through regular exercise, for example), or it might be part of a more encompassing **personal development plan** or individual action plan.

An effective action plan is likely to specify the steps that need to be taken, in the order in which they need to be done, and with reference to specific times or dates. So, for example, part of an action plan for a get-fit goal might be: 'Go swimming after work for 40 minutes every Monday and Thursday beginning next week. On Monday, arrange a fitness assessment at the leisure centre.'

Action plans are also advocated by many trainers to ensure appropriate follow-up action after training, so the order is: training → action plan → follow-up. This will ensure that ideas or skills acquired are put into practice or developed rather than quickly forgotten.

Advocates of action plans see many benefits to them. These include:

- helping to make clear whether an objective is achievable;
- helping to see what resources might be needed if it is to be met;

- helping to make the best use of time:
- highlighting possible difficulties and pitfalls;
- giving the poorly self-disciplined person a structure to which to work.

(See **Goals**)

Actualization

The process of becoming all that we are capable of becoming.

According to Carl Rogers (1961), every organism, including the human organism, has one major drive or tendency: the actualization tendency. This is the organism's tendency both to maintain and to enhance itself. It translates broadly into a striving for growth and fulfilment in relation to inherent capabilities or potentialities. Under the right conditions, actualization processes will lead us to become more open to experiences, flexible in our responses and behaviour, and autonomous, in that we will accept **responsibility** for determining our own behaviour. However, the specific forms that actualization takes varies from individual to individual.

The direction that our actualization (or organismic growth) takes is mainly a function of our valuing process. According to Rogers, we evaluate experiences in terms of whether they are 'right' or 'wrong' for us, particularly in terms of our growth and fulfilment. When we are young, this valuing process is likely to be easy; we know our likes and dislikes. But as we move towards adulthood, we are less able to trust our inner experiences. The main reason for this is that we develop a self-concept (the conscious idea of who and what we are) that is shaped by the approval or disapproval we receive from the people who most matter to us (our significant others). For the self-concept to develop, we require 'positive regard' from significant others. Over time, we are likely to take on board (introject) the values and standards by which others give us positive regard.

In other words, we 'allow' other people, rather than our organismic being, to decide what is 'right' and 'wrong' for us. This may cause us increasingly to lose touch with our organismic valuing process. The tendency towards actualization of ourselves as a whole organism becomes increasingly directed into the process of *self-actualization* by which we strive to live up to and develop the self-concept. If actualization and self-actualization are incongruent, then we are likely to become psychologically unhealthy. We will not be open to or aware of the range of experiences required for actualization. Potentialities outside the self-concept will not be developed. If, on the other hand, we use our capabilities to the full and ensure through close contact with our deepest experiences that the self does not develop at the expense of our organism as a whole, then full actualization is a theoretical possibility. We would become a **fully functioning person.**

The concept of self-actualization is most famously associated with Abraham Maslow who studied what he believed were self-actualizing people who differed significantly from 'normals' or people who never extended themselves to become all that they were capable of becoming. Maslow coined the phrase 'the pathology of the average' to describe this condition. By contrast, Maslow found self-actualizing people to be highly self-aware, self-directed, creative people, able to accept and love themselves and others and engage in a search for personal meaning and fulfilment (Maslow, 1970).

The concepts of actualization and, in particular, self-actualization have unquestionably influenced the many PD writers who share the humanistic conviction in the presence and power of a 'growth urge'. Actualization thinking is based on premises that are pervasive in PD literature: that human nature is basically good, that human potential is considerable, and that the realization of this is what life is all about. We are naturally programmed with the capacity to develop fully all our capabilities, but this does not happen automatically. Actualization theory helps to explain and perhaps provides the theoretical legitimacy for the **positive thinking** that dominates **success** and other PD programmes. There are also many specific connections between the ideas of Rogers and Maslow on the one hand and the concerns of PD writers on the other, just one of which would be an interest in peak moments and **peak performance**.

However, it would probably be fair to say that PD writers have highlighted the concept of self-actualization, celebrated it without qualification, and failed generally to see its relationship to actualization. As we've seen in Rogers' scheme of things, actualization of the self-concept is not necessarily a psychologically healthy process if it occurs without reference to the needs of the whole organism. In other words, actualization thinking implies a holistic view of individual development. Some PD writers, however, have a more partial view, and suggest that self-actualization is an end in itself and is thus unproblematic. In reality, putting all our energies into becoming a 'success' or peak performer in one area of our lives may not be consistent with moving towards fulfilment as a whole person.

Actualization thinking has been over-simplified and distorted in other ways in PD literature. For example, many PD writers suggest that we can program ourselves to become just about anything we choose. However, this could mean trying to actualize something that is not congruent with our organismic development. Maintaining a distorted self-concept might militate against genuine actualization. For instance, if I decide I'd like to become an excellent scientist, I may become anxious and guilty, and I may distort and deny experience when I find I cannot realize this goal in practice because the **potential** is just not there.
(See **Congruence; Holistic Development; Programming; Self Acceptance; Self-Awareness.**)

Adaptability

Our ability to adapt or modify our behaviour to function effectively in a variety of situations is generally regarded as a major life skill.

Personal development is sometimes construed as a growth in what Scott (1968) termed 'General Adaptive Capacity'. It is a capacity that is becoming ever more important since the nature of work technologies and social organizations undergoes ceaseless change.

The implicit aim of much personal development training is to enable us to be more adaptable. In part this means becoming more self-aware, so that we begin to get a clear picture of our rigid habits and positions, and of the behaviours in our active repertoire. It also means being more able to see and make use of a wider range of behavioural choices, ego states and the like; for example, to be able to adapt from working independently or under close supervision to working as part of a self-directed team.

Being adaptable does not mean being unpredictable or inconsistent, though the misguided belief that it does keeps some people back from developing into adaptable adults. Being adaptable means developing a sensitivity to situational appropriateness and behaving in generally the same kinds of ways in broadly the same kinds of situations. For example, an adaptable leader (and the personal development of all leaders needs to entail a growth in adaptability) is able to switch from giving direction to giving support and from intervening in the work of his team to leaving his team to sort out their own difficulties. The subordinate of such a leader will almost always have some sense of why one approach was adopted rather than another.

Studies of 'survivors' (of major illness, of POW camps etc) also show time and again that adaptability is a key quality. 'Excellent' survivors seem to know what is right (for them) in any given situation: it may be to be assertive or to be passive, to accept medication or to refuse it.

Training programs that develop adaptability – of interpersonal communication skills, for example – rest on the assumption that adaptability can be learned, that is, that adaptability is a skill, or a set of skills, not an inherent character feature. In reality, many of us continue to believe that our 'behaviour is a fixture rather than a mixture' (Honey, 1988). Learning for ourselves that our personality may influence, but does not determine, our adaptive capacity is itself a personal development experience. (See **Self-Awareness**.)

Adjustment

A term from psychology concerned with how we as individuals respond to the demands made upon us by other people and the social environment.

Adjustment is a problematic concept, even for those who are comfortable working with it. The notion of 'good adjustment' means different things to different kinds of psychologists (see Napoli *et al*, 1982). It also rests upon value judgements which are neither universal nor constant over time. From a PD perspective, 'adjustment' is particularly problematic. How does it relate to 'growth'? It is a fundamental question, but opinions vary. Some experts regard these concepts as the twin and necessary aspects of development (Napoli, p xi). For others, 'growth' stands in contrast to 'adjustment' (Corey, 1986). When Thomas A. Harris popularized **transactional analysis** in *I'm OK – You're OK* (1970) he decided that TA provided 'a new answer to people who want to change rather than to adjust'.

In contemporary PD literature, 'growth' is almost always the preferred term. Adjustment seems to imply a society where values are generally agreed and stable. It also implies an ideology of social conformance, of meeting or falling short of the norms that other people have set. It may also suggest settling for 'a complacent and dead existence, one that has neither challenge nor excitement' (Corey, 1986). All this goes against the grain of current PD ideology which is centred on the individual (or the team conceived as an individual entity) being considered capable of self-determining, life-long development. Adjustments might have to be made, particularly in new situations and transition states. But adjustment implies deference as opposed to mere reference to circumstances, whereas the essential message of the more popular personal development programs is that decisions rather than conditions make our lives what they are. The current emphasis is also upon setting our own standards or ideals and of acknowledging that our **potential** for growth is virtually limitless.
(See **Development**.)

Affirmation

A verbal tool or technique for **programming** the mind-body. It usually takes the form of a positive, declarative sentence, and it invariably includes the word 'I'.

Virtually anyone who recommends the use of affirmations points out that they should always be positive (ie, state what is wanted, not what is not wanted) and personal (since we cannot affirm for anyone else). Most also suggest that affirmations should be in the present tense, so that the **subconscious** can process them, though the continuous rather than simple present tense may be more appropriate for unfolding or improving situations – 'My memory is getting better each day' rather than 'I have an excellent memory' (Edwards, 1991). A mix of the two tenses may be appropriate for the partly achieved but still improving situation: 'I am confident, and growing in confidence daily'. Other features of good affirmations include: brevity; an absence of qualification; words which evoke feelings or pictures; action words which energize or suggest accomplishment ('I love to ...', 'I effortlessly ...'); and a sense of what we can realize rather than what lies outrageously beyond our capabilities or prospects. Some writers suggest also that we should generate affirmations to cover all aspects of our lives (health, family, job, etc) so that they are collectively broad and balanced.

As programs for the subconscious mind, affirmations are used to effect and reinforce **change**. They can be used to change **beliefs**, induce or access positive emotional states, influence the performance of a technical skill (eg, sporting skill) or enhance our self-image. Some authorities believe that affirmations need to be written down and repeated time and again if they are to work. It is often suggested that they be used in conjunction with other mind-directing techniques, particularly **visualization** (Fanning, 1994; Syer and Connolly, 1991).

Affirmations have many advocates among most of the approaches to personal development, and affirmations form a major part of many development programs.
(See **Self-talk.**)

'Aha' Experience

Any experience which provides us with a moment of insight into ourselves and thus potential for development. The 'aha' suggests that the moment is likely to be sudden and surprising – a glimpse, perhaps, of the private logic which has unknowingly influenced our patterns of behaviour.

An 'aha' experience may be triggered by something we read or hear, but some therapists will work to bring an 'aha' experience about so that their clients/patients gain an insight which might make it possible for them to change in some preferred direction.

'Aha' experiences can also be brought about by design as part of a creative or problem-solving process. In essence, we provide the creative function of our subconscious with a problem to solve. When the subconscious has done its work, it transmits its creative resolutions to the conscious mind as a moment of illumination. We usually call them 'bright ideas'.

Alignment

A term that literally means 'in line with' but is generally accepted as meaning 'pulling in the same direction' or 'moving towards the same end'. Alignment is cognate with **congruence**. If the orchestra is a good image for congruence, then a graphic image for alignment would be a group of planes flying in formation.

Alignment has a number of applications in Personal Development. *Inner* alignment is when the elements of our **inner team** work towards the same end, for example, when our **beliefs**, **values** and **goals** are all mutually consistent. In hierarchical versions of self, alignment occurs when the interests of the Lower Self are not opposed to those of the **Higher Self**.

The elements of our inner team are not equally powerful. Beliefs are generally more potent than intentions, for example, so although we may intend to become more assertive, we are unlikely to be very successful if we have powerful beliefs pulling in the other direction – beliefs that assertive people are pushy and unpopular, for example. Our life goals need also to be aligned to our core values if we are both to achieve them *and* derive gratification from so doing.

Inner-outer alignment occurs when action is aligned to **purpose** – that is, when we do things that will take us closer to fulfilling our purpose. Much activity of individuals and of organizations is unproductive because it is not consistent with the goals that have been set.

Another form of alignment occurs when the ideas or development intentions of an individual are in tune with those of the external world, an organization or the collective consciousness of a community or interest. William Blake's ideas were not aligned to the prevailing ideas of his day but are aligned with much 'New Age' thinking today. An employee is more likely to get promotion if his career plan is in line with his company's own development plan than if it is not.

Misalignment has a number of causes. One cause is categorical thinking, when, for example, our beliefs are kept mentally separate from our values. Another cause is failure to revise 'old' beliefs and ideas when we acquire new ones which may be in conflict with them. Many people, for example, have misaligned **mental maps** regarding money because at different times of their lives they acquired very different beliefs about and **attitudes** towards money. This makes it difficult for them to accomplish financial development goals, however clearly they might have been formulated. Personal development tends to require the appropriate form of alignment. Coming into alignment can also be a developmental process in its own right.

(See **Personal Power**.)

Anchor

An **NLP** term for any stimulus associated with and capable of triggering a response, normally physiological. The stimulus can be anything – a thought, a behaviour, a sound, a picture – which elicits the feelings associated with the 'original' experience. For example, a holiday snapshot could elicit the feelings we had when the photograph was taken – provided the process of establishing a connection (anchoring) has taken place. A song we heard on holiday could have the same eliciting effect, as could a specific memory.

Many anchors are established naturally. For example, a film showing an aeroplane in trouble might remind us of an unpleasant flying experience. Someone might unwittingly touch us in a way which brings to mind how someone touched us in the past and how we felt at the time. Anchors can also be established deliberately. This makes them potentially powerful tools for psychological manipulation – by salespeople, for example.

Anchors can have a significant impact upon personal development. Used effectively and ethically, they can help us to establish rapport with other people and enhance our communication. Positive anchors can help us to access our most resourceful states. Identifying and overcoming negative anchors (those which elicit anxiety, depression, panic etc) can also benefit our relationships and ourselves. Phobias are, in effect, acute kinds of anchors.

'Ask for what you want'

A prescription at the point where assertiveness training meets **transactional analysis** (TA).

Most people occasionally (and some people throughout most of their lives) do not ask for the things they want. We don't say, for example, 'Can I have another helping, please?' or 'Please don't charge me for the excess postage.' The reason is that we've been brought up not to ask for the things we want (because we've been told it's impolite, self-centred) and, worse still, to accept the things we haven't asked for and don't want. In TA terms, it's the voice of the critical parent speaking to us in our head that brings about this situation. From a PD perspective, asking for what you want is psychologically healthy. It establishes **congruence** and **authenticity** and can benefit **self-efficacy** and **self-esteem**. As with **decision-making**, it gets easier with practice. It often 'works', and even when it doesn't, little is usually lost.

Aspire

An acronym that is made from the initial letters of the following words: Assessment, Planning, Implementation, Review and Evaluation.

The words form a sequence and represent a cycle of activity that can be used for **development** purposes. We begin by assessing our current situation and our development needs. We might gather 'information' about ourself (do a **self-audit**, for example) or address the What, Which, Who, Why sequence of **questions** (eg, What are my strengths, my unmet needs, my long-term goals?). On the basis of this, **goals** are set, plans are made, and the 'How' question is addressed. The plan is then implemented and finally reviewed and evaluated to see whether or not it has

been effective. Ideally, evaluation is considered at the very start of the planning process so that it is built in rather than bolted on at the end. This will encourage clear criteria of effectiveness to be devised. Monitoring to ensure that the plan is on course should go on throughout the implementation stage.
(See **Action Plan**.)

Assessment Centres

Not specific places, but rather situations in which people undertake a set of exercises and then have their performance assessed against agreed criteria. The exercises usually simulate some aspects of a job or role, and the criteria are the **competences** required to perform effectively in it.

Some assessment centres are used to select candidates for jobs or advancement. These are also known as selection centres. Assessment centres, whose main purpose is to identify the training and development needs of participants in relation either to their present jobs or those to which they aspire are more often termed development centres or development workshops. The participants may belong to the same organization (eg, all middle managers with the same company) or come from different organizations (eg, all deputy headteachers but from different schools).

In the best development centres, the exercises are designed very carefully to enable participants to show what they can do in relation to the competences, and also to discriminate between participants in terms of current performance levels. The assessors will also be well trained to look for and record the behaviours associated with the competences. For example, if one of the competences is 'interpersonal sensitivity' and one of the looked-for behaviours is 'participant makes eye contact with the speaker', the relevant assessor will record the instances when the participant demonstrates this behaviour in, say, the course of a group discussion. In some development centres, biodata and/or **psychometric tests** are used as part of the evidence base, but the more popular and characteristic kinds of exercise include in-trays, case studies, group tasks or discussions and one-to-one interviews.

At the end of a development centre, participants are debriefed, usually in detail, and may also be given a written report of their performance. Part of this report may be the start of a **personal development plan**, highlighting areas of relative weakness which need to be addressed, strengths to build upon and suggestions for training and development. Participants may have opportunities to plug into a management development program at their workplace or elsewhere and they may also be assigned a **mentor** to support their subsequent development.

As Woodruffe (1993) comments, 'a well-conducted assessment centre is the best way of getting people to buy into and take responsibility for their own development plan.' It can also be an extremely valuable development experience in its own right, offering participants insights into or confirmation of their strengths and areas of need, a realistic preview of tasks they may not yet have tackled for real and opportunities for remotivation and displaying their talents to the people who matter.

Association

The concept of association has a long history in philosophy, psychology and learning theory. The power of association has long been recognized. What, if anything, is new in the systematic application of association techniques to technologies of personal **change**? The impetus for using association techniques is due largely to our growing understanding (or, at least, our preferred models) of how the brain and nervous system function. The more we know about the brain, the more the principle of association is endorsed as crucial to fast, efficient learning, state control and change. As Colin Rose (1985) puts it within the context of **accelerated learning**, 'the more associations and the stronger they are, the easier it is to remember and learn.'

Making, reinforcing and unmaking associations are primary activities in **NLP. Anchoring** is essentially a purposeful association process. Also central to NLP is the practice of getting into or switching between a state of *association* (the 'normal' state of seeing the world from within our body) and *dissociation*, when we see ourselves 'out there' as someone else might see us. Both states have their uses. Being able to get ourselves into or out of these basic states is a tool of **mastery**.

A particularly prominent idea in some areas of contemporary PD literature is the idea that an intellectual commitment to change is rarely enough to effect that change in practice. (The fate of most New Year resolutions attests to this!) According to some PD tutors, the key is to link the idea to strong emotional associations. In particular, associate not changing in the desired direction with huge amounts of pain (or unpleasantness) and changing with huge amounts of pleasure, and the leverage for change may have been achieved. The process of **programming** these associations systematically into the nervous systems is what Anthony Robbins (1992) calls Neuro-Associative Conditioning$^{(TM)}$. (Neuro-Association Conditioning is a registered trademark of Robbins Research International, Inc.)
(See **Anchor**.)

Atrophy

Also known as the *Law of Use*. Memories, skills and facilities wither with the passage of time. We can keep them 'alive' only by putting them to work: 'use them or lose them', as the saying goes. Experienced PD tutors know only too well that exposure to a great idea (such as a technique for personal growth) is a necessary but not a sufficient condition for **change**. Knowledge remains only **potential** power until it is applied, and it is in the application that most people falter. It is the main reason that PD programs include exercises and 'gaps' – so that audience members can apply the ideas they have just received.

Atrophy is not the same thing as over-familiarity, but the effects are similar. Knowing about some concept or activity in PD (goal-setting is the classic example) leads some people to equate knowing with doing.

Atrophy is linked to the *Continuity of Effort* principle which states that, once neglected, a behaviour becomes harder to perform. Hence the advice: 'try not to let a single day pass without taking a positive step towards your next sub-goal' (Sharpe and Lewis, 1976). This is almost identical to the principle of *entropy* which Egan (1994) defines as 'the tendency to give up action

that has been initiated'. We begin a change program, full of enthusiasm, but often we run into difficulties and our enthusiasm wanes, and effort becomes progressively half-hearted. In clinical and therapeutic settings it is called 'relapse', or referred to as the 'ubiquitous decay curve' (Phillips, 1987).
(See **Action; Leverage.**)

Attitudes

Having a 'positive attitude' – towards life, the world and our potential for enriching experiences – is generally regarded both as a prerequisite for personal growth and as an outcome of it. Strictly speaking, this is not so much an attitude as a general orientation towards the world; or a state of mind which endures from situation to situation, and impacts upon the specific attitudes we adopt to things. It is difficult to define 'positive' without being tautological. In the 1960 classic *Success Through A Positive Mental Attitude*, Napoleon Hill and W Clement Stone define PMA as 'the right mental attitude for each specific occasion'.

A positive attitude is closely associated with a general belief in our capacity for self-improvement and achievement. In fact attitudes are like **beliefs**, with the addition of an emotional component which inclines us to respond either positively or negatively to the subject of the attitude.

Attitudes are essential and unavoidable. Without them we should have to respond to people, events and messages on a moment-to-moment basis, and decide each time we encountered them how we felt and thought about them. But the specific attitudes we have, their *direction* (favourable or unfavourable), *salience* (how important they are for us) and *intensity* (how strongly we hold them) can have a very significant influence upon our capacity for development. Indeed, one of the resounding messages in contemporary PD literature is that what matters is not what happens to us in life so much as our attitude towards what happens.

In general, we are more likely to reinforce our attitudes than to change them. This is especially the case with attitudes closely tied to our self-image (sometimes called the *ego involvement* aspect of attitudes) and with *generalized* attitudes – those which underpin structures of attitudes. Changing a generalized attitude (eg, one towards a religious faith or political party) inevitably entails a host of changes to the specific attitudes which relate to it.

Personal development tends to require or imply a re-evaluation of certain attitudes – a shift towards those consistent with our **goals** and aspirations and away from those which block their accomplishment. For example, if we have been raised with a negative attitude towards the rich, then we are unlikely to achieve wealth-related goals until we have altered our attitude. Particularly crucial here are our attitudes towards **change** itself. As it is made clear in the workbook accompanying the excellent Open University course on Personal and Career Development (1992), 'How successful you are in achieving change will be influenced by the attitude, or state of mind, with which you approach the task, and by the existence of "self-defeating beliefs" which can block you from achieving change.'

Personal growth also involves an alignment of positive attitudes and behaviour: for example, taking regular exercise as well as having a favourable attitude towards it; or actually setting goals, not just having a positive view about the business of goal-setting.

Maintaining the 'right' attitudes for development usually involves an active seeking out of like-minded people and of sources of information conducive to our attitudes. It is not unusual for 'serious' personal improvers to immerse themselves in a world of self-improvement tapes, books and speakers to ensure that they are exposed largely to messages in line with their attitudes. Similarly, motivational speakers suggest to their audiences that they avoid newspapers and anything else which might have a negative influence.

Huge claims have been made for having a positive attitude. The 'pay off', claim Hill and Stone, 'will be success, health, happiness, wealth or whatever definite aims you have in life.' Similarly massive claims were made in other mid-century books, though they were often heavy on assertion and anecdote but light on theory and technique. Today's success experts, Jack Black, for example, or Brian Tracy, tend also to emphasize the attitude component of achievement. So what is the link between internal attitude and external achievement? Part of the explanation seems to be that if we have a positive attitude (almost certainly linked to high **self-esteem**) we will be more open to ideas and solutions, and will go on looking for them longer than someone with a negative attitude. Another part of the theory goes like this: we approach a situation (a job interview, for instance) with positive expectations. We think it is going to go well. These expectations give rise to positive attitudes towards the situation, the people in it and ourselves. In turn, we translate these attitudes into the kinds of verbal and non-verbal behaviours (eg, smiling, making good eye contact, being complimentary) which encourage other people to be receptive and positive towards us. Hence, we get the outcome we wanted.

Attribution Theory

A theory about the ways in which we explain the good and bad events we experience. Three attributes or dimensions are especially important.

- Whether the cause was seen as *internal* ('It was down to me') or *external* ('They refused to join us').
- Whether the cause was seen as *temporary* ('I didn't play my best on this occasion') or *permanent* ('I'm useless at tennis').
- Whether the cause was seen as *specific* ('Our row has made us tense with each other') or *global* ('Our row has ruined everything between us').

Attribution theory suggests that how we make sense of everyday as well as major experiences affects our expectations about the future and, in turn, our feelings and behaviour in the present. It is underpinned by the **ABC theory** that an event will activate certain **beliefs** and **values** which give rise to certain feelings and behaviours. The event does not directly determine the feeling; it all depends on the beliefs and values which 'intervene' between the event and the feelings and behaviour.

Those of us with a generally pessimistic attributional style are likely to construe the 'bad' events which befall us as permanent, global and beyond our control. Not surprisingly, this style is associated with depression, stress and a sense of hopelessness and low motivation.

Attribution theory forms the basis of some forms of cognitive therapy and the training programs which use cognitive therapy approaches. These can address the development needs of stressed and depressed individuals and of demotivated work groups. The ultimate goal is to develop values, attributes and beliefs which enable those concerned to be hopeful, resourceful, resilient and successful.

(See **Cognitive Distortion; Meta Model; Negative Thinking.**)

Authenticity

This is usually defined as the ideal of being true to oneself irrespective of circumstances.

Some PD programs stress the importance of authenticity as a guiding principle in **development**. It serves as a touchstone by which we can gauge whether particular behaviours are 'right' for us. If we are authentic, then we won't develop in the 'wrong' ways for the 'wrong' reasons. For example, we won't pursue a particular career just to please our parents.

Authenticity is not the straightforward concept it might seem. It implies a single, stable self, whereas many PD specialists see the self as multi-dimensional. It is also difficult to square the concept of authenticity with the process of development. How is it possible for a fixed entity to develop? What if that aspect of the self to which we were once 'true' has now developed out of all recognition? Authenticity is also difficult to reconcile with the concept of communicative competence – the capacity to vary our talk and behaviour to take account of the people we are with and the 'requirements' of the situation as we understand them to be. Displaying situational sensitivity is normally regarded as a mark of personal effectiveness. Not to display it is more likely to be seen as boorish egoism or social ineptitude than as authenticity.

The notion of authenticity seems to make more sense when the self is construed as a process rather than as a solid entity. Authenticity then becomes 'a gradual ongoing process of self-understanding' (Van Deurzen-Smith, 1990), a striving to make our behaviour consistent with the person we understand ourselves to be at the time.

Awareness Continuum

A concept associated with Gestalt psychology that draws attention to a familiar aspect of subjective experience – that in any situation we can be *more* or *less* aware of the features of the situation and of what we are experiencing.

Very often we are not *in* that situation in that our 'mind is elsewhere'. Quite often we worry about what has already happened or what might happen. Not 'being in the situation' or not living in the **here and now** is a serious problem for some people. It seriously prevents their living life to the full by dulling their experiences. There are awareness continuum techniques for keeping in a situation, the simplest of which is just to make a deliberate habit of noticing and focusing upon particular things in the environment or particular sensations of your own body.

Beliefs

Thoughts of some certainty about ourselves, others, things and situations.

Beliefs often have a feeling dimension, hence Sue Knight's description of them as 'emotionally held thoughts' (Knight, 1995). Beliefs can also be defined in terms of function. They provide the filters by which we perceive and organize reality, and they also guide us. Anthony Robbins (1992) sees them as the guiding forces that inform us of what will lead to pain or to pleasure. Beliefs can be 'found' at a deeper neurological level than behaviour – ie, beliefs are further away from the 'surface' and closer to the core of our sense of identity. This has major implications for personal development for it means that **change** must often be effected at the fundamental level of beliefs if it is to last. Merely changing behaviours may not be enough if the new behaviours are out of line with existing, unchanged beliefs.

Belief is one of the most frequently discussed concepts in PD literature. Writers from all quarters of the PD field emphasize its importance. From where does this conviction about the importance of beliefs come? The short answer is another belief: that it is our thinking, not reality itself, that determines our behaviour. That is, we act in accordance with what we believe rather than with the way things 'really are'. Except for some authorities on **enlightenment** who believe that reality can be apprehended without mediation by beliefs, the general view in the PD world is that beliefs affect, if not govern, our perceptions of ourselves, our abilities, potentialities and opportunities. They also determine our perceptions. For example, if we believe that life is a struggle, then we shall probably struggle. If we believe that life offers us endless opportunities for advancement, then we shall probably see and seize them. If we believe that we are unlovable, then we shall probably behave in ways to ensure that other people confirm our beliefs.

Central to our understanding of personal development is the relationship between belief and experience. The conventional wisdom of social psychology is that we acquire our beliefs from experience and other people. It is summed up in the view that beliefs are 'conclusions that you have reached based on experience' (Honey, 1988). This view is not discounted in **NLP** and other popular approaches to PD, but the current emphasis is on the opposite point of view. Not that seeing is believing ('I can believe I'm bright because I've passed my exams') but rather believing is seeing ('I passed my exams *because* I believed I was bright'). The most extreme form of this view can be found in the teachings of some of the 'new spiritual' and holistic psychology writers. Gill Edwards (1991) states it boldly: 'Beliefs create experience, not vice versa.' Jill Hall (1990) suggests that beliefs in contact with the deepest levels of consciousness 'have the power to create our reality'. Colin Turner (1994) makes a similar point from a human potential perspective: 'The universal law of belief states that what you really believe in with feeling will become your reality'. The mechanism for this process is usually taken to be the *Law of Attraction* working either through the subconscious or some more mysterious individual or collective unconscious. At the simplest level of explanation, this is a matter of beliefs making our minds more aware of whatever it is that will confirm them. This may create the effect of our minds acting like magnets. A less straightforward explanation is that beliefs cause our minds to produce energies which somehow attract or resonate with energies in the world beyond the mind.

PD literature includes abundant advice about how we can optimize our development opportunities. The main recommendation is to identify our core beliefs – those central to our **decision-making** and behaviour. They are likely to include global beliefs about ourselves and life which form the basis for hosts of more specific beliefs. 'I am hopeless at sports' and 'People will help you if they can' are global beliefs which could have considerable implications for anyone who holds them. Other key beliefs are criteria beliefs (or rule beliefs) about the conditions that need to be met before we can attain a state, such as success, or freedom, or happiness. 'I'll be happy when I'm a millionaire' is a criteria belief.

Once we have isolated our core beliefs, we need to consider what they do for and to us. The advice generally given is to change them if they are not helpful, supportive or empowering. This in turn implies that beliefs are a matter of choice. As Alder (1995) puts it, 'You can believe whatever you want'. In contrast to the orthodox view from psychology that beliefs are resistant to change, particularly if they are central, the NLP view is that 'old' beliefs can be taken out and new beliefs installed with no great effort. (The process of replacing one belief with another is sometimes called 'belief negation'.) There are also techniques for fixing and intensifying beliefs – **affirmation**, use of submodalities etc. The function of such techniques, broadly speaking, is to cut out and then irrigate new neural channels, leaving the old ones to dry up.

Another area of advice concerns **modelling** the beliefs of people who are exceptional performers in their fields. This might include stepping into the **mental maps** of exceptional people to ensure adoption of some common, empowering beliefs (eg, that every problem has a solution).

Advice is also targeted at PD professionals. Teachers need to know about belief systems critical to efficient learning: for example, that most fast, proficient readers believe that reading is important, purposeful and that it can be fun (Van Najel *et al*, 1985). Counsellors and psychotherapists need to be aware of the more common beliefs that hinder effective living (Egan, 1994; Ellis, 1987).

It is hard to over-estimate the importance accorded to beliefs in contemporary PD, just as many PD tutors take the view that it would be hard to over-estimate the **potential** of anyone with a quiver of empowering core beliefs. Although some authorities on **enlightenment** see beliefs as 'an impediment on the path to understanding' (ITC, 1987), PD tutors generally view them as inevitable, necessary and powerful. It's our responsibility to ensure that our beliefs support rather than hinder our **development**. Not surprisingly, perhaps, the truth value of beliefs is not of primary concern to many current PD tutors who take a more pragmatic view. Since we cannot always be certain about what 'really is', it makes sense to err on the positive side and hold beliefs which empower and help us. In this sense, beliefs (as operating assumptions) are our servants rather than our masters

– provided we have hired the right ones!
(See **Attitudes; Change**.)

Body Awareness

Consciousness of the mind-body relationship, with an emphasis upon the body and its crucial role in growth and **well-being**. Body awareness activities promote appreciation through direct experience of what our bodies can do to and for us.

The range of mind-body disciplines, therapies and exercises is considerable and increasing. In addition to massage and breathing activities, there are manipulative therapies that work directly on the body's muscle, tissues and joints (eg, Rolfing, polarity therapy, biodynamic massage), movement-based disciplines (eg, rhythmic dance, dance therapy, tai-chi), voice and sound work, disciplines that work on the flow and balance of the body's energy (eg, Reiki, bioenergetics) and cross-disciplinary forms such as biodanza (a mix of dance and music) and yoga, which is truly multi-disciplinary.

Engaging in body awareness activities is not just about taking care of our bodies. Health and fitness programs can help us to do this, but won't necessarily do much for our body awareness. More fundamentally, it is about reconnecting with our bodies, and experiencing them as an integral part of our being. Authorities in body awareness believe with Lucy Liddell (1987) that for 'much of the time in adult life, our energy is predominantly in our heads, and we exist out of contact with parts of our bodies.' The deeper **beliefs** are that we cannot know who we are until we know fully what we feel and what we have the **potential** to feel when our bodies are at one with our minds and **emotions**.

Disconnection from our bodies and senses can result in diminished experiences (numbed senses, a lack of vitality etc), tension, stress and even illness. And because these 'conditions' can be chronic, we may not even know we have them.

Another belief that supports body awareness activities is that the body has a wisdom of its own. The body is not simply a machine, or even a machine at all. Its intelligence is not the rational intelligence of the brain, but it may be a more sound and trustworthy intelligence. This is sometimes attributed to the body's direct contact with the earth and, by extension, reality itself. Our feet are 'planted on the ground' whilst our heads are 'in the air'. Another view is that the very cells of our body are 'thinking' cells, a view maintained by Deepak Chopra (1987). When we get a 'gut feeling', we are being sent signals from cells that trust themselves more than those in the brain.

The promotion of body awareness can also be seen as a reaction to the forms of therapy which predominated during the first two-thirds of this century. We experience the world through three main modes (auditory, visual and kinaesthetic) and yet most psychotherapies and most development programs emphasize spoken language (auditory) or written language (visual), rather than the bodywork of the kinaesthetic mode. Body awareness disciplines offer alternative or complementary pathways to development from those which are predominantly verbal and cerebral. Many personal development books and programs are still based very largely on applied cognitive psychology and other brain-based disciplines.

The body awareness disciplines also differ from approaches to personal development that emphasize **success** and achievement in terms of their key values. Whereas *doing* and *having* values are generally paramount in the latter, *being* values are paramount in the former. In practice, this means that the body awareness disciplines show deference for 'simple', 'ordinary' experiences such as walking, breathing, touching and being alive in the moment – whatever and wherever this may be.

If we enjoy high levels of body awareness, then the mind and the body will be more or less equal partners. In any situation, our actions are likely to give the same messages as our emotions and our words. We won't do one thing and feel and think something else or, if we do, we shall be aware fully of the lack of **congruence**. We will feel intensely both pain and pleasure. It will be common for us to experience both relaxation and vitality, to have a mind that's quiet and yet senses that are highly alert. Our movements are likely to feel free, rhythmic, spontaneous, and yet we shall also feel grounded. It won't be easy to throw us off balance – literally or psychologically. We may find it easier to relate to other people and be less concerned with their view of us from the outside. Above all, we will feel that we fully inhabit and know our own body.

There are many specific techniques and exercises that we can use to raise our body awareness. Some of these are designed in part to ease us into a receptive state of body and mind in order to explore ourselves (for example, progressive relaxation and attitude work). Ideally, our **attitudes** should be as relaxed as our bodies, ie, unfixed by presuppositions. Feeling a sense of adventure is much better than feeling very self-conscious or over-concerned with technical correctness.

If we are relaxed, then we can begin to release the grip of our conscious, chattering mind, and focus upon staying aware of the present moment. This may involve sitting or lying quietly and 'observing' our thoughts rather than resisting them or following them. Resistance is better explored than ignored or suppressed.

Many simple actions can assist with body-befriending. Touching ourselves, self-massage, giving ourselves a hug, running our fingers through our hair and enjoying the sensation are among the ways of getting closer to our bodies. To awaken dulled senses, we can notice sensory information normally screened out by our **reticular activating system** because it is too 'mundane'. To enhance sensory awareness, we can concentrate upon one sense, open ourselves to multi-sensory experiences, and alter the nature of 'ordinary' experiences to renew our attentiveness to them. For example, we can see what it feels like to wash the dishes at half the normal speed or how our body feels when we take a slow-motion shower. We can touch ordinary objects in a slow, deliberate, exploratory way, again focusing upon the sensations.

Getting to know the parts of us that we have generally taken for granted or 'ignored' can be an important element of a body-work program. For many of us, this may include most of our 'bottom halves'. Connecting with our legs and feet and lower torso can begin to make us feel more stable, solid and **centred**. Work on improving our posture can improve not only our health but also our freedom of movement. In body awareness terms, 'good' posture means having excellent potential for movement.

Becoming more familiar with our own bodies can increase our acceptance of and liking for them. Some people experience this as a kind of self-compassion. Knowing our bodies as intimates, and acquiring an insider's view of our bodies through exploration of our inner space, can make us less concerned with external appearance and ultimately with other people's view of what we look like. A relevant technique here is self-gazing – looking at our (naked) bodies in the mirror without feeling awkward or guilty.

The aspect of body awareness generally considered of overriding importance is breathing. Breathing is considered to be the bridge between mind and body, and one of the most effective tools for altering how we think and feel. More specifically, learning the disciplines of breathing can increase energy levels, improve circulation, strengthen our immune systems, promote digestion and elimination, and help us to focus and feel more centred. Learning how to breathe from the abdomen rather than the upper chest, how to breathe fully and freely and how to breathe through alternate nostrils, are among the disciplines advocated by authorities in the area.

Linked to breathing is voice work – exploring the full expressive range of the voice, including projection, singing, chanting and laughter.

There are many more active forms of body awareness involving movement, dance, martial art disciplines and bodywork with a partner. One of the things they share is an intent to heighten awareness generally through enhanced body consciousness. As Bija Bennett has said, 'The fate of our body can only be changed by awareness' (quoted in McGovern, 1995).

Doing exercises that enhance our consciousness of our bodies is not always a comfortable experience. Some initial discomfort is often positive because it indicates that energy has begun to flow, and that old frozen ways of moving, holding ourselves or experiencing our bodies have begun to thaw. We can sometimes experience real physical pain when direct bodywork releases the fluids (and, some authorities would say, emotions) trapped between muscles and nerves. In the world of body awareness disciplines, as in the related world of holistic **healing**, things can often appear to get worse before they get better.

Body awareness also plays an important part in approaches to personal development that aren't primarily about enjoying the benefits of reconnecting with our bodies, for example, in **NLP**. Physiology is important to NLPers for rather pragmatic reasons. They are interested in how we can use our physiology to change our state. Anthony Robbins (1988) regards it as the most power-ful means we have of doing so. We can get ourselves in a more productive state, for example, simply by changing our posture or how we breathe.

More generally, NLPers are interested in physiology and body language because of the part they play in self-communication and communication with others. Gestures, breathing patterns, eye movements etc, provide ways to access internal states and preferred modes of thinking (visual, auditory or kinaesthetic). We can establish **rapport** with another person only if we are sen-sitive to and skilfully match their physical actions and tone of voice. Sensitivity to the meanings of the words they use is only a small part of the process. Similarly, **modelling** someone else requires us to elicit and adopt their behaviour patterns.

The body as a set of signifying systems is also of interest, though sometimes at a less subtle level, to authorities concerned with personal presentation. There are many popular books and programs on impression management, or presenting an attrac-tive, marketable self-image. These usually deal with internal matters (eg, how to build self-confidence) but there is also a heavy emphasis upon appearance and body language.

In most respects, this kind of body awareness is the antithesis of that fostered through the mind-body disciplines. A major concern of personal presentation is how our bodies are per-ceived by others, rather than considering how our bodies feel to us, and the 'look good' factor ranks alongside the 'feel good' fac-tor. Also, emphasis on external appearance inevitably implies comparisons with others. The heavier the emphasis, the more likely presentation work is to develop body *self*-consciousness rather than body consciousness, and to leave us estranged from, rather than befriended with, our bodies.
(See **Holistic Development**.)

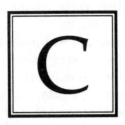

Career Development

This has been defined as 'the process of individual growth, learning and development in relation to work' (Ball, 1984). It is especially important nowadays to view career development as a dynamic relationship between the individual and work in its broadest sense. A person's employment history with the high points highlighted is *not* career development and is of little interest from a PD perspective. The areas of interest from this perspective include: the development of **self-awareness** at and derived from work; self-concept in relation to work; the **choices** that have or have not been made; an individual's sense of control over life events related to work; and the individual's readiness to seize or make **opportunities** for development through work. Contributions to these and other matters come both from career development specialists and from **self-help** tutors whose ideas apply as much to career development as to any other area of PD. Work in all its forms (full-time, part-time, casual, voluntary, etc) clearly affords many people opportunities for developing and expressing personal identities. For some people it is the *main* vehicle for personal development. The reverse is also becoming true. 'Personal development is the key way in which employees can guarantee their continued employability in an uncertain market' (Holbeche, 1995). The themes of contemporary career development thinking reflect current realities: a complex, volatile work environment, partly the result of rapid social and technological change, and a trend towards smaller organizations offering fewer possibilities for promotion. Hence, the idea of a career as a life-time **commitment** to one job with the expectation of employment security and regular advancement is giving way to the notion of 'employability': individuals making sure that they acquire the skills and experiences to market themselves successfully when their current employer no longer requires them.

In the light of this, there are two main themes centred on the notion of **responsibility**. Firstly, companies need to provide substantial infrastructures for supporting the personal development of staff. These might include career **counselling** services and career shops; opportunities for staff to train and develop; opportunities for staff to develop laterally – ie, move between functions or units to broaden their experience and skills bases; competency schemes to highlight similarities between apparently different jobs.

Secondly, individuals must take (almost) full responsibility for their own careers. They must clarify their own career **goals** and be clear about their underpinning **values** and motivations. They must be self-aware and conduct **self-audits** (of strengths, development needs, etc) and skills inventories. They must plan and manage their careers proactively rather than reacting to external events (eg, re-organizations, redundancies). They must take the initiative to seek out advice and career counselling, network, get the training and development opportunities they need to remain marketable, and keep records of their personal development activities. They may need also to develop generic skills such as **decision-making** and establishing **rapport**.

From a PD point of view, an ecological perspective (seeing one's career in relation to the other areas of one's life) is also important.

(See **Action Hobbies; Adaptability; Assessment Centres; Competence(s); Continuous Development; Ecology; Personal Development Plan.**)

Centredness

This concept is associated with Gestalt therapy and with psychospiritual approaches to personal development that emphasize *being* as opposed to *doing*.

Being centred is a state of mind or being, and development is construed as a movement from experiencing our being from the centre rather than the periphery. Centredness is characterized by stillness, dynamic calmness, clarity and awareness. It is not an intellectual or ego state. Indeed, if we experience the world from our intellect or ego, then we are almost certainly not centred.

When we are centred, we experience the world 'objectively' in that our personal needs or desires are not overwhelming. In this state we 'deal with the circumstances of our lives as they present themselves, according to the dictates of healthy functioning' (Latner, 1986). We don't feel that we have to manipulate or exert control over our environment (including other people) in order to function effectively or feel at home in the world. Being centred enables us to assimilate and evaluate situations and to know what to do with our feelings – express them, simply acknowledge them etc.

Gestalt therapists regard centredness as a kind of situational maturity – a state of being in which we do not have to strain either to give meaning to experience or to relate to the environments in which we find ourselves. Fritz Perls (1969) himself said that 'achieving a centre, being grounded in oneself, is about the highest state a human being can achieve.' He argued also 'that identification with the centre automatically sharpens awareness and fosters actualization of inner potential' (in Bloomfield et al, 1976).

Centredness appears to be a figurative extension of the concept of *centring* which has the more literal meaning of being in the 'centre of our mass'. This is also called the 'one point', the spot located just below and behind our navel. Being at the centre of our mass gives us a feeling of being balanced, and consequently we feel calm, confident and in control. We are receptive to stimuli and our thinking is clear.

Not surprisingly, the concept of centring comes from the martial arts but is also highly relevant to other kinds of performers, including athletes. If an athlete isn't able to centre, perhaps because of unwanted thoughts, then he is unlikely to perform at his optimum. Feeling centred is brought about by the centring processes of breathing and attentional re-focussing.
(See **Here and Now; Self-Awareness.**)

Challenge

In the PD field, a challenge is what a problem becomes when it is positively redefined. It is a problem perceived to offer **opportunities** for personal development.

A challenge can provide both the impetus and the incentive for personal change. It is very much a personal thing; one person's challenge is another's routine behaviour. If there is a 'test' or trial involved then it is within the individual. Personal development is about challenging oneself rather than competing with others, though a competition may provide the context for it (eg, a sports event for athletes). There is general agreement in the PD field that succeeding at a challenge may be less important in growth terms than taking it on in the first place and learning from it.

Personal development can issue from seemingly unsolicited challenges, like family disasters, but dedicated personal developers will also deliberately seek them out. They know that growth comes from having ideas and beliefs challenged, and not from trying to confirm them at all costs. As M Scott Peck puts it in *The Road Less Travelled* (1990): 'The only way that we can be certain that our map of reality is valid is to expose it to the criticism and challenge of other map-makers.' Serious self-improvers are not defensive; being 'right' is not important to them if being 'wrong' or being 'less right' can lead on to being 'more right'.

Not surprisingly, challenge is considered, 'central to counselling and therapy' (Egan, 1994). Professional helpers challenge clients to find the perspectives from which they might identify their blind spots and **cognitive distortions**.

Any challenge can disturb our psychic order, and most challenges involve either exploration and/or transformation of ourselves. Some of the more common challenges dealt with and encouraged in PD programs include: challenging ingrained **habits** and taken-for-granted **beliefs**; overcoming fears of trying new experiences; finding the courage to make tough **choices**; breaking negative thought patterns; gaining control over aspects of our lives that previously we didn't even realize we could control. Some PD books/programs specialize in specific challenges – those presented by public speaking, for example, or by other situations requiring high self-confidence (eg, Davies, 1995).

Although personal in terms of how they are experienced, challenges can be structured systematically. For example, **enlightenment** and **meditation** programs are typically sequential and progressive. Each stage of consciousness offers a new and higher challenge. The same is true of other spiritual, psychic and metaphysical systems – developing through experiencing higher levels of universal energy, for example (see Roman, 1986) – as well as of the more prosaic challenges built into qualification systems.

(See **Comfort Zone; Risks.**)

Change

There can be change without **development** but not development without change. Even more-of-the-same kinds of development (getting better at swimming, say) involve changes of a sort. The importance of change can be gauged by the fact that most of the entries in this book are concerned with change in some way or another. The same is true of all books on personal development, some of which deal exclusively with the change process. *I Want to Change but I Don't Know How* (Rusk and Read, 1986) is one of many examples. The majority of personal development books, tapes and other programs fall into one (or both) of two very broad categories. One is the 'how to change' category. These books focus upon the processes of change, sometimes prescribing step-by-step procedures for changing, and describe the factors which both inhibit and facilitate or promote change, including **attitudes** and **beliefs**. Increasingly, they also present specific techniques or technologies for effecting change. Some books specialize in the latter. *Using Your Brain For A Change* (Bandler, 1985) and *Visualisation for Change* (Fanning, 1994) are examples. A second category deals with *ways* of changing – with how we can change and, perhaps, why we should change. A number of 'New Age' spiritual and metaphysical books are concerned with possible and preferred directions for change. Many personal development books straddle both categories – many books on success and personal **healing**, for example. Still other personal development books offer reflections upon or accounts of individual 'journeys' of development. These are also, inevitably, books about change.

In addition, there are substantial bodies of literature on individual change processes within psychology, psychotherapy, **counselling**, education and management/business studies. A key theme in the latter two disciplines concerns individual development within the context of organizational development, and includes staff development and the management of change. Much popular personal development literature draws upon concepts from psychology and psychotherapy, and some make accessible the theories of personal change within particular approaches, such as Gestalt therapy and **transactional analysis**. *I'm OK, You're OK* (Harris, 1970) and *Breaking Free* (James, 1981) are examples of the latter. Contemporary psychotechnologies, including **NLP**, are also influencing the change models within 'conventional' psychotherapy.

Within the PD world there are two views about change. One is that change is a multi-dimensional, highly complex process, too complex and messy to be reduced to a strategy. The other view is that change seems complex and messy only when you don't have some effective strategies for it. In other words, it's as complex (or straightforward) as you want it to be. The extreme position here is that you can reduce the model of change to the briefest of injunctions: 'Just do it!' would be one. Another would be the 'Rhinoceros' model of change: 'Charge!' (Alexander, 1980). The NLP view is that the 'secret' of effective change is knowing what to do that works. This includes knowing what to do to get sufficiently motivated to take the necessary action. Psychotherapists and counsellors tend to see change as a more complicated and difficult process, but these professional helpers differ considerably in terms of how they conceptualize change, what they look for, what they regard as important etc. There are, for example, very big differences between how a behavioural psychologist sees change and how a Freudian psychologist sees it.

The term 'change' itself has many applications. It can refer to here and now changes of state (eg, moving from a depressed to productive set of emotions), to a specific behavioural change (eg, eliminating a habit) or, at the furthest extreme, to a profound change of perspective – from a negative to a positive 'world view', for example.

Change can occur in the same direction, by building upon and extending something that is already happening, or it can represent a change of direction. It can be discretionary or non-discretionary, though the view of some PD writers is that we are responsible for bringing into our lives even changes which appear to occur without our consent. Some people also distinguish between remedial changes and changes which build upon strengths.

Given these different kinds of change and the variety of perspectives on it, it is not surprising that there is no one accepted model of change. However, there is general agreement about some features of change.

Generally, PD tutors regard change as natural, inevitable and predominantly life-enhancing. It is presented primarily as a gain process (self-discoveries, etc) rather than as a loss process, in that each change adds to rather than depletes our stock of experience. However, it is acknowledged also that the majority of us tend not to see most change in these ways. Rather, we see it as scary, threatening and risky. We prefer equilibrium to disequilibrium, even if we are miserable in our equilibrium. We also see it as hard work, hence the challenge which many PD tutors take on of packaging change to make it seem more attractive. Coaching their 'students' to gain **leverage** and giving them recipes for successful change management are two of the most popular packaging devices.

There are some dominant themes in current PD literature about the process of change. One of these is that we as individuals already possess all the most important resources we need to effect change. For example, we are all capable of **programming** our minds, of inducing pain, of imagining what it would be like to change and of substituting one **habit** for another. A second key message is that no one can be made to change in any significant sense; change has to be self-motivated and self-directed. A related theme is that of personal **responsibility**. Notwithstanding the support we might get from others, we must be our own change agents and advocates. We must sell the idea and benefits of changing to both our conscious and **subconscious** minds, and we need also to compliment and congratulate ourselves for the progress we make.

Perhaps the single most important process theme is that

change is predominantly an inside-out activity. This is especially the case with change that needs to make a major impact on
our lives. Physiology and actual behaviour can certainly affect
our state, and the reactions we get from other people can also
help us to change internally. Nonetheless, the key to meaningful, lasting change is to work first on the inside (on beliefs, on
the self-image, on defining goals etc) and then to behave consistently with them. The supposition is that we are more likely to
change if we have first convinced ourselves that we are, say, a
non-smoker, than if we stop smoking in the hope that our mind
will make the appropriate adjustments. It won't. It will continue
to tell us that we are a smoker who isn't (at present) smoking.

There is general agreement about the conditions under which
we are most likely to make personal change effective. The following points are especially important:

- *We are committed to the change at all appropriate levels of ourselves.* This belief is linked to the crucial concepts of personal
  alignment and **congruence**. Some changes can quite happily
  be effected at one level – some habits, for example. But others
  may require aligned changes at more than one level of being
  or consciousness. For example, we may need to change a
  belief before we can consistently change a behaviour (as in
  the smoking example above). If we do not effect change at the
  appropriate level(s), then one part of us will sabotage another part. A multi-layered model of the self certainly seems better able to account for familiar experiences of 'mixed feelings'
  or 'being in two minds' or even of feeling enthusiastic about
  making a change, but finding that some of our behaviour
  seems to be working against the change.
- *The change (and the time of the change) seems 'right' for us.* Some
  books on personal change suggest that we can change ourselves or our lives in any ways we want to – if we want to
  badly enough. This may be so, but almost certainly some
  kinds of change are going to 'feel' more appropriate to our
  present needs and interests than others. The general view is
  that we need to be sufficiently self-aware and self-monitoring
  to know what these are. (This is related to the concept in
  Gestalt therapy called the Paradoxical Theory of Change
  which suggests that change occurs when a person 'becomes

what he is when he tries to become what he is not'.) Using willpower to try to force ourselves into a change or allowing an external agent, however well-meaning, to encourage us to change in a way which doesn't feel right, is almost always counter-productive.

- *Both desire and dissatisfaction are sufficiently intense.* Change is much easier to effect when we know that we want it, know why we want it and have a compelling mental image (**vision**) of what it will be like when we have achieved it. Associating the consequences of changing with pleasure is important, but making the consequences of not changing painful can be even more important. The theory here is that most of us will do more to avoid pain than we will to acquire pleasure. **Dissatisfaction** with the current (pre-change) situation is the motor of change. A number of PD coaches offer specific strategies for inducing pain and increasing dissatisfaction. Anthony Robbins' Neuro-Associative Conditioning [TM] is an example of this.
- *We have a clear and precise idea of what we want as well as of what we don't want.* Unsuccessful change is often linked to not having anything to replace whatever has been eliminated or deleted. It is unsuccessful because 'incomplete'. Effective change is nearly always defined positively and constructively, even if it also involves 'destruction' of some kind.
- *Pressure and support are appropriately balanced.* This is linked to the previous propositions. **Leverage** and urgency are important forces, whether we apply them to ourselves or (less effectively) others apply them to us. But we need also to look after ourselves, praise ourselves for small successes, remind ourselves that we don't have to be perfect etc. Support from others can be very helpful. The pressure/ support mix can vary according to need. Pressure may be especially important to initiate change, support to sustain it.
- *We feel good about ourselves and believe we are worthy of respect from others.* For many PD coaches, the first requirement for major discretionary change is at least a degree of self-love and **self-acceptance**. Self-love has huge benefits. It enables us to acknowledge our defects and fears, and thus to free ourselves from them, at least in part. It helps rid us of the guilt that somehow we don't deserve the rewards that change might

bring. It makes us less concerned with living up to the expectations others may have of us, and more able to see through personal changes when others make it hard to do so.

- *We know what we need to do to effect change.* For some kinds of change we need plans and strategies, but sometimes we just require skills and techniques that work. These might include NLP methods, 'brief therapy', the constructive use of pain, self-hypnosis etc. So often, as NLP practitioners are fond of reminding us, our attempts at changing falter because we just don't know what to do that works or, worse still, the 'experts' who are meant to be helping us are equally clueless.

- *We are change-oriented.* Making changes, like making **choices**, appears to get easier with practice. One of the familiar exhortations in programs on change is to make lots of changes. They can be minor and inconsequential, like taking a different route to work or switching from coffee to tea, but accumulatively they establish the habit, or even the mind-set, of change. The key is to take action without being paralysed by over-analysis and without mistaking insight or understanding (of our situation) for **action**.

Although there is consensus on a number of themes about change, there are divergent perspectives on others. For example, there is what might be called the 'capability v motivation' issue. Much of the popular literature on **success** and self-development implies or asserts that it is inadequate motivation rather than capability that prevents most of us from bringing about changes in our lives. The psychoanalytical viewpoint, by contrast, is that our present capability is very much affected/constrained by our past experiences, particularly those lodged within the unconscious mind. And while there might be general agreement about the influence of past conditioning, there are debates about the relevance of this to the present and the probabilities of being able to counter this conditioning effectively.

A related issue concerns the time it takes to change. Until fairly recently, most PD coaches believed that change was inevitably a gradual process. Some still believe this. For example, it's not unusual for psychotherapists and counsellors to work on change with their clients for months or years. Even a very specific change (eg, getting used to a new haircut) can take weeks, at least according to some PD coaches, who are still quoting Maxwell Maltz's assertion that it usually takes a minimum of 21 days to effect any perceptible change in a mental image (Maltz, 1960). The literature on change also includes a number of models of change (sometimes presented as graphs) showing a sequence of stages over time. These can apply to life transitions or to change following a trauma, crisis or loss.

In recent years, some PD experts have seriously questioned models of change which come with fixed time sequences. The relevant factor here is our growing appreciation that the brain works in leaps and bounds, not in a steady, evenly-paced way. **'Aha' experiences** can move learning, and thus change, forward in an instant. But the major challenge has come from psycho-technologies that work directly on the brain – hypnosis and NLP, especially. Their exponents argue that they can effect very rapid changes, which are measurable in hours or even minutes, rather than days, weeks or years. What is needed, they say, is an understanding of the mental structures of whatever they are involved in helping to change (a phobia, grief etc). That knowledge tells them what techniques are needed to effect the relevant changes.

A final matter on which PD specialists offer divergent advice concerns what we do about uneasy mixed feelings that appear to constrain us. On the assumption that they distract from or debilitate the change process, some tutors suggest we focus so intensely upon the change target that all 'competing' stimuli are bracketed off. This view, or more refined versions of it, is common in how-to books on **success**. The alternative view is that we ignore internal resistance at our peril. It is there to teach us something, to encourage us to explore further. One writer calls it 'a thread to the unconscious belief system' (Hall 1993). A third option is to make use of both approaches one after the other. First we must listen to doubts, explore these to ensure that the change we wish to undertake is right for us (consistent with our deepest **values**, for example). Then, once we are certain, we must focus fully and not allow anything to deter us. This might be called the 'know what you want, then go for what you want' approach.

(See **Development; Will.**)

Change Personal History (CPH)

An **NLP** procedure for enabling individuals to alter their perceptions of past situations or recurring behaviours.

Experiencing growth, or just getting on with our lives, can be hampered by haunting memories of unpleasant past events. The same is true of bothersome behaviours which we continue to experience. Although we cannot change the actual events of the past, we can certainly change how we perceive and feel about them. We can even install 'memories' of events that never really occurred. Indeed, we can invent whole new personal histories for ourselves. The founders of NLP advocated this: 'The more personal histories you have, the more choices you'll have available to you' (Bandler and Grinder, 1979).

CPH is especially concerned with bringing about perceptual alterations which will help us to be more resourceful in the present and future. Its exponents believe it to be more effective than conventional methods for addressing a past experience which 'has been designed to either have the person "work through it" or ignore it' (Van Nagel *et al*, 1985). There are a number of specific steps to CPH, but the process essentially involves selective anchoring and the use of resource states to change our perceptions of the earliest relevant experience associated with the event or behaviour (see O'Connor and Seymour, 1993).
(See **Anchor; Time; Timelines.**)

Child (Within)

The part of us distinguished by such qualities as freedom, joy and creativity.

The belief that we each carry a child within us is basic to theories and therapies that accept that it is normal to have multiple selves. The Inner Child is variously defined as a sub-personality (psychosynthesis), a mode of being (metaphysics) and an ego state (**transactional analysis**). The latter is the most fully theorized version of the concept, and needs to be understood in relation to the ego states of Adult and Parent. Gestalt therapy and hypnotherapy also recognize the concept.

The term 'Inner Child' refers generally to a self which relates in some way to the actual child each of us was, though it can be used to symbolize certain 'childlike' (but *not* childish) capacities.

A major '**healing**' theme in PD literature concerns the importance of getting to know and love our child within. Doing so can be 'an immensely powerful way of changing our lives' (Edwards, 1991). Failure to do so can leave us as adults 'greatly diminished and handicapped' (Hall, 1993). In practice, connecting with the child within can mean ministering to its wounds, for most of us are to some degree wounded by parenting styles that are over-critical, over-protective, emotionally over-demanding or negative in some other way. It may more positively involve recovering and releasing the 'natural' child, the free spirit who is the source of our life's '**aha' experiences** and who 'can contribute to the individual's life exactly what an actual child can contribute to family life: charm, pleasure and creativity' (Berne, 1968).

Those of us who have over-adapted to the needs and expectations of others or who are over-devoted to work and duty (and dismissive of 'frivolous' play) may most need to find and love our Inner Child. In **transactional analysis** terms, becoming a 'strong adult' in part means becoming sensitive to the child within us and within others (Harris, 1970). Encouraging that child to 'develop more of its joy of life and creative potentiality' (James, 1981) is a major part of the TA process of self-reparenting. There are various specific ways of connecting with the child, including the psychotherapeutic process of reliving the child ego-state in the present.
(See **Emotions; Time.**)

Choice

Making choices is probably the single most important personal development 'activity' and one inextricably linked to central concepts such as **personal power** and **responsibility**. Some PD books and programs are devoted exclusively to it – Shad Helmstetter's *Life Choices* (1989), for example. Many others invite us to reflect upon the choices we have made and the effects these have had. This is sometimes done in a very systematic way in the many humanistic (mainly American) course books on personal development, such as the aptly-named *I*

Never Knew I Had a Choice (Corey, 1986), and in the rethink-your-life books for those in mid-life. However, virtually all PD programs are in some way concerned with extending our perceived range of choices and fostering a choice-maker's mentality.

To take two examples: **NLP** emphasizes the many choices we have when we select words to use, assign meaning to events, adapt positions from which to perceive situations and control our submodalities. Personal effectiveness courses frequently help people who typically 'choose' to be aggressive in frustrating situations to generate alternative options – passivity or assertiveness, for example.

The common messages about choice include the following:

- *Choice is better than no choice.* This is an NLP aphorism, but it has general currency.
- *We have choices in almost every situation.* Since there are very few 'have tos' in life there must be options. It's just that we don't often *acknowledge* that there are – or else we don't see them as options because they are all equally unpleasant. Some problem-solving exercises are intended to generate options (eg, lateral thinking and brainstorming exercises).
- *Choosing is a facility. The more we do it, the easier it becomes, the better we get at it and the more choice seems to operate in our lives.* Why should this be? Choosing effortlessly implies and may further reinforce a state of internal **congruence**. Also, making choices inevitably drip-feeds into the brain the idea that we are choice-makers. In exercising choice, we are choosing to program ourselves as choice-makers.
- *To choose is to program.* The choices we make tend to be seen as the result of the programs we have 'chosen' to allow other people and ourselves to install in us. But choosing is itself a form of **programming** that enables further choices to be made with relative ease. As Helmstetter puts it: 'choices create programming … choices create change.' **Self-talk** is one of the techniques to make the programming effective.
- *What we 'get' in life is the result of the choices we make.* This view is promulgated through most **'success'** manuals. It applies, for example, to states. If we are generally unhappy, then it is because we have chosen to be. We could just as easily have

chosen to be happy. Choice, much more than chance, determines the direction and the degree to which we develop.

PD writers are hard on those who argue to the contrary or offer excuses. To 'arguments' such as, 'I had to stay married because of the children', or 'I can't look for another job at my age', they present an implacable: 'That's your choice'.

Another theme on the subject of choice is following-through. This is a major difficulty for some people. The more powerless we see ourselves, the more difficult we find it to choose. Then the more difficult we find it to follow through without sabotaging our own efforts in a torment of muddled thinking and imagined fears. Cudney and Hardy (1991) point out that 'it takes more effort to choose a self-defeating behaviour than it does to choose a winning behaviour.' The brief explanation for this is that we only have to make a single choice to move forward but we must continue to make choices if we 'opt for the road to self-defeat'. (See Cudney and Hardy for a detailed analysis of this.) Some writers believe that the complexities of choosing, including the common experience of non-choice, can be understood in terms of a much more sophisticated model of the mind than seems often to be assumed in psychology and PD literature. For Jill Hall (1993), this must be a 'multi-dimensional' model of consciousness, and it can only operate in a multi-dimensional reality.
(See **Decision-Making**.)

Climate (for Development)

'Climate' (or 'atmosphere' or 'organizational culture') refers to the conditions of a situation or setting under which development is likely or unlikely to occur. Some conditions are inimical to development, some are conducive to it. Among the key features of a positive psychological and emotional climate for development are the following.

- The climate must be low in stress and threat, high in **challenge** and opportunity.
- Experimentation should be encouraged. It is all right to make

mistakes and take **risks**; these can even be encouraged.
- There should be **opportunities** to learn from experience, and there should be minimal direction or rescuing by others. Reflection should be encouraged. Time should be allowed to 'discover' personal insights.
- Respect for and acceptance of the individual should be shown. There should be a non-judgemental, 'person-centred' approach to individuals, and a 'definable climate of facilitative attitudes' (Rogers, 1974).
- The climate should be supportive and warm. Support needs to accompany and balance pressure and there should be an emphasis on accomplishment.
- Openness and trust are needed, and a degree of freedom to express pain and feelings without fear of rebuke, resentment or over-sensitivity. We should be able to have confidence in the responses of others to our behaviour.

(See **Team (context)**.)

Coaching

A helping and guiding process that can lead to personal development in the form of improved performance.

When we are coached, the key processes for us are planned learning and review. As a result of coaching, we might make 'fewer mistakes' and achieve 'more successes' (Honey, 1988), but we might also understand why we are able to do something well in the first place. In this respect it is linked to **modelling**. **NLP** practitioners and writers operate in a coaching mode when dealing with modelling – when coaching **rapport**, for example. Coaching is also like **mentoring**, but more specific and focused upon performance, and usually shorter term.

Gillen (1995) describes coaching as 'a concept whose time has come'. It fits in both conceptually and practically with learning organizations and customer-oriented companies in which one of the main jobs of managers is to coach subordinates to ensure effective performance by everyone. The principles underpinning coaching also fit well with personal development thinking: the belief that you can help someone learn but you can't teach them to develop, for example.

Cognitive Distortions

Distortions in the ways we process and evalute information leading to psychological and emotional disturbance.

Instead of interpreting a situation by making the 'best', most rational use of the information available to us, we give undue weight to a belief we have carried with us. This predisposes us to feel about it in a certain, usually negative, way. In effect, we are thinking and feeling in ways which are 'fair', neither to ourselves nor to anyone else involved.

A number of cognitive distortions have been identified by Beck (1979, 1982), Dattilo and Padesky (1990) and others. They include: blowing things out of proportion (magnification); thinking and talking in extreme either/or terms (absolutist/dichotomous thinking); focusing upon only one feature of a situation, and ignoring other, more salient features (selective abstraction); making general statements and conclusions on the basis of isolated occurrences (over-generalization); and assigning generalized, indicting labels to people (global labelling).

Uncovering cognitive distortions requires self-monitoring of the 'automatic thoughts' that are triggered by certain events. Recording these thoughts and the feelings they evoke against the events themselves is the first step in challenging and changing them.

Cognitive distortion can inhibit personal development construed as a journey into higher levels of emotional and psychological **well-being**. Certainly, cognitive distortions breed or are associated with a good deal of negative and critical **self-talk**. They can seriously damage interpersonal relationships and are linked to high levels of anxiety and emotional disorder. Conversely, identifying and sorting out our cognitive disorders can promote **self-awareness**, **self-esteem** and the development of coping and problem-solving skills.
(See **ABC Theory**; **Musturbation**.)

Comfort Zones

The areas of thinking and experience to which we confine ourselves so as not to feel uneasy or 'out of our depth'.

A comfort zone is the perceptual equivalent of the shallow end of a swimming pool to a swimmer who lacks confidence. It can also be described as a **mental map** of some area of our life projected from the self-image. As a rule, we 'stay' within the familiar areas of the map. Unless our **self-talk** is deliberately challenging, it tends to keep us there.

Venturing beyond a comfort zone puts our system into tension because the reality we experience is at odds with how we see ourselves. We often experience this when we take on new roles, for example, on becoming a parent or a manager for the first time. To begin with we feel like strangers in unfamiliar territory. We feel uncomfortable with the role and may try to get back to a more familiar one. Personal development, however, comes from venturing beyond and expanding our comfort zones – ie, re-drawing our mental maps to make the familiar areas bigger.

There are two ways of doing this. The obvious way is to 'have a go' at the unfamiliar until it feels familiar. The theory here is that successful experience teaches our self-image that it has nothing to fear from a bigger confort zone. A number of contemporary PD specialists regard this approach as needlessly stressful and inefficient. Their belief is that even if we do unfamiliar things successfully, we may still not convince our self-images that they should change. As Colin Turner (1994) points out, 'our comfort zone knows us better than anyone and hits us on our Achilles' heel.' We see this in sports people who 'throw away' chances after putting in an exceptional performance. It's as though their self-image is telling them that they aren't good enough to sustain the new performance level, so they revert to the comfort zone level. The second approach is to work first of all on changing the self-image using **programming** techniques such as positive self-talk and **visualization**. The advocates of this approach believe that we need to 'see' ourselves operating successfully beyond current comfort zones before we can bring our behaviour consistently into line with the new self-image. It's a good example of inside-out **change**.

Comfort zones feature prominently in a number of self-development programs, including Jack Black's *Mindstore* and the *Investment in Excellence* program presented by Lou Tice of the

Pacific Institute. Both programs recognize that 'the power of the Comfort Zone to keep us where we are is the biggest single hurdle to moving forward and in particular to goal-setting and what can be achieved' (Black, 1994) Realizing that we have comfort zones which may limit our development are clearly important outcomes of and reasons for becoming more self-aware. It's important also to recognize that comfort zones can account for some of our self-sabotaging behaviour. Hence the need to distinguish between, on the one hand, genuine reasons for keeping within a comfort zone and, on the other, rationalizing why we should do so. For example, we may opt not to learn to drive because we believe we would be a menace on the roads. (Some comfort zones are necessary to our well-being.) But we may offer various false reasons for not learning to drive simply to stay within our comfort zone.

One of the other important things to understand about comfort zones is that they are not always pleasurable. Sometimes, the associated experience is painful, but at least it's a *familiar* pain. This preference for the familar over the unfamiliar (even when the unfamiliar has the potential to offer so much more) helps to explain why many of us stick with jobs and partners who do not make us happy, or settle for the vicarious 'pleasures' of television entertainment rather than **risk** the more intense pleasures (or hazards!) of live entertainment.

Turning comfort zones into *dis*comfort zones is one of the major **challenges** for teachers of self-improvement, and has prompted some to 'create' specific change technologies, such as Robbins' Neuro-Associative Conditioning (TM). The emphasis here is on making the pain of staying within the comfort zone more intense than the pain of leaving or expanding it. Other teachers, such as Tice in the *Investment in Excellence* and *Strategic Thinking for Strategic Planning* programs, place more emphasis on envisioning to induce **dissatisfaction** with the current situation or comfort zone.

Commitment

This has been called 'the essence of our growth' (Covey, 1992). The generally accepted view is expressed by Hopson and

Hough (1973): 'there can only be personal growth and career development if there is commitment.' Anthony Robbins (1988) also says that abiding success comes only with commitment.

PD writers have much to say about what commitment is, why it is important and how we can recognize it. Harry Alder (1994) distinguishes commitment to a goal from mere interest in it. But there may be degrees of commitment. Deciding to pursue a goal is a form of commitment, but being prepared to do whatever it takes to achieve it is clearly a more intense commitment.

Commitment is shown in a variety of ways, but above all in specific pieces of action. Progress comes from learning, committing and doing – in that order, says Covey. Self-help writers suggest that commitment is likely to be followed through when action is diaried – when, say, meetings are arranged with dates, times and venues all agreed. Commitment can also be shown (and strengthened) by making it public and by closing off all escape routes so that there can be no turning back. If we start a new job, or get into a new relationship with the idea, 'If this doesn't work out, then I can always ... ' then we have not fully committed.

A distinction is sometimes made between initial and sustained (or ongoing) commitment to plan a goal. Initital commitment will show itself in action, but ongoing commitment requires not only progress towards our goals but also, as Egan (1994) observes, moving forward again after failures. This relentless movement forward is what Colin Turner (1994) doubtless had in mind when he wrote that 'the instant you commit yourself to something is the instant you start achieving it.'

Strength of commitment appears to be related above all to three things: the perceived attractiveness of the goal or plan; understanding the **purpose** for committing to it; and ownership of it, which comes from an involvement in deciding or defining it. People rarely commit to goals or causes that other people impose upon them. Too often, as self-help specialists know well, people often fail to commit to their *own* goals; some of these specialists make a major issue of keeping the promises we make to ourselves (see **Contracting**).

In the last 30 or so years, a number of commentators have suggested that the problems many people have making commitments, or of 'willing' as the existentialist philosopher Rollo

May termed it in *Love and Will* (1970), is a symptom of a wide-spread modern neurosis. There is little hint of this belief in popular PD literature where the assumption is made that the individual can commit to virtually anything if he so chooses. Self-help writers supply some tips on **leverage** to lubricate the process.

Competence(ies)

Competence is about achieving successful results on a consistent basis in relation to a specific role or activity. It implies knowing what to do and knowing the factors to take into account. For example, communicative competence has to do with knowing the strategies that lead to successful **outcomes** in a range of communication situations. These would include establishing **rapport** and the ability to adapt the form and content of our 'messages' to the audience, our purposes and the constraints of the situation.

Some self-help books concentrate on techniques to enhance competence in relation to particular subjects, such as negotiation or making presentations. Others focus upon more general kinds of competence – the ability to switch into a resourceful state, for example, or to influence someone else's state. Nowadays, many training programs emphasize the outcomes that show competence rather than, say, the processes we experience. So completing a course successfully is more likely to mean demonstrating competence (ie, achievement of intended outcomes) than finding the course content absorbing or producing results that the trainers weren't looking for.

The notion of 'looked for' outcomes is basic to the current technical use of the term 'competence'. Burgoyne (1990) defines competence as 'the ability to perform a task', but the performance is usually judged in relation to the skills and/or standards set down by other people or bodies. In some situations, the onus is upon the individual to provide the evidence to demonstrate competence.

There has been much debate over the term 'competence' and related or equivalent terms. One distinction is between *areas of competence* which is a label for the areas of work or the roles at which the individual is competent, and *competency* or 'the dimensions of behaviour that lie behind competent performance' (Woodruffe, 1993). 'Staff management' would be an area of competence; 'sensitivity' would be an example of a competency. Some authorities (eg, Boak, 1991) prefer to distinguish between *skills* (the behaviours behind competencies) and *standards* (the performance levels expected of a competent person).

The competence movement clearly impacts upon personal development in relation to jobs and roles and training for them. Personal development can even be defined in competence terms, as can different levels of **development** or performance. A *novice*, someone who currently lacks competence, can be distinguished from an *effective performer*, who performs at a minimum or threshold level of competence, who in turn is distinguished from a *superior performer* who demonstrates **mastery** or **excellence** in the relevant competence.

From a user's point of view, competence frameworks (lists of competencies) can be useful. They tell the individual manager, for example, what competencies are considered relevant to his level of job. Individuals can assess themselves against the relevant competencies or receive **feedback** from assessors or appraisers in the light of them.

There are obvious parallels between the competence movement approach to improving the effectiveness of management (and other occupational roles) and the **NLP** process of **modelling**. Boak summarizes the aims of the former: 'to learn what qualities and skills are possessed by effective managers and then, through selection, training and development, put effective individuals in all key posts.' One difference between the two approaches is that NLP concentrates on excellent performers, whereas the competence approach tends to identify both highly effective and below standard performers. The assumption is that comparisons make it possible to identify the key aspects of competence which discriminate between effective and ineffective performers.

Competence is assessed by collecting evidence which demonstrates or supports claims to it. Methods include direct observation of actual jobs, tasks or simulated job tasks within an **assessment centre** context, and examining evidence assembled in a portfolio (see **Writing**).

One of the hot debates in the competence movement centres on whether or not some competemcies are generic or universal. Is it possible, for example, to identify a set of management competencies applicable to all managers in all positions in all kinds of organizations? Or are some competencies peculiar to, say, senior managers or to managers in particular kinds of organizations (eg, schools)? And if some competencies are generic, then how is progression to be defined? One response to this is that the competencies may be the same for managers at different levels, but that the contexts in which they are applied differ significantly.

Another distinction sometimes made is between what Esp (1993) calls 'underpinning' and 'overarching' competencies. The former are basic skills (literacy, numeracy, some IT skills, etc) that support competent performance. Overarching competencies include the capacities of learning from, adapting to, anticipating and creating changes.

All competencies, even technical ones, offer scope for personal development, but some competence frameworks focus specifically upon personal effectiveness. An example in the British context is the Management Charter Initiative framework called the Personal Competencies Model. This includes four clusters of personal competence: planning to optimize the achievement of results; managing others to optimize results; managing oneself to optimize results; and using intellect to optimize results. Linked to each of these are the discrete dimensions of the competence. The managing oneself cluster, for example, has the dimensions of: showing self-confidence and personal drive; managing personal learning and development; and managing personal emotions and stress. Each of these dimensions has its attached behavioural indicators, so individual managers can see what they need to do to demonstrate personal competence.

A number of reservations have been expressed about the competence approach to development and performance. Some critics say that it reduces real people to identikits or fragments, and complex roles to sets of discrete tasks. It can appear to be narrowly prescriptive, whereas in reality there may be many 'right' ways to achieve results.

The actual outcomes of behaviour may also be richer, more varied and less predictable than the expected, 'looked for' out-

comes. These may not be acknowledged. Similarly, some fundamental aspects of a role, including a person's **beliefs** and **values**,
may not be included in the framework. It has also been said that
the competence approach can make the measurable important
rather than the important measurable. What can't easily be
assessed (eg. **intuition, creativity**) may be ignored. A great deal
of knowledge tends also to underpin competence, and this
might not be assessed.

A quite different shortcoming of many competence frameworks is that they are designed for individuals whereas a great
many people actually work in teams. The collective competence
of the team may be the proper level of focus, unless the contributions of individuals to team performance can be assessed
with accuracy (see **Team Context**).

Finally, the competence approach is about being judged
against criteria determined by other people. This might be seen
as opposed to the idea that **self-acceptance** doesn't require validation by others using external criteria, but validation by oneself using personal criteria.

Congruence

The state in which the different parts of ourselves are in harmony and devoted to a common cause.

The 'parts' can be variously construed. At the most general
level, they are mind and body. This congruence has been
defined as 'that state of alignment when you believe in what
you are doing and your body and mind are working towards
your goal' (O'Connor and Prior, 1995). A rather more elaborate
(tripartite) system includes feelings – ie, mind, heart and body
(or behaviour). In **NLP**, the 'parts' tend to be the elements of the
neurological system including behaviour, beliefs and values in
relation to intentions. From the viewpoint of psychosynthesis,
internal incongruence is a condition arising from tussles
between our subpersonalities, those 'psychological satellites'
which coexist 'as a multiple of lives within the overall medium
of our personality' (Ferrucci, 1990). The metaphor of an '**inner
team**' of multiple personalities either pulling against one
another or working congruently has also been developed by
NLP specialists (see Alder, 1994).

Many common expressions suggest that getting our inner parts congruent is no easy matter. Doubts and uncertainties can be traced to the intellect ('I was in two minds'), the **emotions** ('My heart wasn't in it'), **beliefs** ('He doesn't believe in himself'), **values** and desire ('I didn't want it badly enough', 'It wasn't that important to her') and **goals** ('I didn't know what I wanted'). Ignoring or attempting to override the doubts that give rise to incongruence is rarely a sensible thing to do. It's more likely to lead to behaviour which sabotages rather than promotes **development**. Better to accept that one part of you is letting you know that it is not happy, that it can't go along with the majority verdict. As O'Connor and Seymour (1993) say, 'being able to detect incongruence in yourself will save you from making many mistakes.'

Congruence facilitates personal development and is the ideal state for which many people strive. It is often considered a prerequisite for peace of mind and sustained happiness, and for some psychotherapists and PD teachers, congruence is a sign of individual maturity. Myra Chave-Jones (1989) represents this view when she says that 'a well-balanced and mature human being has all his or her component parts – the mind, heart, will and body – informing one another and being regarded as of equal value.' Our development as learners is also greatly enhanced if we undertake activities that are congruent with our learning styles (see Honey and Mumford, 1986).

Few of us are entirely congruent all of the time. However, to live in a state of chronic incongruence, or to lack congruence in regard to major **outcomes** we seek in our lives, can seriously interfere with personal development and **well-being**. Incongruence makes it hard to make and follow-through with decisions and personal **action plans**. **Goals** are difficult to define precisely, let alone achieve, if they conflict with the interests of one or more of our parts. When a lack of congruence inside manifests itself as mismatch between what we say and our non-verbal behaviour, then it is difficult to establish and maintain **rapport**, trust and credence with other people. By contrast, congruence is the basis of **personal power**. Congruence produces synergy produces strength.

Finally, the term 'congruence' is used in more specific senses within particular systems or theories of personal development.

For example, within the personality theory of Carl Rogers and the form of non-directive therapy to which it is linked, 'congruence' is used to describe the state in which our potentialities (our inherent capacities) are consistent with our self (the conscious notion of who and what we are). This is the ideal state for moving towards self-**actualization** – for Rogers, the basic creative life force that accounts for our personal development activities.

Continuous Development (CD)

An approach or attitude to development, particularly within a workplace context, which emphasizes learning as a lifelong, self-directed activity.

CD is fast replacing the idea that managers or trainers 'know best', that employees have to have their training needs determined and provided for them by third parties. Where CD operates, 'each individual is encouraged and given resources to accept responsibility for their own learning as the job holder is seen as uniquely placed to understand their own learning needs' (Peel, 1992). CD acknowledges that needs may vary considerably even between people doing the same job. There are many variables, including perceptions of need and learning style preferences.

CD stands in contrast to the intermittent learning associated with occasional doses of training. Employees in CD contexts may still opt to go on courses or meet their needs through other standard staff development practices, but the choice is theirs. Most learning is likely to be work-related. For example, it may result from solving a workplace problem or taking on a new role within a self-directed team or anticipating the skills that may be required for a future role. Learning is integral to work.

It is not hard to see why CD is in the ascendant. At a social level, 'people are less willing than they were to accept authority unquestioningly and more willing to be responsible for themselves' (Wood, 1988). Within organizations, the pace and extent of change can make it virtually impossible to meet individual development needs through a centrally organized training program. And organizations themselves can survive only if their employees are able to respond effectively to new situations and challenges. 'The CD process helps individuals to develop, and this helps the organization to achieve its objectives, through the intimate association of improved learning and improved performance' (Wood, 1988). CD is clearly consistent with the philosophy of the so-called Learning Organization. Indeed, one definition of the Learning Organization is: 'Creating an environment where the behaviours and practices involved in continuous development are actively encouraged' (in Mumford, 1993). It is also related to the continuous improvement objectives of organizations that put Total Quality Management into practice.

It is debatable whether CD is the same thing as personal development. In work-place situations, CD is not a clarion call or **challenge** to experience personal growth, though it is an experience-based approach to learning that may have consequences for growth. However, asking ourselves regularly what we are going to keep and what we are going to change in our lives is clearly a CD process linked to the desire for improvement.

(See **Career Development; Personal Development Planning**.)

Contracting

Making an agreement with ourselves or someone else based upon a decision. In PD contexts, that agreement can be with ourselves and usually involves a decision about making a change or committing to a PD programme.

Self-contracting is consistent with the philosophy that underpins many books on personal change in which the fundamental message is that we have to take care of ourselves before we can do the same for others. (The **transactional analysis** term for this is 'self-reparenting'.) Contracting has been called 'a vital career and life management skill' (Hopson and Scally, 1991) that can enable us to clarify our objectives, explore alternatives, make **choices** and follow through with our commitments. It is a psychological contract so it doesn't have to be formalized in **writing**, though many advocates insist that the more a contract looks like a semi-legal document, the more seriously we will take it. Contracts for personal development purposes usually consist of questions and answers; the latter are always the individual's, though the process can include another party – therapist, adviser, teacher etc. Informal contracting is commonplace in counsellor-client relationships, though some counsellors prefer a less legal-sounding term. Egan (1994) suggests 'working charter'. A 'learning contract' has also been seen as an ideal way of managing a productive relationship within a **mentoring** context. 'The person being mentored writes down his or her aims, what he or she hopes to achieve, and the specific, practical advantages he or she hopes to make' (Cunningham, 1992). Some employers require staff to agree to a learning contract as part of a training and development package; and a number of self-help books and programs 'invite' their readers/participants to make a contract agreeing to complete the exercises set and commit to the **goals** set. However, as Egan has noted, no contract can be perfect and some people insert their own 'covert codicils' as get-out clauses! (See **Commitment; Personal Development Planning**.)

Core Skills

Key skills common to many jobs or roles, as opposed to skills peculiar to specific jobs or roles. Giving aircraft pilots landing instructions is a skill distinct to air traffic controllers, but communication is a skill required in nearly all occupations and social roles. Other skills currently considered to be core skills include problem solving, improving learning and performance, working with others, applying number and information technology. In Britain, core skills are being built into and promoted through a range of learning programs and examination courses for students in schools and colleges. However, they are likely to be present in more learning programs, academic as well as vocational, and experienced through informal, personal and social learning as well as through formal education.

In vocationally-oriented courses, students are expected to demonstrate through evidence that they have acquired core skills. Core skills may provide the basis for developing more specific technical skills, such as IT skills relevant to a particular job.

Given that core skills are fundamental, have wide application and are generally considered necessary for functioning effectively in contemporary society, it can be argued that they make a significant contribution to personal development. Significantly, considerable emphasis is given to four core skills (communication, problem solving, improving our learning performance and working with others) in the Open University course *A Portfolio Approach to Personal and Career Development*. (See **Competence(s)**.)

Counselling

A process of helping others to help themselves. For the client, it is 'an opportunity to explore, discover and clarify ways to live more resourcefully and towards greater well-being' (BAC, 1991). Counselling is also defined as the process of helping others 'develop programs for constructive change' (Egan, 1994) and attain 'a higher stage of personal competence' (Hopson, 1986).

Some forms of counselling are largely reactive and 'crisis'-centred. That is, the focus is mainly confined to the presenting problem, and the client's stock of concepts and skills is not significantly expanded by the experience. However, counselling can, and nowadays often does, have a much more developmental emphasis – as the above definitions suggest. The supposition which supports this emphasis is that many of us have considerable resources which we are under-using, and that a skilled other can be as valuable in helping us to develop our resources and opportunities for growth as in helping us to sort out our immediate problems. It's another contemporary demonstration of the idea that we don't have to be ill to get better.

A still unusual but excellent example of positive development counselling is the guidance sought by some pre-marital and newly-wed couples. The purpose is not to find out how to assuage suffering or 'mend' a broken relationship, but rather to receive guidance on maintaining happiness. Leslie Cameron-Bandler (1985) poignantly describes this kind of counselling as an 'uncommon, joyful experience'.

In development counselling generally, helpers are likely to assist their clients to: sort out their thoughts and feelings, and perhaps their **values**; define the dimensions of the **challenges** they face and the options open to them; set their **goals**; and take action to move them forward. Counsellors also help clients to appreciate the opportunities available to them and to recognize that they have **life skills** and coping skills that can be built upon. Development counsellors want their clients to be capable of taking full **responsibility** for their own destinies. At its most positive, development counselling is a substantial learning experience – including, on occasions, for the counsellor as well. Indeed, a contemporary theme in counselling literature is the personal development of the helper. Dryden and Feltham (1994) argue that counsellors need to follow the lead of psychotherapists in undergoing 'personal therapy' (ie, counselling) themselves, partly to experience and thus gain insights into the client's role, and partly to understand themselves better, among other reasons.

Although counselling has become a professional, institutionalized activity, virtually any of us can assume an informal counselling role for work colleagues, friends and family members. Some professional counsellors are happy not only to acknowledge this but also to demystify the phenomenon that counselling has become. Hopson (1986) for example, makes it clear that counselling skills do not constitute a separate group of skills but are 'what people use to help people to help themselves'.

Creativity

Within the context of PD, creativity is primarily about using our own psychological and emotional resources to produce results, bring about **change** and find unusual or high quality solutions to problems. PD is very much a creative enterprise, and 'create' is a favourite word of PD writers. We read about 'creating our own reality', 'creating future scenarios', 'creating a sense of urgency' and so forth. The dominant metaphors in contemporary PD are that we are the authors, artists, designers and makers of our lives, ourselves and our subjective experiences.

'Creativity' and 'development' share a common vocabulary (eg, 'insight', 'intuition') and a common theoretical base.

Nowadays, creativity, like personal development, is thought to owe more to cognition than to chance or divine inspiration. David Perkins (1981), a leading theorist on creativity, writes: 'Creating concerns what we do with our abilities. Any normal person can be creative in terms of whatever abilities he or she has or can acquire.' Similarly, Jane Henry (1991) hypothesizes that 'creative action is not so much a *personality trait* as a *state of mind* which can be learnt.' These views exactly parallel the dominant view in PD that we all have the mental resources we need to bring about the results we want. The critical factors are belief, knowledge and application. We need to know that we have creative resources and how to use them effectively. And we need to use them in reality. Hence, much PD literature offers us the technologies to make best use of our creative capabilities, including creative **visualization**, the creative use of **questions**, **mind mapping** and the deliberate use of metaphorical thinking. Meditative and 'passive' methods, sitting still, alone and in silence for some time, for example, can also be highly creative. Many **NLP** technologies, such as **reframing** and working with submodalities, are also creative and exploit the mind's natural creativity.

The cognitive approach to creativity, which suggests that creativity can be explained in terms of normal cognitive processes such as recognition, understanding and insight, fits in well with brain-based approaches to learning and development. A specific example would be the NLP technique of 'creative synthesis' which uses some of the cognitive processes of insight (selective combining and synthesizing information) in bringing together **modelling** and visualization to solve a problem or develop a skill. In general terms, if creativity is just another name for making effective use of cognitive processes, then what Patrick Porter (1993) terms 'Controlled Creativity' – the ability to turn on creativity whenever it is needed – must be a strong possibility.

Another popular explanation of creativity, the theory that the **association** of ideas is fundamental to mental life and learning, also links strongly with PD technologies. It justifies divergent thinking techniques such as lateral thinking and brainstorming, used to solve problems and generate ideas or options. Moreover, the conscious association of pain or pleasure to the things we wish to change, and other examples of self-conditioning that work by creating new neural associations, are now established techniques for personal change.

The structure of creativity may also parallel the structure of self-development. A four-stage model of the creative process was suggested by Wallas (1926). 'Preparation', including information gathering, preceded an 'incubation' stage in which the problem was not consciously addressed. During the 'illumination' stage there is an initial insight into the solution which is carried forward and tested out in the 'verification' stage. This model can be and has been applied to problem-solving and goal-setting in PD contexts. In part, it involves defining a goal or problem then handing it over to the creative part of the **subconscious** which will either suggest a solution or way forward to the conscious mind or else lead us to 'see' **opportunities**. (Relevant here is Louis Pasteur's comment that 'Chance favours only the prepared mind'!)

Not surprisingly, the characteristics ascribed to people who seem most creative are similar to those which seem to characterize committed self-developers. These include independent thinking, acceptance of ambiguity, flexibility, optimism and confidence, verbal fluency and curiosity. Creative people also 'appear comfortable with risk taking, are open to new experiences and exhibit a high degree of perseverance and discipline' (Henry, 1991). Similarly, the common barriers to being creative are similar to the barriers to personal development. They include fears (of failure and making mistakes), rigid habits, self-defeating behaviours, an overriding concern with feeling secure and relatively poor control over the mind and its resources (see Adams, 1974; Egan, 1994).

Finally, some therapies for **healing** and **development** are themselves creative, such as art therapy which encourages self-expressive creativity. However, all forms of therapy and **counselling** require creative approaches on the part of helpers as well as clients, if only so that helpers can find creative ways of assisting clients to be more creative themselves. Which brings us back to the very close relationship between creativity and development.

Current Reality

The way we perceive ourselves and our situation to be at the present time.

From a PD perspective there are two universal **beliefs** here. One is that current reality is never the way things have to be. We are not fixed-for-ever entities. Only the timescales over which current reality can be changed would be in dispute. The other belief is that current reality is not a set of objective facts. At most, it's a set of perceived facts or images. In other words, we play a part in creating or constructing 'reality', including reality as we currently experience it. The extreme position is that we are whatever we consistently think about, and that we can bring about a different reality in part by changing the **focus** of our thinking. The only major constraint is our self-belief system. If we can see ourselves being or doing something, then we can make it a reality. If we cannot convincingly 'sell it' to ourselves, then we probably cannot realize it in practice.

The concept of current reality is important because it stands in contrast to future 'reality' or to our **vision** of what we want to be. Much PD coaching is about getting us in the right frame of mind to close the 'gap' between our perceived present and our preferred future. It's about making us feel motivated rather than dispirited by the gap, and about giving us the beliefs, skills and strategies to close it.

Where PD coaches disagree is on the question of how much attention we should give to our current reality. One view is that it is psychologically healthy to confront or at least acknowledge those aspects of ourselves that we wish to change. An associated position is that we can only plan sensibly for change if we have accurate, detailed information about ourselves at the present time. A quite different argument for taking a good look at our current situation is that this can generate so much **dissatisfaction** in us that it gives us the **leverage** we need to bring about change. This is particularly the case if we look at current reality from the perspective of our preferred future – rather like looking at the plateau we are stuck on from the peak we hope to reach.

An opposing viewpoint is that dwelling on current reality serves only to keep us locked in it. It reinforces the very representations of reality we wish to alter, and may make us feel so overwhelmed by our present plight that we are unable to take **action** to change it. The better strategy, it is argued, is to bring the preferred future into the present – to act as if it were here already (see **Acting 'As If'**). (Hence, the advice to state affirmations positively in the present tense.) We should say to ourselves, for example, not 'I feel lousy but I hope to feel excited soon', but rather 'I feel really excited about the day ahead!' In theory, that's how we should very soon feel.

What is certain is that the relationship in our minds between current reality and our future **vision** is a very crucial one for our **development**. Almost certainly our images of the latter need to be stronger than those of the former if we are to achieve our development **goals**.

Decision-Making

This is a major topic in PD, reflecting the widespread assumption that our lives are determined by the decisions we make or allow others to make for us. We are not always required to make decisions, but we cannot escape the consequences of not making them. The other widespread assumption is that we can (and should) all learn to be more effective decision-makers.

There is general agreement about a number of matters, including the following:

- A good decision is one we make ourselves. It is important to accept **responsibility** for the decisions we make. Accepting responsibility tends to make us less tense about making them and less angry when things go 'wrong'.
- Deciding is not enough: we must commit and follow through. **Commitment** is crucial.
- Commitment shows itself in **action**, in blocking up escape routes ('I can always go back to my old job if this doesn't work out' is *not* commitment) and in a refusal to countenance any possibility of not following through.
- Commitment is easier when **values** as well as **goals** are **congruent** with the decision made, when the decision feels right at the deepest level, when **self-talk** is consistent and constructive and when we do not take decision-making *too* seriously, whatever the decision may be about.
- The very act of deciding makes things start to happen.
- The more decisions we make, the easier deciding becomes and the better we get at making decisions. Some writers use a muscle analogy: the more we use it, the stronger it gets.
- We've got to be prepared to make 'poor' decisions before we

can become proficient at making 'good' ones.

- Being able to make decisions quickly and effortlessly is generally a good sign. In most cases, we do not make better quality decisions just because we've taken more time to reach them. Being decisive *is* different, and *feels* different, from being impulsive. The latter may feel right at an initial, surface level, but may not be consistent with our deeper feelings.
- Indecision results mainly from a lack of self-trust, a lack of clarity about key values, a mismatch between goals and values and a fear of making mistakes. The latter can include fear of the consequences which flow from 'good' as well as from 'bad' decisions.
- Ideally, if paradoxically, commitment should go hand-in-hand with flexibility. We need to feel sure when we make a decision but still be willing to think again if something inside us tells us we should.
- Effective decision-makers are not tormented by the process, and may even enjoy it.
- Decisions made by the subconscious or in what Schwartz (1959) called 'managed solitude' tend to be right for us.

When it comes to models of decision-making, there is more diversity of opinion. Different writers have different preferred approaches, though the rational model is rarely one of them. This is the approach that assumes a logical, linear set of steps, which usually includes defining the 'problem', generating options, gathering relevant information, analysing it, making a considered choice, implementing it, then monitoring and evaluating the results. The rational approach can be useful as a frame of reference, which is how professional helpers tend to use it with their clients, but it rarely describes what we actually do when we try to make decisions. Taking a rational approach isn't 'sexy', and may not even be an effective model, even for those willing to follow it.

The **NLP** approach is to find out how we as individuals make decisions and then, if our procedure doesn't get good results, suggest a new program to run in our heads. For example, if our 'problem' seems to be that we are not generating sufficient options from which to select, then a program might be installed to allow us to visualize new as opposed to only remembered possibilities. If our 'problem' is not so much a lack of creativity as a tendency to select any option at random, then we might be given a program which demands that we consider each option in turn, evaluate them and then select the first option that makes us feel good about it.

Perhaps the main point of difference in the suggested approaches to making decisions concerns the importance of **outcomes**. Most approaches have emphasized outcomes - the consequences of making a 'poor' decision in particular, and hence the importance of trying to predict outcomes. Some writers even suggest using a balance sheet for assessing the likely gains and losses (Irving and Mann, 1977; Nelson-Jones, 1989). This approach reflects a right/wrong view of decisions (or at least a view that some are 'more right' than others!) and emphasizes the need to anticipate setbacks and difficulties.

Opposed to this approach is the one which emphasizes opportunities. Susan Jeffers (1991) is one of the better known champions of this view. The focus here is upon the opportunities for experience, learning and growth to which any decision gives access. If we choose Path A rather than Path B, then we may end up with a smaller salary, but that is of less consequence perceptually than what we might learn in the process. Jeffers refers to this as the No-Lose Model. There is no 'right' or 'wrong' decision. There are only alternative paths and 'each is strewn with opportunities – *despite the outcome'*.

A related point of difference concerns the importance of having an action plan to implement the decision. Rationalists and those who emphasize outcomes tend to advocate plans to make them happen and to deal with expected difficulties. Those who stress opportunities are less hung up on planning which they associate with the angst of trying to control the future and avoid 'mistakes'. PD tutors like Jeffers think in terms of 'goodies' (her word) not mistakes. They trust that the 'hows' will disclose themselves if the decision is followed through with commitment. 'Trust in yourself, then trust in the future' might be the motto here.

(See **Choices**.)

Deficit (model)

Any approach to personal **development** which construes it as a process of 'making good' rather than 'building upon'.

The starting point for improvement is the question: 'What is lacking here?' An example would be a training program which set out to highlight and then remedy the 'deficiencies' of those concerned.

Opposed to the deficit model is the *growth* model, neatly summed up by the expression, 'You don't have to be ill to get better'. In most of the fields concerned with personal development, the emphasis today is very much upon growth. **NLP** psychosynthesis, good job appraisal schemes and most healing therapies all share both an underpinning conviction that we already have the resources and **potential** for development, and a belief that we get whatever we **focus** upon. Focusing upon our potential for wholeness, say, is very different from focusing upon our 'brokenness'. NLP advocates focus upon our psychic resources, and castigate some traditional psychotherapies for emphasizing psychic disorders.

There is some hard evidence that playing to our strengths is actually more productive than working on our weaknesses. Follow-up studies of people who have been through **assessment centres** indicate that they make more progress in their 'strong' than their 'weak' **competencies**. That is, we tend to get better at what we are already good at, and continue to do less well at what we found difficult to start with.

Deletion

The process of blocking out some potential experiences so that we can **focus** upon others.

Because the conscious mind can attend to only a limited amount of information at any one time, it is necessary for the brain and nervous system to screen out much of the sensory data available to us. In other words, our experiences of the world are highly selective. The nature and quality of our experiences depend upon what we select and what we delete.

In effect, most courses in personal development provide an

education in deletion. We learn to recognize the factors most critical in determining what we select and delete (eg, our **beliefs**, priorities and **goals**) and to consider whether they are currently serving our interests – empowering or disempowering us, for example. We learn consciously to delete to our advantage, focusing upon the things that help us feel good, inspire us etc, and screening out the things that don't help us. Deletion is a major process in self-**programming**. When deletion becomes a discipline we call it **meditation**.

Another important area of deletion education is language. In language, deletion is the process of leaving out at the surface level, the level of utterance, some of the words and meanings represented in the underlying structure. For example, 'Their relationship broke up' deletes any reference to the agents who brought about the breaking up. Our use of deleted, simplified language structures has enormous implications for our communication and interpersonal relationships. An education in deletion helps us to recognize deletions (ours and others') and to notice how they affect our perceptions and feelings, and the extent to which we can share our experiences and representations of reality with other people.
(See **Meta Model**.)

Development (personal)

The process of experiencing and perceiving personally meaningful change.

This definition may be neither particularly helpful nor particularly contentious. Every PD tutor would acknowledge that development involves **change**, and most would accept that change is inevitable and generally to be welcomed. The majority would also concur with the following propositions:

- Each of us can shape our development to a significant degree. Our environment is never fully determining.
- We are individually responsible for initiating and managing the bulk of experiences through which we develop.
- Although we can benefit vicariously from other people's experiences, we can develop only through engaging *internally* with our own experiences.

- Development is a process, not just a 'product' such as reaching a goal or destination. The process may occur in spurts but it is rarely 'one off'.
- 'No growth' is not a tenable option. As George Land (1986) puts it: either we grow qualitatively speaking or we die psychologically speaking.
- Much of what we need *to* develop, and much of what we need *in order* to develop, we already have.

There is also general agreement about some of the main requirements or conditions for personal development. They include the following:

- Some level of **self-awareness** and **self-acceptance**, though development can also foster both. To elaborate crudely: self-awareness without self-acceptance is self-condemnation; self-acceptance without self-awareness is denial. Neither condition augurs well for growth.
- A willingness to accept full personal **responsibility** for growth (or the lack of it).
- A willingness to commit to and take appropriate action. 'Development' does *not* mean 'having an intellectual understanding of development'.

There are doubtless other requirements for development. For M Scott Peck (1990) the acceptance of death is one, without whose 'wise counsel' we cannot know how best to use our time. But there is no way of establishing whether there is general recognition of this and other specific requirements.

In reality, personal development is construed differently by different authorities, depending on their perspectives and interests. A management consultant specializing in personal development training is unlikely to view development in quite the same ways as a motivational speaker, a psychotherapist or someone who might accept the label 'New Age seeker'. It's not always easy to see where the common ground lies between people who would all regard themselves as experts in the PD field. And yet, it is neither easy nor valid to categorize or, worse still, polarize them, and creative partnerships can and have taken place (eg, between NLPers and psychotherapists, and between meditation teachers and 'brain scientists'). Identifying some differences in emphasis is one way forward.

One such difference regards the number of areas of development considered. In theory, most PD authorities would agree that we develop along many dimensions, including the physical, mental, emotional and social. In reality, though, many approaches are anything but holistic or multi-faceted. Some ignore or dismiss the spiritual dimension; for others, it is the most important dimension of all. Some approaches have a largely cognitive focus, some are emotion-dominant. Some virtually ignore the body, others see body and mind as inseparable and equal.

Another major difference of emphasis is between *being* and *becoming*. 'Being' approaches rest on values relating to the **here and now** and to wholeness. Development is more likely to be related to *fulfilment* (feeling 'full' as a person) than to **success**. The priority is knowing ourselves – or reconnecting with ourselves. From a 'becoming' perspective, development is more likely to be construed as a *making* than as a *knowing* process – ie, as a cumulative process of gaining more skills, attaining more goals, and generally 'adding' to ourselves and our lives. Key values include **excellence** and success.

Generally speaking, the distinction between being and becoming correlates with the distinction between a multi-dimensional view of the person and an ego-dominant view. Many popular PD programs assume a unitary, conscious self. But at least some approaches accept that there is much more to each of us than the conscious self that we present to ourselves and the world. Development, indeed, involves exploring and confronting the many layers of the self, some of them shadowy. If we take this view, then we are unlikely to feel comfortable with a rational model of development (eg, **Aspire**) which implies a straightforward linear process centred on the ego. We are also likely to construe behaviours which seem to sabotage our development as indicators that some parts of ourselves are unhappy with the way things are rather than as troublesome behaviours to overcome.

Virtually all approaches to personal development acknowledge the central importance of the mind or psyche. What characterizes particular approaches is what they highlight additionally. On this basis, we can identify broad differences of emphasis within the PD field without pretending that it can be cut up into discrete plots.

One area of emphasis might be termed *psychoneurological*, because of its emphasis upon the 'hardware' of the brain, or *psychotechnological*, because of its focus upon the 'software' of techniques and strategies that we can run on it. **NLP, accelerated learning, timeline** therapy and probably hypnotherapy and some cognitive therapies would be included here. Development is construed mainly as a matter of neurological mastery – discovering and learning to control the many capabilities of the brain. The benefits of this may be far more than cerebral, and might include **state management**, improved interpersonal relationships, **healing** and many others besides.

Another label might be *psychosocial*. The emphasis here is as much upon the growth of *inter*personal as upon *intra*personal effectiveness. For at least some PD tutors, personal development is always in part *inter*personal development. That is, we cannot know ourselves except in relation to other people or, as Karen Hanson (1986) puts it: 'recognition of self requires recognition of others.' Development is construed partly as a matter of understanding ourselves as social beings and becoming effective in the world, and partly as a matter of realizing our **potential** as individuals. In both cases, it's about 'getting better' as a person – becoming more competent, empowered, efficacious, more capable of making choices and more willing to accept **responsibility** for our lives. The emphasis may also be on success and achievement, and the techniques of the psychotechnologies may be employed to this end. Processes such as goal-setting and planning are seen as important.

The term 'psychosocial' might be used to cover a disparate range of PD related activities including **transactional analysis, counselling, success** programs, **personal development planning, life skills** programs and most books that offer guidance on improving our relationships and taking charge of our lives.

A third area of emphasis is the *psychospiritual*. A major assumption here is that an exclusively psychological view of the person is inadequate and impoverished. We are 'whole', and our wholeness includes a spiritual dimension. Indeed, this dimension is paramount. Development is construed in terms of recovering or enhancing our wholeness, becoming more fully integrated as a person and more fully aware of our whole being, not just our ego. Growth might also include an expansion of consciousness on the path of **enlightenment**. In terms of the communication processes involved in development, the emphasis is upon the *intra*personal and the *trans*personal. 'Living in the flow' and seeking truths will be more important than striving after success. Expressions of the *psychospiritual* within mainstream PD include the declaration by M Scott Peck (1990) that 'the growth of the human spirit is the end of human existence', and the statement of the Borysenkos (1995) that 'our task as human beings is to discover and live from that place of wholeness.' Psychospiritual approaches include psychosynthesis, transpersonal psychology, the enlightenment technologies and many New Age interests.

A fourth area is what might be termed the *psychophysiological*, although it is integral to some psychospiritual approaches and associated with other approaches, including NLP. The emphasis here is upon the partnership of mind and body. Development is construed in terms of greater 'mind/body' awareness, with all the benefits which flow from this. Examples of psychophysiological approaches would be yoga, the martial arts and many **body awareness** and healing disciplines.

Some definitions of development cut across at least some of these areas of emphasis. One of the most dominant concerns 'taking charge'. This rests on a number of assumptions: that development might not happen if left to chance and circumstances; that it ought to be volitional and purposeful; that we *can* take charge of it because we have the mental and other resources to do so; and we *must* take charge to ensure that other people don't direct our lives in line with their interests.

'Taking charge' can represent a philosophy of **personal power**, but it can also be motivated by fear and anxiety. A number of PD tutors who write from personal experience see taking charge as an insurance policy against being hurt or let down by other people. It can be motivated by harsh economic as well as emotional realities – the need to remain marketable. As Holbeche (1995) puts it: 'Personal development is the key way in which employees can guarantee their continued employability in an uncertain market.'

A variant of the 'taking charge' definition is the self-help definition, also very common in current PD. Margaret Caldwell (1995) presents it from a provider's perspective: 'Personal development is about helping people to help themselves.' From the 'receiver's' or 'self-provider's' viewpoint, it is about becoming more effective at helping ourselves.

Another way of defining development that fits well with much current thinking is in terms of improving the quality of our personal, interpersonal and, perhaps, transpersonal experiences by improving the quality of our self-communication. This would include greater self-awareness, better state management and improving the use and control of our thinking and self-talk.

Another definition that would secure widespread agreement would be about decreasing or eliminating the 'have tos' in life and increasing the 'choose tos' and 'want tos'.

There is no shortage of theories of human development. We can find plenty of them in any decent book on Adult Development (AD), but they don't help us much when it comes to understanding 'development' in PD contexts. AD and PD are not the same thing. AD is a branch of developmental psychology (enriched by perspectives from other disciplines such as medicine and sociology) concerned with identifying and making sense of the life changes of adults in general. Some AD theorists (eg, Jane Loevinger, 1976) suggest that our development is characterized by increasingly mature ways of thinking and making sense of experience. Other AD theorists suggest that our lives are paced by predictable life events (eg, the impetus to establish social roles). They look for discernible age-related stages, variants of Shakespeare's Seven Ages of Man. For example, David Levinson (1978) suggests four stable periods with transitions in between them.

AD models have been used to formulate staff development programs (see Oja, 1989), and AD and PD share topics of common interest – **self-efficacy** and **self-esteem**, for example. Doubtless, AD has potentially much to contribute to PD, while PD might productively challenge AD models. Currently, however, there is little evidence to suggest any significant degree of intercourse between the two areas.

In the main, PD programs are not informed or underpinned by explicit AD theories. In fact, PD tutors tend to work from a very different set of assumptions from AD authorities. Most PD books and programs are pitched at adults in general, and so variables such as age, life stage, social setting and gender are largely immaterial. There are exceptions on both sides. Some AD theorists (eg, Neugarten, 1987) believe that age has little relevance, while some PD programs are customized for particular cohorts - 'mid-lifers' reviewing their futures, for example, or materials pitched only at men or at women.

PD tutors have different interests from AD theorists. They are less concerned with general patterns of change or behaviour than with offering prescriptions or guidance on intentional, volitional, personally-initiated and enhancing change. Many PD books offer bootstrap programs for personally meaningful change. AD has important practical applications (eg, within the caring professions) but it is not practical or advocative in the ways in which PD programs are.

Semantics may offer no more help than Adult Development in clarifying 'development' in PD contexts. In theory, we could distinguish nicely between 'development' and 'growth', but PD tutors do not make a consistent distinction between them. We could also distinguish between 'development' and 'improvement', reserving the latter for qualitatively progressive development of 'getting better' forms of change. (Some forms of change – trying out a new lifestyle, for example – might be developmental without being improving). In reality, the distinction is not consistently maintained in the literature.

This is not to say that the world of PD is linguistically homogenous. The different areas of emphasis identified earlier are not discrete enough to have their own 'community' languages, but they do have some linguistic peculiarities. Words like 'mastery', 'state management' and the technical terms of NLP distinguish the psychotechnologies. A quite different set of terms ('reconnecting', 'shifting', 'moving', 'unblocking', etc) characterizes approaches which emphasize mind/body/emotion links. Development can translate to 'healing' in some PD contexts.

We started by defining 'development' as 'personally meaningful change'. The word 'personally' is clearly critical. If we use other people's indicators of development, then they have to make sense to us. If we 'devise' our own, then there is no limit

to the number of possible ways by which we can define personal development: becoming more self-reliant; feeling generally
more alive; not feeling 'something missing' in life; being able to
feel good at will; having more love for ourselves and others;
being able to solve more and bigger problems; being able to
stand up for ourselves at work – the list of indicators of success
criteria is endless.

If we accept the view that all gain involves loss (see Lessem,
1987; Cooper, 1991), then some of our indicators may legitimately be less than positive. Needless to say, the tenor of PD
programs is overwhelmingly positive: development is seen as a
very 'good thing' indeed.

Disidentification

The conscious process by which we distance ourselves from old
habits, concepts, **beliefs** and self-images. In psychosynthesis, it
is the process of detaching ourselves from a subpersonality and
observing it from the 'outside'.

Identification is the process by which I come to sense that I
and aspects of my consciousness are one and the same. I come
to believe that I *am* my back pain, my habit of apologizing, my
harsh critic subpersonality, my socialist beliefs, etc. As Ferrucci
(1990) points out, this is an illusion, but it may take a process of
heightened **self-awareness** to shatter it.

Disidentification is frequently an important stage in personal
change. Syer and Connolly (1991) place it after *awareness* and
before **reframing** in their strategy for **change**, and see it as a necessary but not sufficient process for personal change. 'By
disidentifying from the old, you prepare the ground for experiencing the new.'

PD tutors may help us to disidentify by, for example, helping
us to gain insights into ourselves or see that we have the
resources to manage change. They may also give us techniques,
such as verbal disidentifiers ('I am not X') and **mental rehearsal**,
but only we can actually bring about disidentification.

Dissatisfaction

A force for personal **change**, sometimes a necessary one. We tend not to change unless we are frustrated with the current situation. Hence, many success and development programs set out to induce or intensify our dissatisfaction. The **focus** can be on the pain of the present or the anticipated pleasure of the desired future. A focus on both at more or less the same time can be especially powerful because the perceived discrepancy between what we have and what we want can amplify the dissatisfaction and activate our creative energies to find a way forward.

Dissatisfaction can be negative. Hill and Stone (1960) distinguish between 'negative' and 'inspirational' dissatisfaction. The former is turned into the latter by a positive mental **attitude**, which in turn makes success more likely. Perhaps 'productive dissatisfaction' would be more precise than 'inspirational dissatisfaction', for it is *action* as well as a positive attitude that brings about change. An example of productive dissatisfaction would be the process of **disidentification**.

Ecology

In PD terms, ecology concerns the ways in which any new **development** activity we undertake connects with and has possible consequences for many other things in our lives. Ecology implies systematic thinking. We see ourselves as made up of interrelated parts, and we see ourselves in relation to our social environments in terms of complex webs of interconnections. A change to one component within these systems is likely to have effects for other components, only some of which may be obvious and predictable. One of the more obvious effects is displacement. If, for example, we choose to do a course in our leisure time, this will clearly displace other activities (we might watch less television, for example) but it may also have an emotionally displacing effect on family members if they feel put out by our decision. If, as a result of the course, we develop, say, greater self-confidence, then this may alter the way we relate to ourselves as well as to other people. If one of our subpersonalities 'grows', then this might alter the dynamics of the whole **inner team** of subpersonalities, as well as having implications for the dynamics of our family and work teams, for example.

How we distribute our energies is clearly a critical factor in ecological terms. For some of us, development means spreading our energies more widely (if, for example, we see our 'problem' as narrow specialization or workaholism), while for others it may be channelling our energies in a more focused way. PD tutors suggest that whenever we make a decision about our development, particularly about an outcome we wish to pursue, then we should carry out an *ecology check*. That is, we should ask ourselves a range of questions to determine the nature and significance of the consequences that our decision is likely to have. Sometimes, the consequences we foresee may be unacceptable

to us, in which case we then need to think again.
(See **Decision-Making**.)

Emotions/Emotional Development

There is general agreement in PD that emotions are subjective feeling states related not to external events but rather to our evaluations of them. Our feelings reflect what is going on in our minds in relation to the things that most concern us. For example, we do not get upset because someone shouts at us. We get upset because of the meaning we give to their shouting, because we allow ourselves to feel upset and because we choose to **focus** on the shouting rather than upon something else.

These assumptions run counter to those with which many of us operate, but PD books and programs tend to be based upon them. This is true of general PD programs which include an emotions element, specific programs with an emotions dimension, such as assertion training courses (eg, Hare, 1988) and programs exclusively devoted to emotions (eg, Chave-Jones, 1989; Sutherland, 1993).

PD programs which deal with emotions vary in emphasis. **NLP** approaches emphasize emotional control or **state management**; using our brains to get the feelings we want at the required intensity. Programs rooted in psychotherapy emphasize emotional development or emotional 'literacy', including getting to understand and distinguish between emotions, and expressing how we feel, often with attention to our personal histories.

The following are among the more important recurring themes on emotions in relation to personal development. Some are universally accepted; others are more approach specific.

- Emotions are massively important to us. They enrich our interactions, facilitate communication, prepare us to act, give us pleasure and enhance our **well-being**. If we do the 'wrong' things with them, they can also torture and disable us in many ways. Some PD mentors contend that our emotions determine the quality of our lives and that what each of us seeks is a particular set of feelings to enjoy on a consistent or at-will basis. We may *think* that what we want is a big car or a top job or a successful relationship, but what we *really* want are the feelings we associate with these things.

- We should neither submit to nor dismiss our emotions. Giving into emotions indiscriminately can make us feel good at the time, but it can also spell disaster if it happens consistently. We can't learn anything from an emotion if we give into it unthinkingly; nor can we find a better way to utilize it. We need to educate and be educated by our emotions. That means allowing ourselves to experience them, listen to them, discriminate between them, acknowledge them and then choose what, if anything, to do with them beyond this. Ignoring, disparaging or suppressing emotions can be even more damaging. As one writer puts it: 'buried feelings are buried alive' (Hare, 1988). It is often appropriate and sufficient to acknowledge a feeling and then withdraw attention from it.

- Developing as a person means experiencing and accepting the full range of emotions, allowing them to flow through us and acknowledging even those that we might prefer not to have. Resisting an emotion or feeling guilty because we are experiencing one thing (sadness) when we 'should', we think, be feeling another (happiness) consumes valuable psychic energy. It is also counterproductive, because when we resist an emotion it tends to fight back and so persists. Moreover, we cannot hope to come to terms with, let alone master, an emotion that we refuse even to acknowledge. Acknowledging an emotion can sometimes weaken it.

- The better we understand our own emotions and ourselves as emotional beings, the better our chances of understanding the emotions of other people.

- Understanding our emotions, including those which trouble us, offers huge **potential** for personal growth.

- Although emotions are morally neutral, neither 'good' nor 'bad', some are disabling and disempowering and we need to develop strategies to modulate from these to more empowering emotions. For example, we need to have the choice of moving from a state of disappointment or despondency to a state in which we feel positive and productive.

- To a significant degree, we are responsible for how we feel.

We choose how we feel or, at least, we can learn to decide how we feel by learning to control our minds, since it is easier to manage our feelings by managing our thinking than by working on feelings directly. Emotional management and **mastery** involve various techniques: controlling how we represent experiences internally; regulating the submodalities of our internal images; **visualization**; controlling focus etc. Bodily action (movement, painting) can also play a part. The NLP viewpoint is that we can choose to feel more or less whatever we choose to feel. We do not have to wait for some external event to trigger the desired emotion. The 'secret' is the brain's inability to distinguish the strong, clear signals we send it internally from the sensory data it gets from the external world.

• Emotions play an important part in learning. They tell the brain what to pay attention to, which has major implications for motivation and helps explain the vehicles we choose for our personal development. We are more likely to recall events if they are congruent with our mood at the time. We also attract thoughts congruent with our mood, which then reinforce that mood. If we are in a depressed state, depressing thoughts are likely to come into our minds. Cutting into this self-reinforcing cycle is a challenge for therapists working with depressed and anxious clients. Clearly the same self-reinforcing cycle works with more positive states, which indicates why mood management is so important.

From some '**enlightenment**' perspectives, the drive for emotional gratification is characteristic of a pre-enlightenment consciousness. The emotions are seen less as a source of enrichment than of turbulence, constraint and an insistent concern with the ego or personality. Detaching from our emotions, and making them much less of a priority in our lives, is to move nearer to an early stage of enlightenment.

Encounter Groups

Relatively small groups offering opportunities for individuals to find out more about themselves and how they relate to others by means of intense but 'honest' interactions.

Encounter groups are expressions of the human potential movement. They are not so much therapy groups for the emotionally disturbed, as self-improvement groups for 'normal people who want to get more out of life' (Napoli et al, 1982). The emphasis is very much upon positive extension and enhancement rather than upon deleting the negatives (getting rid of neuroses, for example).

Encounter groups tend to be facilitated rather than led, but to be relatively unstructured. Individuals are allowed or encouraged to explore and express feelings honestly, directly and physically (eg, hugging rather than just talking about hugging). If they are conducted in a positive atmosphere, without excessive hostility of expression, then individuals can be encouraged to try out new thoughts and feelings and to get the support of the group.

Encounter group participation can be disturbing and discomforting as well as uplifting and improving. Facing up to old fears, newly uncovered feelings or the candid perceptions of others can be both painful and developmental. On balance, encounter groups should increase the actualization of participants. As Robert Nye (1992) writes with reference to encounter groups and the humanistic psychology of Carl Rogers: 'encounter group members should be more fully functioning after this intensive group experience, and there should be less incongruence between their self-concepts and their organismic experiencing.'
(See **Emotions; Fully Functioning Person; Self-Help Groups**.)

Enlightenment

States of consciousness associated with heightened levels of awareness.

The awareness enlightenment brings us has been variously defined, and includes the following: an apprehension of true reality; a 'consciousness without content, which nonetheless permits all content to exist' (ITC, 1987); extinction of the self and integration with all things; seeing into the mind itself rather than the psychic's ability to be 'in touch with an area of mind inaccessible to ordinary consciousness' (Kapleau, 1980); 'understanding the perfect poise of being-and-becoming' (White, 1984); 'absolute peace' (Watson, 1991); and awareness of higher energy realms.

Perhaps the one matter upon which all enlightenment 'experts' agree is that the concept is ineffable and can only truly be understood by direct experience. Put more graphically: 'Reading about enlightenment is like scratching an itch through your shoe' (Kapleau, 1980). There is general agreement also that enlightenment is not a one-off revelation, but a progressive and endless process.

It could be argued that enlightenment is the most radically transforming of all personal experiences, the most profound form of personal development available to us. It could also be argued that with enlightenment the notion of *personal* development ceases to be meaningful, since consciousness seems to move beyond the personality. It's human, but it's not strictly personal. Certainly, it differs in a number of ways from other personal development pathways. We can't see **goals** and make plans for achieving enlightenment in the way that we can for achieving **success** in most areas of our life. We can hope only to discover it. There seem to be no short-cuts or guaranteed enlightenment programs that we can go through, though as John White (1984) observes, 'there has been a veritable explosion of psychotechnologies and consciousness-altering devices claiming to induce mystical, transformative and "enlighted states".' We would have to include here the 'chemical enlightenment' of hallucinogenic and psychedelic drugs (Storm, 1991). In contrast to many current approaches to personal development, where the emphasis is upon the ease of achieving it (provided the relevant 'how tos' are followed), the 'advocates' of enlightenment stress how difficult it is, how it requires discipline and strenuous practice. There are enlightenment technologies, chiefly **meditation**, but these may be 'manifestation of enlightenment rather than a way towards it.' (Fontana, 1992). Moreover, the mental resources, including rational thinking, that we use to develop in other areas can be positively unhelpful in a quest for enlightenment.

In a number of respects, enlightenment is clearly a 'special case' within the field of PD. To see it as simply another item on the personal development menu would trivialize it.

Enlightenment has its own (very long) history, and substantial literature. It has connections with the world's major religious and spiritual traditions, and yet in some of its forms (the Shambhala teachings, for example) offers a secular pathway to uplifting personal existence (see Trungpa, 1984).

'Exaggerating the mistake'

A technique for helping us to **change** a behaviour pattern that involves making the unwanted behaviour more pronounced. (Not surprisingly, the technique is also known as *paradoxical intention*.)

This technique is sometimes used by therapists whose clients resist at one level the change they want to bring about at another. Getting them to magnify the behaviour can give them an insight into it and may motivate them to change. The technique is specifically used to demonstrate our conscious control over behaviours we thought were controlling us. For example, if we tend to shout rather than talk at other people, then we can show ourselves that this is not beyond our control by deliberately shouting still louder. If we can increase the volume one way, then we ought to be able to decrease it the other.
(See **'Aha!' Experience**.)

Excellence

The ability to do something exceptionally well on a consistent basis.

'Exceptionally' implies a level of performance well above that required to demonstrate a minimum level of **competence**. The gap between the two levels is popularly called 'the difference that makes the difference'. 'Well' tends to mean quickly, effortlessly and, sometimes, elegantly. 'Consistent basis' implies the ability to achieve the same (high) results more or less at will by reproducing the processes and behaviours responsible for them. Finally, 'ability' refers to whatever particular set of mental and other processes are required to produce excellent results. They could also be called (and are) the 'strategies of high achievers'.

They include particular kinds of thinking, **beliefs**, feeling states, ways of using our voices and physiology and other physical behaviours (see **Body Awareness**). We may not be conscious of how we are using these strategies, or even that we are using them at all.

Very rarely in PD literature is excellence considered to be peculiar to particular individuals, a unique talent. An exception on the margins of PD but with major implications for aspects of it would be recent studies by Howard Gardner (1995) of 'individuals who are truly extraordinary'. Excellence is explicable, not mysterious. That, at least, is the assumption underpinning **NLP** which is often described as the study of personal excellence, 'a way of coding and reproducing excellence' (Knight, 1995). Excellence has a content (the component processes which make it up) and a structure (the way these components are put together). We can elicit and model the content and structure of excellence and get the same results as an excellent practitioner. At least, that is the theory.

Virtually any area of human activity provides examples of excellence. Some of the areas most frequently discussed in popular PD literature include general models of **success**, establishing **rapport**, self-motivation and the motivation of others, and 'technical' skill areas such as those of spelling and reading. But we can demonstrate excellence in the most unlikely areas. For example, we can be exceptionally 'good' at getting ourselves depressed or show remarkably good learning skills in relation to a phobia.

Excellence very definitely does not equate to perfectionism. Excellence is related to the concept of **continuous development**. It is about being very good at something and trying to get even better at it, which sometimes involves making mistakes. Perfectionism is about not making mistakes. Paradoxically, this abhorrence of mistakes and shortcomings, compounded by the accompanying anxiety and the intolerance of self and others, often means that those of us who strive for perfection are less 'excellent' than those who strive for (achievable) excellence.
(See **Mastery; Modelling**.)

Failure

In contemporary PD, the one unpardonable sin is not to 'have a go' at whatever it is we want to do or achieve. PD mentors also take a dim view of those of us who habitually **focus** on failure, allowing it to limit what we try, sicken our thinking and incline us to expect only negative experiences. The dominant connotations of the word are also considered unfortunate; some writers suggest we banish it from our vocabulary.

In virtually every other respect, however, failure is very positively regarded. To understand this we need to appreciate that to call something a failure is not to state a fact but to make a judgement, a negative evaluation based on negative belief criteria. For example, if we go for a job but don't get it, have we experienced failure? PD mentors would say that this depends on us. If we believe that there is only one criterion of **success**, being offered the job, then we will probably say we've failed. But if we believe that there are other criteria of success, including learning something useful from the experience, then we will doubtless say we haven't failed.

The very widely promulgated view is that failure is not the opposite of success but rather a necessary part of it and often a precondition for it. In this sense, failure is something we should welcome. It provides us with opportunities to grow and to learn. Not getting these opportunities is a cause for concern. It probably means that we're not taking enough **risks**. In this situation we need to make the shift that Susan Jeffers made: 'from being afraid of making a mistake to being afraid of *not* making a mistake' (Jeffers, 1991).

This positive view of failure is expressed across the PD spectrum. In **NLP**, 'failure' has been neutralized, drained of its negative associations, and semantically reframed as 'information' or **feedback**. Further development depends upon the information we get from making mistakes and 'failing'. From the quite different perspective of Personal Construct Psychology, though (like NLP, an area concerned with how we codify and construe experience), failure is a process of invalidation that can lead to growth. When our acquired way of making sense of experience no longer seems valid, we have to look for fresh ways. Or as Bannister and Fransella (1986) put it: 'development can be seen as occurring largely when anticipations fail.' Cognitive therapists also see failure as functional if we are able to deal adaptively with it, for example, if we can become better problem-solvers by assessing our performance and resolving not to repeat the 'failed' aspects of it. (Not being able to do this can be a sign of psychological disturbance.) Encouraging failure might be perverse, but creating the conditions in which mistakes are positively allowed is becoming a norm in some contemporary organizations. Learning organizations require people who are allowed and willing to make mistakes. The imperative to get it 'right first time' is being seriously questioned (McCrimmon, 1995).

More generally, the current approach to failure is to construe it as a positive collaboration with the inevitable. Everyone has setbacks. The trick is to 'learn to see them as a form of behavioural judo, turning the force of disappointment to your own advantage' (Sharpe and Lewis, 1976). Surviving or developing from failures is not a matter of chance but a matter of perceptions based on our **beliefs**, including those concerning ourselves.

Linked to this is a central, if often implicit, theme in PD literature: that we should program ourselves to succeed, rather than program ourselves either to fail or to avoid failure. This involves setting **goals** and going after them. It involves doing all we can to learn from the mistakes other people have made and even to use our imaginative powers to visualize the mistakes we could have made. It involves **modelling excellence**. It involves **programming** our minds until we 'accept that success is basically no more difficult than failure' (Poissant 1989).

We need to be very careful about the criteria we set for success and failure. If our success criteria are unrealistically high, then we may be programming ourselves to fail. If the criteria apply only to specific **outcomes**, rather than to processes, then we may be damaging our chances for development and **well-being**. If 'winning' or 'achieving' is ultimately less important than 'trying' or 'learning', then our chances of failing are very low. This is another example of when it is vital to be clear about our key **values**.

The one strand in current PD ideology which doesn't square easily with failure philosophy is the 'do whatever it takes' approach to achieving goals. If we refuse to countenance the possibility of not succeeding, then we may be more likely to succeed, but it may blinker us to the effects our efforts might be having upon us. The costs may be very high. The achievement of the goal may not bring with it the expected good feelings. When setbacks occur we may simply stiffen our resolve rather than review our progress, give ourselves credit for the efforts we have made and consider whether achievement of the goal is still of paramount importance. In other words, 'success' in one respect can be failure in another, and seeming failures can be successes in disguise.

Faith

Belief without conclusive evidence for it, particularly in ourselves and our ability to bring about the situations we desire.

Faith is also the 'control' mechanism for strengthening and intensifying **beliefs** and their impact upon the **subconscious**. The mind believes and does what it is consistently told. Having faith involves repeatedly sending the same strong instructions to the subconscious mind which will seek to carry them out, particularly by leading us to perceive and believe in line with these instructions. **Affirmations** are the key tools for inducing and intensifying faith. **Visualization** can also make instructions seem real and realizable. Many PD mentors suggest specific programs for developing faith (eg, Maltz, 1960).

Faith has long been considered crucial to **success** and **development**. Napoleon Hill devotes a full chapter to it in *Think and Grow Rich* (1966), describing it as 'indispensable'. This is not surprising given that personal development, by definition, concerns states and accomplishments which are immaterial and

potential. They exist only in our minds and their realization may seem remote in all senses. Moreover, we cannot see or examine the main capacities and processes for their realization. We may just have to trust that they are there. We may also have to develop faith in actions which on the face of it seem illogical or tenuously connected with our goal. For example, wealth creation mentors advise their clients to give away significant proportions of their wealth and trust that it will come back to them many times over. We all need at times to take **risks** which seem like leaps in the dark, and put our faith in the problem-solving and planning abilities of the subconscious when the temptation is to find conscious solutions.

Feedback

Information that helps us to judge how well we are doing. In relation to development objectives, feedback tells us whether we are on target or whether adjustments may be required.

Originating in cybernetics, the concept of feedback has long enjoyed a central place in communication theory. Not surprisingly, it has acquired a place of equal significance in communication-based technologies of personal change, including those of **transactional analysis** and **NLP**. Learning, sustained performance, **self-awareness**, goal development – none of these is fully achievable without feedback. Nor are many more specific **outcomes** – those of **rapport** and elicitation in NLP, for example - without the feedback competence that Anthony Robbins (1988) calls 'sensory acuity'. Giving and asking for feedback are processes facilitating development; they are also the behaviours of a developing person. Giving feedback is a particularly skilful activity requiring 'courage, skill, understanding, and respect for yourself and others as well as involvement' (Johnson, 1981). Many PD books and programs offer guidance on this area (eg, Johnson, 1981; Honey, 1988, 1992).

Feedback tends to be thought of as disclosures from other people, but it can take a myriad of forms. Technically speaking, 'positive' feedback does not mean 'good' feedback but rather information that tells us we are on course; 'negative' feedback is not necessarily 'bad'. Indeed, since it informs us that we need to take corrective action – or just to try something else – it is rarely unwanted. But as Maxwell Maltz (1960) noted, excessive negative feedback can be inhibiting; it can stop us trying to get better. NLP encourages us to see all feedback as neutral or helpful. It is simply the information which tells us that we have not been successful – yet. It is what **failure** becomes when it is reframed.

Worth mentioning here is a newish trend in Human Resource Management (HRM) called 360° feedback. It refers to a process of giving employees (usually a manager) a rounded picture of their behaviour from the feedback pooled from relevant managers, peers and subordinates. Responses tend to be collated and fed back by a third party, usually for a report. The idea is to provide the manager with feedback which is straightforward and difficult to deny or dismiss. This can be the basis of a learning experience leading to **personal development planning**.

Focus

Focus, or the ability to concentrate on one thing to the exclusion of all others, is one of the great integrating concepts in PD. Whatever we understand PD to be, we are certain to believe that there can be little of it without focus.

At the level of general activity, focusing equates to prioritizing. It means putting the bulk of our efforts into the few things that really make a difference. This is the 80:20 (or Pareto) principle applied to PD. If we believe, for example, that having a clear set of **values** is one of the four or five keys to achieving fulfilment, then we may need to put 20 per cent of our time into values-related thinking. We might then apply the 80:20 principle to values themselves – ie, focus on the few things about values that make a difference.

At this level, focusing means concentrating upon the particular image, thought or **goal**. One effect of this is the deletion of all other images, thoughts and goals, because the mind can dwell upon only one thing at a time (at least, at the level of immediate consciousness). For most PD tutors, this 'simple' fact has enormously significant implications and benefits. It means that we can exclude negative thoughts merely by keeping our mind on positive ones. It makes it possible for the mind to be the goal-seeking mechanism that so many PD coaches insist it is. And the related view that the mind can quite literally realize whatever it dwells sufficiently upon has very wide acceptance. It's one of the beliefs that **success** gurus and personal mastery tutors have in common with those whose view of PD is more metaphysical and psychical. They agree further that focusing can create, attract and accelerate the attainment of goals and states. The ability to focus is central to **personal power**, however it is defined. From a metaphysical perspective, focusing enables the mind both to sense and to direct universal energies. From some **enlightenment** through higher consciousness points of view, development comes from shifting the focus of awareness from the personal self to the transpersonal self. Focusing is generally considered the key to **meditation**, particularly a focused awareness on breathing. Cultivating the focusing 'muscles' has high priority in psychosynthesis. Many of its exercises and techniques for development are intended to improve our capacity to focus on one or more of our senses. This includes 'reflective meditation', the 'process of deepening our mental abilities to the point where new powers and states become available to us' (Ferrucci, 1990). The process starts with an increase in focus, and then the mind is firmly but gently re-focused any time it begins to 'stray'.

There is clearly an art or skill to effective concentration, and it appears to have little to do with bullying our minds into obedient attentiveness. What we know from fields as apparently disparate as **accelerated learning**, sports psychology and some Eastern philosophies, is that concentration is more a **letting go** than a desperate clinging to of conscious control. It's trusting in the subconscious program, the state of unconscious competence or the power of the mind when it is relaxed but receptive. 'This state of concentration seems to be a suspension of doubt and self-consciousness, a way of clearing the mind of all distracting rubble and trash' (Rusk and Read, 1986). Our **peak performances** are invariably associated with such states. Using **willpower** to concentrate seems counterproductive: it simply generates tension and provokes our mind into talking back to us. The familiar exhortation by teachers to their students to 'concentrate!' probably does more harm than good.

NLP and the new mind technologies offer techniques for

enhancing concentration. For example, having observed that 'the key factor in concentration is interest', Patrick Porter (1993) suggests we use the state associated with really enjoyable learning experiences to enhance concentration when we feel less motivated to learn.

Negative focus, focusing upon what we don't want (fears, obstacles, self-defeating behaviours, etc) rather than what we do want, is frequently cited as the main reason we do not achieve our goals in life.

Fully functioning person

We may come close to being fully functioning if we enjoy an extraordinarily high level of psychological health, and if we are moving along a path of ever-increasing growth and fulfilment. Carl Rogers used 'fully functioning' to refer to an ideal condition or process in which we give ourselves unconditional positive regard, feel fully in contact with even our deepest feelings and realize fully our potentialities. These are not restricted by or in conflict with our self-concept.

Few, if any of us, reach this ideal, but if we are comparatively fully functioning then it is likely that as we grew up the people who mattered most to us did not make their regard for us conditional. We didn't have to do or feel certain things in order to feel loved and accepted. It's probable also that we didn't judge our own worth in terms of meeting or of not meeting certain standards. We didn't, for example, beat ourselves up if we didn't achieve top marks in an exam.

If we are fully functioning and psychologically healthy then we are almost certainly **congruent**; in particular, our self-concept is likely to be harmonious with our deeper, organismic needs and experiences. We won't for example, strive relentlessly to achieve career goals in line with our self-concept if we sense that our more basic needs as an organism have to do with maintaining intimate relationships. We trust what feels right. And if we are in touch with our organismic experiencing, which can include rational thinking as part of the whole, then we will trust ourselves as decision-makers. Clearly, then, we will be open to experience and aware fully of what we are experiencing.

We will be unlikely to avoid, distort or deny experiences, behaviours and feelings that seem discordant with the self-concept we are striving to maintain. And because we are fully aware at a feeling level and receptive to experience, we will be able to live fully in the moment (see **Here and Now**).

Few PD writers appear to have adopted Rogers' term 'fully functioning person'. Even so, as a concept it has undoubtedly been highly influential. It reflects a positive and optimistic view of human potential which is now omnipresent in mainstream self-help literature. The defining features of the fully functioning person have also become the 'goals' or measures of progress towards psychological **well-being** found in many PD programs and used by professional helpers influenced by Rogers' client-centred approaches to therapy (counsellors, social workers, priests etc). If a flesh-and-blood fully functioning person existed, then he or she would be the walking embodiment of many of the terms and themes of this book.

(See **Actualization**.)

GIGO

Garbage In, Garbage Out is a term from the field of computer science/IT that self-help teachers have applied to personal rather than computer **programming**. It is usually offered as a warning to gate-keep our minds so that we don't allow too many negative and disempowering messages to get in. If they do get in, then we are likely to think and utter negative ideas. According to one self-development authority, 80 per cent of our thoughts (on a good day!) are likely to be negative (Milteer, 1990).

In its crude form, GIGO is clearly an extreme and untenable version of mental determinism: given A (messages), then B (thoughts, beliefs) follow. Our minds are more active than this, and all kinds of variables intervene between the reception and the perception/organization of messages in our brains. Even so, the advice to screen the ideas that come to us, and even to avoid sources of 'garbage', including people with highly **negative thinking** patterns, may well be sensible on a practical level.

Goals

A goal is anything we set out to achieve. It can be a state of being, an action, an accomplishment, a thing, a level of knowledge or a relationship. It is something for which we take both **responsibility** and **action**, which distinguishes it from a dream or a wish.

No self-help book or **success** manual would be complete without a section on goals and goal-seeking. PD messages concerning goals have been remarkably consistent for decades. The chief of these is that goals are 'as essential to success as air is to water' (Schwartz, 1959). Authorities on success are unanimous that 'it is an inability to state their goals in life correctly which prevents many people from realising their true potential' (Sharpe and Lewis, 1976). It is also generally acknowledged that we are goal-striving mechanisms to whom goal-setting ought to come naturally. This is only a seeming paradox, for the issue is not about goal-setting so much as setting and pursuing goals effectively.

Goals are considered crucial to PD, largely because they give direction and purpose to our lives and actions. They keep us focused, mobilize our energies to make us purposeful doers rather than aimless dissipators, and incline us to be more persistent and resourceful. By putting us in search mode, goals stimulate us to be inventive in finding strategies to take us forward. PD tutors tell us that we are many more times more likely to get what we want from life if we set clear goals. It would even seem that having goals can help us to live longer. For instance, there are many stories of people who have 'deferred' their own deaths until a cherished goal has been achieved.

The literature on goals deals mainly with the rules for selecting, setting and stating goals. Rules guiding selection include the following:

- Begin by generating a long list of goals. Include big and small goals, and goals that cover different time periods (weeks, years, a lifetime).
- Reduce the long list to a prioritized shortlist in line with your **vision** and **values**.
- Spend as much time as necessary clarifying *why* you want to achieve these goals and making certain that they are worthwhile.
- Run a number of checks on your goals. Ensure they are sufficiently broad and balanced in the areas of your life they cover. Ensure they are goals over which you have personal control. Ensure they are consistent with one another. Ensure you can accept the 'costs' of pursuing and achieving them.

Rules for actually setting and formulating goals include the following:

- State the goal positively so that it expresses what you want, not what you don't want.

- Be as specific as possible.
- Decide the success criteria, or the evidence that will tell you your goal has been achieved.
- Ensure the goal is realistic for you. Can *you* see yourself achieving it?
- Contextualize the goal. Specify the situation in which it would be achieved. (Don't say, 'become more assertive', but 'become more assertive in team meetings'.)
- Write down the goal. Some authorities say that goals written down are over 20 times more likely to be achieved than goals not made explicit (see **Writing**).

After goals have been set, some kind of planning needs to take place. Some experts consider detailed **action plans** prerequisites for successful achievement. Others say that if goals have been set 'properly' and with total **commitment**, then we will find the 'hows' to achieve them. The means may emerge, for example, through the good offices of our creative **subconscious**. At an early stage, **faith** may be more important than strategy. Certainly, though, no goal is achieved without action. Our goals need also to be reviewed regularly to check with ourselves that they remain relevant, aligned to our vision, within our sights. Some PD tutors suggest that we reward ourselves when we achieve our goals. Celebrations help sustain motivation and momentum for the goals we are still pursuing.

Seasoned self-improvers are (over-) familiar with the standard prescriptions for goal-setting, which poses a challenge to PD tutors who know they must continue to preach the gospel of goal-setting. They know also that many of us do not in reality practise what they preach. We may set goals, but pursuing them with vigour is another matter. A fair quantity of current literature on goals attempts to account for and to get over this 'know but don't do' situation (see **Atrophy**).

The key issue seems to centre on motivation and **leverage**. We want to achieve our goals, but not enough, perhaps, to get us to take sustained action. This may be a matter of size. Our goals may be too small to inspire us or too large to seem really achievable. It may be that we can't keep our goals consistently in **focus**. Or it may be that we can't fully *feel* what achieving or not achieving our goals would really be like. The challenge for PD tutors is to help us to help ourselves to take the action to overcome the inertia of doing nothing or very little. The 'solution' offered is usually more effective self-programming. Anthony Robbins' Neuro-Associative Conditioning (TM) procedure is a case in point (Robbins, 1992).

To challenge the orthodoxy of the goal-setting gospel may seem like heresy, but there may be a shadow side to setting goals, or at least alternative perspectives on the process. There are glimpses of this in approaches to PD less concerned exclusively with success and achievement, but it would be wrong to suggest that they amount to a counter-theory of goals.

One misgiving about a heavy emphasis on goals is that it can lead to a lack of flexibility and spontaneity in our approach to life. We take our goals too seriously. We are not prepared to do things that appear to deflect us from them. And yet, as various writers have observed, we can sometimes move closer to our goals if we are relaxed and really enjoying the **here and now** or if we follow our **intuition** rather than our plans when it feels right to do so. Goal-setting in a highly conscious, systematic way seems to suit some of us better than others. Some of us appear to get what we want with only an informal approach to goal-setting and planning.

Another 'problem' with goals is that they inevitably preclude certain possibilities. If we commit to one goal then we may not in reality find it possible fully to achieve another goal - which may be a problem if we value them equally. Juggling career- and family-related goals is a familiar example. What Egan (1994) says in a counselling context has general application: 'although liberating in many respects, goals also hem clients in.'

Finally, defining success exclusively in terms of achieving our goals can be psychologically unhealthy. If we have additional success criteria, such as learning valuable life lessons, and expanding aspects of ourselves, then the pursuit of a goal can be developmental irrespective of whether or not we achieve it fully. Moreover, and this point is too infrequently considered in the literature, 'failure' to achieve a goal may be in our own best interests if we view ourselves holistically. If I go after a goal which is not really 'me', which is not aligned to my core values, say, then a deeper, wiser or more authentic part of me may recognize this and sabotage my conscious intentions for positive reasons and with beneficial effects.

'Going with the flow'

Following our impulses and **intuition** as opposed to doing things which may not feel 'right' but appear to be requirements of our **goals** or situations.

The image is the stream - the river of life, the stream of universal energy etc. 'Going with the flow' implies an effortless journey of **development** – effortless because our inner intelligence, working through our intuition and impulses, ensures that we move with the dominant flow of the stream. At any moment, we trust our inner intelligence to guide our actions and know what is best for us.

Going with the flow does not mean a moment-to-moment approach to life, though it does link very closely with the idea of living in the **here and now**. We can still set goals and plan ahead, indeed we need to do this if we are to 'flow' rather than 'drift', but we do not charge at or struggle towards our goals by the shortest, quickest route possible. To do so would be to miss out on the joys of the journey and, almost certainly, to 'force' things to happen. Moreover, if we invest too much emotional energy in going after our goals, then we may channel some of that energy into irrigating the channels of fear (the fear of not attaining them) which is clearly counterproductive. We need, as Shakti Gawain (1995) puts it, to hold onto our goals 'lightly'. We need to have plans but to be flexible about their implementation. Sometimes, we will achieve more, as well as feel better, by following our feelings rather than by sticking rigidly to plans and schedules.

PD tutors tell us that the tell-tale sign of not going with the flow is a feeling of resistance. If we feel that we are forcing ourselves to make something happen, or pushing open a door that seems to want to stay closed, then we may need to desist. There may be a better way.

The idea of going with the dominant energy flow appears elsewhere in PD. For example, it's implicit in the idea of assuming a positive intention (eg, that someone intends to be helpful rather than hurtful), for then we can work with rather than against them. It is also present in the concept of 'channelling' energies - not trying to block anger or aggression, say, but rather finding positive forms of expression for them.

Going with the flow (or 'living in the flow') is associated also with Eastern philosophies and **enlightenment** technologies. The emphasis here is upon not 'interfering' with the unfolding of reality, for interfering is an act of self-will opposed to the natural flow (see **Will**). Accepting the things that happen to us is considered a step towards enlightenment. This would seem to be a rather more passive attitude towards 'the flow' than is generally suggested in PD literature, where 'going with the flow' is presented as a responsive and ultimately creative process, a heightened sensitivity towards the **alignment** between the direction of our own lives and the direction of the universe of which we are a part.

Habits

Patterns of activity that we perform automatically; programmed or routine ways of thinking, behaving and speaking.

In some cases, habits are skills performed with unconscious competence. Personal habits have also been thought of as the smallest building blocks of character. If character is destiny, then the cumulative effects of our habits can indeed be profound.

From a PD standpoint, habits are both useful and unhelpful. On the positive side, they can free us to turn our minds to more important matters, and allow us to do so while we are engaged in mundane routines (like walking and dressing). If we had to think afresh about every habitual behaviour, then we'd have no time or mental space to be creative, to consider 'higher' things such as personal development. Habits also make aspects of our lives straightforward, smooth-running and secure.

On the negative side, habits blunt our awareness, making us operate on automatic pilot and less likely to live intensely in the **here and now**. If we always respond to the same situation (getting up, entering our work place, etc) with the same thinking pattern, the chances are we're always going to feel the same way about it. Also, if we are not aware, then we can't learn. Habits inhibit learning.

Habits can also be 'bad' for our functioning and development in at least three ways. First, they can be 'unhealthy' physically, psychologically or emotionally. Smoking is an obvious example. Less obvious is using a negative phrase in a habitual way ('It's boring', 'I'm just surviving'). Second, habits can be relatively inefficient ways of performing an activity. For example, our typing skills may be habitual, but they may be inefficient if we were poorly tutored. Third, habits can be ill-matched to new external requirements. They may have been efficient or appropriate at one time, but are now outmoded or inappropriate. The speed of change is making this increasingly common. For example, teachers who encourage only habits of individual study (ie, who regard collaborative study skills as unimportant or 'cheating') are out of touch with the requirements of many business environments.

PD programmes which tackle habits tend to do the following:

- Help us to become more aware of our habituated natures, and to appreciate the effects of habits upon us.
- Help us to see that we always have **choices**, and that sometimes we need to jettison a habit in order to see that having it was a choice. Acting automatically often means acting as though there were no other option.
- Help us to distinguish between habits which are worth having and those which are not. Worthwhile habits are enabling, either because they free us to concentrate on 'higher' things or because they empower us to help us produce the **outcomes** we want.
- Help us to break old and make new habits. PD tutors invariably argue that no habit is necessarily fixed forever. Any habit *can* be broken, though breaking it can be very painful and difficult. (Covey talks of the 'tremendous gravity pull' of a habit.) **NLP** offers technologies for making and breaking habits, of which **modelling** excellent performers is one. Some PD tutors offer specific strategies, such as Patrick Porter's strategy for building 'genius habits' (Porter, 1993).

Probably the best-known PD book with 'habits' in the title is Stephen Covey's *The Seven Habits of Highly Effective People* (1992). Actually, 'habits' as Covey conceives them are much more like principles or strategies for effective living. Hence, his definition of a habit ('the intersection of *knowledge, skill* and *desire*') is appropriately peculiar.

Healing

From 'New Age' and 'holistic' perspectives, healing and personal development are very nearly synonymous. Some healing therapies are concerned primarily with making the body better, either in the sense of making sound again or improving the state of physical **well-being**. However, in PD contexts healing applies less to the recovery of good physical health than to the recovery of our wholeness as human beings. The key words here are 'wholeness' and 'being'. Some approaches to personal development are concerned mainly with *doing*, and with what we achieve by doing; self-help books on **success** generally fall into this category. Within this frame of reference, the concept of healing does not make much sense. But when personal development is conceived largely in terms of restoring and achieving our full 'being-ness', then healing comes into its own, for healing is any process that enhances our physical, mental, emotional and spiritual well-being.

In this broad sense, healing usually implies a holistic model of the person. We are not an assemblage of separate parts that can be treated or 'mended' on their own, but rather an interrelated mix of physical, mental and spiritual systems which collectively constitute our wholeness. The ideal conditions are invariably considered to be equilibrium and integration, which may be natural but are not in reality inevitable. We may need healing to bring body, mind and spirit into **alignment** or into a state of 'ease' rather than 'dis-ease', and to develop all aspects of ourselves to the full. Healing, then, is both restorative and generative. More specifically, healing can help us to: recover and enhance our vitality; achieve a state of balance, so that none of our dimensions dominates or exerts detrimental effects on other dimensions; accept that our consciousness is itself multi-dimensional; begin to own what we once rejected about ourselves – certain emotions, for example, or our spirituality; release and unblock old patterns of thinking and behaving, old formative energies and the positions we have taken against past wounds. Healing may also involve giving ourselves the love and care we gave only to others (or to no one) in the past. This is the personal development process known in **transactional analysis** circles as self-reparenting.

From an emotional and/or spiritual point of view, healing may be largely a matter of letting go of fear, anger or past hurts. As Gerald Jampolsky (1979) suggests, taking his lead from *A Course in Miracles* (1975), healing is a matter of choice: of choosing forgiveness and peace rather than anxiety and fear. The Borysenkos (1995) put it rather differently and graphically. Healing in spiritual terms, they say, 'is the process of harvesting the teachings from our wounds.'

For some healers, healing also implies attunement with universal energies. Usually, this does not require beliefs in a divine force. Generally speaking, healers think of themselves as either channels for pervasive energies or as tutors and supportive others for the people they help. They tend not to arrogate to themselves extraordinary healing powers. Indeed, a widespread assumption within the healing arts is that each of us has the resources (and the responsibility) to be the primary agents of our own healing.

The New Age interest in non-Western systems of thinking and practices has had a major impact on the healing movement. Ancient healing arts from the East and elsewhere (eg, native North American cultures) have been 'recovered' and are now offered in 'pure' forms or else blended with conventional Western practices. An example would be the bringing together of modern medicine and the ancient Indian healing art of *Ayurveda*. Some world-famous figures in the PD world have helped to build their reputations from forging such alliances. A good example is Deepak Chopra, author of *Ageless Body, Timeless Mind* (1993).

Synthesizing hitherto separate approaches to healing, or working on one level (eg, the physical) in the expectation of impacting upon other levels, have been major trends in the healing 'movements'. They enact at the level of the healing arts and therapies the very processes that healing is intended to bring about within the individual. It could be argued that this is necessary because within the West, spiritual and religious practices have largely been split off from healing ones, which has made impossible an integrated approach to suffering and its causes. This has been exacerbated by divisions within the medical world itself – most obviously between doctors who concentrate on the body and those who concentrate on the mind (or brain). This fragmentation has not made it possible to approach healing in a holistic way, nor to work with a connection theory of what we may lack or need for wholeness.

Currently, however, illuminating connections between the

mind and the emotions on the one hand and physical functioning on the other is an area of massive and burgeoning interest.
Some of the best-known names in PD, including Bernie Siegel,
Carl Simonton, Louise Hay, the Borysenkos and the late
Norman Cousins, have written extensively about the connections. The power of the mind, and of positive states such as hope
and joy, to effect bodily changes is a major theme of healing literature, where stories abound of people who have healed themselves of serious diseases like cancer.

From a healing point of view, illness is not seen as simply a
malfunction of a particular 'part' of the body or an arbitrary
affliction, but rather as a manifestation of disharmony between
body, mind and spirit. Clearly, then, healing is not about eliminating our symptoms; it's about trying to make sense of them in
the light of what else is going on in our lives. This is another
way of saying that illnesses are meaningful, even allegorical,
and that healing arts such as Reiki can help us to 'read' them.
Similarly, the books of Louise Hay suggest correspondences
between physical problems and emotional conditions that
amount to what Fanning (1994) calls 'metaphorical symptomol-
ogy'. For example, a bad back can signify not being supported
at an emotional level by someone else, not giving ourselves
emotional support or 'supporting' problems that are too
weighty for us.

The idea that each of us is at some level of our being 'responsible' for our illness is now widely accepted but clearly has
much potential for misunderstanding and harm. To say that we
'choose' to be ill because illness seems to offer some kind of
solution to a problem or because it meets a need (for a few days
off work, for love and attention, for a 'resolution' to an ongoing
emotional crisis) is very likely to make us feel guilty at a conscious level, which is not what 'responsibility' in this context
means.

The number of healing arts, therapies and techniques now
available is substantial and the list is growing. They include
image-oriented methods (eg, creative visualization, dream-
work), meditation and awareness raising methods (eg, Silva
mind control, autogenic training, yoga), methods emphasizing
memory and catharsis (eg, primal scream, rebirthing, past life
regression), and a huge number concerned with

bodywork/energy/movement and action, including psy-
chodrama, shamanic ritual, Reiki, bioenergetics, acupressure,
yoga, polarity therapy, massage, cranio-sacral therapy, Rolfing,
reflexology, biodynamic massage, colonic irrigation, kinesiolo-
gy, aikido, tai chi chuan, eurhythmics and the Alexander technique. There are many other healing therapies, including irid-
ology, colour therapy, flower remedies, herbalism, crystal/gem
therapy and sound/voice therapies. (This is not an exhaustive
list, nor are the categories watertight.)
(See **Body Awareness; Emotions; Holistic Development.**)

Here and Now

The view that we should live predominantly in the present, and
not in the past or the future, is central to some perspectives on
personal development, most notably that provided by Gestalt
therapy. From this viewpoint, we can develop personally only if
we are highly aware of what we sense, feel and think on a
moment-to-moment basis. Staying stuck in our memories or
expectations is considered unhealthy, since it keeps us from connecting with ourselves and our feelings, and of acting upon
them. Living totally in the moment enables us to contact our
lives generally and so deal with our problems. As Latner (1986)
puts it: 'The more we are aware of ourself, the more we contact
the world, because discovering oneself opens us to new experiences.'

Awareness of the moment is linked to trusting our organismic
experiencing, being open to experience and willing to respond
to it in a fresh way rather than forcing it into preconceived categories. 'What am I feeling right now?' is the kind of question we
might ask ourselves if we live in the here and now.

Living in the present is not a denial of the past. Rather, as
Gestalt therapists point out, we experience past events not
directly but in our awareness of them in the present. 'Present
conditions regulate and redefine past experiences and its application to the present moment' (Nevis, 1987). This applies to
learning. Full awareness of the present can help us see more
clearly how we can apply past learning to present circumstances.

If we can recall a past event, then it must have some signifi-cance in the present moment. If it concerns unfinished business, then living in the here and now may not be easy, for as Korb *et al* (1989) observed: 'Incomplete experiences draw energy away from the present functioning, thus inhibiting the ability of the individual to participate fully in present experience.'

The idea that we can experience the past in the present moment is found in the literature of **enlightenment** and spiritu-al development. In Shambhala teachings, for example, '*Nowness*, the magic of the present moment, is what joins the wisdom of the past with the present' (Trungpa, 1984). Because 'it is always *now*', personal development is most intense when it is focused on the now.

It isn't hard to appreciate the view that living in the past is psychologically unhealthy. PD specialists vary in their respect for the past in terms of its determining effects upon us, but the fashionable view in self-help circles is that the past does not equal the future.

Accepting that living in the now is healthier for our develop-ment than being future-oriented may be more difficult. Many self-help writers do not preach the living in the moment mes-sage. Rather, they emphasize goal-setting, planning to achieve **goals** and techniques such as **mental rehearsal** that enable us to experience the future by proxy, as it were. Indeed, much current PD literature positively celebrates the capacity of the mind to escape the present. Re-editing memories and visualizing future life scripts are examples of this.

There are, then, differences in emphasis within the PD com-munity on the matter of living in the here and now. To over-sim-plify, we might say that living in the present is of paramount importance to those who emphasize Being, whereas to those who emphasize Doing and Having (eg, most success gurus) the future is a major **focus** of attention.

(See **Awareness Continuum; Body Awareness; 'Going with the Flow'; Healing; Time**.)

Higher Self

The part of ourself which transcends the comparatively petty and often negative preoccupations of the 'everyday' plane of existence. There are numerous associated or alternative terms for the Higher Self, including higher conscious, superconscious, innate intelligence, divine love, infinite self and **intuition**.

The term 'Higher Self' appears frequently in many forms of PD literature. It seems logically to imply a hierarchical model of the self in which there is a Lower Self and possibly other aspects of the self. The best known of such models is probably Roberto Assagioli's egg-shaped psychosynthesis model (Assagioli, 1990). (Freud's concept of super ego is psychosocial rather than psychospiritual, and so not equivalent to the Higher Self.) Quite often, however, the Higher Self is not part of an explicit, formalized model of the self. At its least specific, it represents a level of personal existence or that sense of complete fulfilment that many of us seek, but rarely find, because we seek it outside rather than inside of us – in relationships, achievements, acquisitions and the like.

The Higher Self is endowed with infinite wisdom that makes it an ideal, guide and tutor. It can solve problems for us or present us with a higher **vision** of the problem (if it still appears as such). The Higher Self is also believed to be the source of inspiration, **creativity**, love, abundance and **well-being**.

For some PD tutors, finding and staying in touch with our Higher Self is the principal purpose of personal development, and perhaps of life itself. According to psychosynthesis, there are seven paths by which we can journey towards the Higher Self: the heroic way (eg, through service to others); the way of inner illumination and love (eg, through meditation); the way of active involvement in the world; the aesthetic, scientific and devotional ways; and the way of ritual and ceremony, if spiritual consciousness is awakened. Mystical experiences can give us glimpses of the Higher Self and our responses even to fairly ordinary events can have their source in the Higher Self (eg, a sudden rush of love for someone or something).

The more immediate conditions for contacting the Higher Self include stillness of mind and a focus away from the everyday. **Meditation** and **visualization** are the obvious means of achieving these conditions.

Holistic Development

Whole-person as opposed to part-person development.

Any approach to education, healing or personal development generally can claim to be holistic if it acknowledges the inter-relatedness of body, emotions, mind and spirit. In practice, of course, we can and should recognize the distinctiveness of particular systems or aspects of ourselves. The whole self can be developed through particular attention being given to one system (the body, for instance). The holistic principle is violated only when we seek to develop one aspect of ourself in isolation from and at the expense of other aspects. Examples would include academic learning that ignores everything but 'left brain' intellect, and being preoccupied with body building for its own sake.

Holistic approaches to **development** emphasize the **values** of oneness, personal integration and fullness of being. The **focus** is upon the individual, which means 'undivided' as much as 'individual'. Wholeness tends to be regarded not as a new state to be achieved but as a natural state to be realized or recovered. That is, we all have an intrinsic potential for harmony and internal balance. And when it grows holistically it is multi-dimensional, looking 'like an expanding sphere rather than like a straight line' (Ferrucci, 1990). This kind of development is impossible when we mistake the whole self for a part (the ego, in particular), or with a social role, such as parent, partner or employee.

At one time, 'holistic' tended to signify New Age and 'alternative lifestyles' approaches to personal development. This is no longer the case. The links between whole person and whole planet thinking are still strong, but holistic approaches and techniques are now 'respectable' in education and medicine, and increasingly in management and business as well as in PD generally. To a degree, holistic approaches have developed so as to 'put back' what some modern disciplines have left or thrown out. For example, psychology has been accused of discarding the spiritual dimensions to human existence (which helps explain the development and influence of psychosynthesis and transpersonal psychology), and formal education in the West has traditionally attached too little importance to **emotions** and mind-body links for example (see **Body Awareness**).

Holistic principles underpin accelerated learning systems, not only because the principles appeal but also because the evidence increasingly shows that we learn most effectively when mind, body and spirit are all engaged. In practice, this means paying attention to a multitude of factors including **beliefs**, feelings, **self-awareness**, personal problems, diet, breathing, posture, imagination, intuition, and use of both 'left' and 'right' brains. Holistic thinking also informs stress management programmes, partly because relaxing the mind can relax the body and relaxing the body can relax the mind. Holistic principles are massively important in many forms of medical treatment and **healing**.

Holistic approaches to development are inevitably associated with a healthy scepticism for causal thinking. A holistic approach to helping an individual, an organization or any other complex system is likely to involve a search for connections rather than 'simple' causes. Holistic (or systemic) thinking also recognizes that a development initiative in one area might have consequences in some other part of the 'system' which may be hard to predict or trace (see **Ecology**).

Ideal Model

A technique for **mental** (mind-body) **rehearsal** in which we imagine ourselves in the mind and body of an excellent performer. We are likely to use this technique if we ourselves have little relevant experience of the skill or activity in question. For example, we may visualize ourselves as a specific television newsreader and try to think and feel *as if* we were that person. (See **Acting 'As if'; Excellence; Modelling.**)

Ideal Self

In self-concept theory, the ideal self is the person we should like to be. Since most of us would like to be 'better' than we currently are, we nearly always judge our ideal self more favourably than we do our 'actual' self.

Clearly, the impulse for personal development can be 'explained' in terms of our desire to move closer towards our ideal self. There are also clear links with other key concepts such as **self-acceptance**, which in this context involves tolerating, if not approving, our actual self in the light of our ideal self. The gap between the two selves can generate the productive **dissatisfaction** that leads to growth.

One of the messages promulgated in much PD literature is that many of us have an ideal self which does not do us justice. In other words, we underestimate our **potential** for development. One effect of going through a PD program can be to revise dramatically our ideal self-concept. We 'come out' expecting more of ourselves and anticipating further self-development. A quite different outcome of going through a PD program can be to make us aware of the extent to which our ideal self has been shaped by others' expectations and by our **programming**. As a result, we may decide to revise our ideal self or to find much more about our actual, present self that is acceptable to us.

Imprinting

The process by which an experience or an action exerts a significant impression upon us.

Some experiences have a massive impact upon our self-image, subsequent experience or our **well-being** generally. This impact can be positive or negative or both. **NLP-ers** call these experiences 'imprint experiences', and recognize the potential value both of real (ie, remembered) imprint experiences and of important experiences constructed and modelled on actual, positive imprint experiences. The latter can be used as a resource and to reframe relevant remembered experiences. For example, we might be able to 're-write' unpleasant childhood memories by installing an imprint experience that makes us 'remember' and feel differently about them.

An imprint experience can also help us to confront more resourcefully **challenges** we have yet to experience.

'Imprinting' is used also to describe the process of assimilating **affirmations** into our **subconscious** mind. The theory here is that formulating affirmations is not in itself sufficient to ensure they bring about the desired results. Somehow, we must impress them on the subconscious. To do this we need to use words which evoke powerful pictures and feelings. If the subconscious is impressed, then we may shape our self-image, effect inside-out **change** or achieve whatever other goal we are after.

(See **Change Personal History; Reframing; Time.**)

Inner Team

Many PD tutors now take the view that each of us is an 'I' made up of a number, possibly an indefinite or infinite number, of little 'Is' which are known variously as aspects, parts, levels or subpersonalities. Collectively they constitute the inner team. Developing the inner team by getting the 'Is' to work harmoniously or productively together can benefit our overall development.

Inspiration for the concept of an inner team has come from a number of sources, including Assagioli and other exponents of psychosynthesis, psychologists interested in multiple personalities, sports psychologists, team role theorists such as Meredith Belbin and experts on thinking such as Edward de Bono, authorities on visualization, NLP authorities on dynamic and **accelerated learning** (Dilts and Epstein, 1995) and psychotherapists and others for whom models of the psyche are consistent with how we experience reality. Also relevant is Jung's concept of the 'shadow sides' of ourselves that we keep 'in the dark'.

One way to think of the inner team is to see it as made up of the same types of 'people' we have as friends and acquaintances in the external world. Among these we may count people who can give us wise counsel, help us with practical tasks, encourage us to have fun and so on. Different friends or functions may be dominant at different times, but we would be diminished and disadvantaged if any one of these was dominant all of the time.

The inner team concept can be powerful at an explanatory level. For example, it can help us explain seemingly 'irrational' behaviour, or when we appear to sabotage our own efforts at advancement. From a multi-dimensional or inner team perspective, this is one part of ourself in conflict with the **goals** and interests of another part. (The adventurous part of me may co-operate with my goal to go on an an expedition to the Arctic, but the cautious part may induce me to scupper my plans.) The inner team model can also help us to explain why we may both like and despise at different times the same side to our personality, just as we may both like and dislike someone we know.

The basic message of PD tutors is that we should first acknowledge and then seek to become more familiar with our different parts or subpersonalities. What we must not do is try to deny or get rid of the parts we would prefer not to acknowledge. Rather, we must begin to understand that every part has some valid quality and positive function to serve, even if it has become 'degraded' over time. For example, we may not like the part of us that is mean spirited, but we may come to recognize that this part helps us to survive, to look after our own needs, to be cautious etc. In developmental terms, one of our challenges is to 'elevate' the degraded function – to develop the Scrooge into a wise but charitable chancellor, to develop the over-critical 'friend' into an encouraging and appreciative judge etc.

Another developmental challenge is to get our inner team interacting in ways which benefit our growth and lives generally. For example, we may be able to resolve a problem or make a decision more effectively if we engage different aspects of ourselves and encourage them to work together. Dynamic interplay may sometimes be in our interests more than either antagonism or cosy consensus, just as it is with 'real' teams.

To contact and work with our different parts, many PD tutors suggest we use guided imagery and **visualization** techniques, imagining our inner team as a dinner party, for example, or a 'subpersonalities bus' (Syer and Connolly, 1991). Listening to our inner voices and using **self-talk** techniques can also help us to access our inner team members.

(See **Congruence; Decision-Making.**)

Instant Preplay

The **mental** (or mind-body) **rehearsal** of a performance immediately prior to the performance itself. Athletes routinely use this technique, but we can all benefit from it, particularly if we anticipate a difficult or anxious experience. One benefit is that it can help the 'real thing' to go more smoothly. For example, patient-doctor exchanges can be more satisfactory for both parties if patients have sorted out in their minds what they want to tell the doctor.

Instant Replay

Rehearsing or experiencing again in your mind (or mind/body) a performance you have just executed (see **Mental Rehearsal**). The intention is to program the performance into your mind or mind/body so that you can achieve a faithful structural reproduction on subsequent occasions. In **NLP** terms, the challenge is to codify the states, strategies, behaviours, submodalities etc, in the correct sequence. Clearly, the instant replay technique should not be used when we have just performed badly, otherwise we shall be fixing a pattern we don't wish to repeat. Unfortunately, many of us do precisely this as a form of self-punishment.

Intuition

The knowledge that comes to us without conscious cognitive effort on our part. Alternative or related terms include the sixth sense, the third eye, insight and gut feeling.

Intuition is variously considered mysterious or ordinary or a blend of the two. When the mysterious is emphasized, intuition is identified with the **Higher Self** or a transpersonal source and is thought of as beyond the normal dimensions of time and space. A less esoteric explanation is that intuition comes from being able to make exceptionally efficient use of all the relevant information available to us. This might include a host of memories and bits of information that come through non-verbal, chemical and other channels of communication, but not through language itself.

Ferrucci (1990) declares that intuition has been 'universally neglected'. This may be generally true of its recent fate in the West, but within the PD world it is held in high regard, particularly among PD tutors with holistic perspectives. Intuition is generally regarded as an innate human ability, but one which most of us need to recover and strengthen. Getting ourselves into the right condition for intuition to operate, and tuning into our intuition when it comes, are commonly seen as valuable personal development processes. They involve finding ways to subdue the 'noise' within and around us so that we are able to listen to the small quiet voice within, or to pick up signals from what Deepak Chopra calls the 'thinking cells' of our body. The routes to intuition include **meditation**, guided imagery and 'sitting for an answer' in a state of deep relaxation. There is also some evidence that intuition can be primed and cultivated by **modelling** the appropriate physiology (see Clynes, 1977).

The word most often used with reference to becoming more intuitive is 'trust'. We can be intuitive only if we trust the messages we apprehend directly and effortlessly from within. Some

PD tutors say that the more we trust, the better intuition seems to work, and that trusting ourselves is being true to ourselves as well as being open to truths about or from ourselves. Hence, to become more intuitive is to become more fully ourselves. 'In a sense, in using and strengthening the part of your mind, you are strengthening the integrity of your nature as a human being' (Ostrander and Schroeder, 1979).

PD tutors tend to see intuition less as an occasional flash of insight than as a more-or-less persistent guiding force. The authors of *Awaken Your Inner Power* note that intuition means 'inner-tuition' (Johnson and Swindley, 1995). Similarly, Helmstetter (1992), who rejects the idea that intuition is a 'mystical guiding force', recognizes it as 'a set of highly important protective programs that help us to make better choices.'

There is general acknowledgement that intuition has a very valuable part to play in **decision-making**, learning and personal growth. If we are tuned into ourselves, the argument goes, then we are better able to sense when we are taking the 'right' or the 'wrong' life paths. For many PD tutors, it is a skill we can develop and use more or less at will. Presumably, they either don't know about or are unconvinced by the evidence from cognitive psychology which indicates that intuition is very far from infallible and subject to predictable biases.

Karma

A doctrine originating from Eastern religious and **enlightenment** technologies, but now also in evidence in transmuted
forms within the more spiritually and metaphysically inclined
section of the PD world of the West.

Although a very subtle doctrine, karma is essentially the law
of cause and effect - the results we get from the choices we
make. This does not operate as a crude form of moral retribu-
tion. We produce 'good' and 'bad' karma, but we are not in any
obvious sense rewarded or punished for the choices and actions
we make. Rather, every thought or emotion we have and every
action we take is consequential. Put another way, who we are
and everything we experience has been set in motion in some
way by our past thoughts and actions. The present moment reg-
isters the karmic consequences of past choices etc, and sows
consequences for the future, so it offers us an opportunity to
understand the workings of karma in our lives. Some authorities suggest that we can end suffering and negative karma if we
can understand and never repeat the choices that initiated them.
Recurring patterns of difficult experiences indicate that we have
lessons to learn from our karma.

By nature an intricate doctrine, karma has become more complicated by its adoption and adaption to Western PD contexts.
Some original elements appear generally to have been played
down, or rejected. Some Westerners find the notion of 'fixed'
karma linked to race and sex hard to square with current equal
opportunities thinking. Others have objected to the potential for
ideological abuse within the karma doctrine of reincarnation, in
that it can be used to legitimate exploitative and repressive
social and political systems. (The rich and ruling elites are simply reaping the karmic consequences of good previous lives.)

At the same time, Western users have added to the meanings of karma ('heavy' karma, meaning a major karmic debt, is an example) and channelled it in directions that resonate with prevailing PD thinking. In what Gill Edwards (1991) calls 'the new understanding of karma', the emphasis is upon karma as personal choice rather than karma as an implacable universal law of reality. The emphasis seems to be on self-determination and future-orientation rather than upon consequences for past abuses. This fits in well with the general importance attached in PD to individual accountability, and the capacity each of us has to decide our own destiny rather than have it decided by fate. The doctrine of karma seems also to fit well with the growing field of human consciousness studies which focuses upon the power of the mind to make things happen in and outside the body.

Letting Go

The process of releasing whatever may be hurting us, holding us back or diminishing us in some way.

Letting go is an especially important concept in the area of **emotional development** and attachment. PD tutors in this area emphasize the damage we can do to ourselves when we don't relinquish negative feelings. Holding onto a grudge, or to anger or resentment, sometimes for years, can be both imprisoning and disempowering. As Sutherland (1993) observes, releasing or expressing these feelings can bring 'freedom, relief and self-respect'. For some PD tutors, letting go in the sense of forgiving or 'correcting our misperception that the other person has harmed us' (Jampolsky and Keeler, 1979), is the key to happiness, for only when we forgive can we see only love in others. The letting go of a painful or unrewarding relationship is also a well-rehearsed theme in the literature on emotional development. It is another example of where we need to exercise personal authority, and to acquire skills to do so effectively (see McKay *et al*, 1994).

A second kind of letting go concerns acknowledging the limits of our personal control. There are many situations that seem to defy any attempt to change them, and yet we may go on trying to manipulate and control them. This can bring us misery and frustration and prevent us getting on with our lives. Getting out of the situation is one response but another is to accept it and experience just being in it. It can be liberating and, as Shakti Gawain (1995) points out, expose us to the benefits of living in the **here and now**.

A third aspect of the letting go concept in PD contexts relates to the paradox of having something by letting it go, or, at least, by holding it only lightly. For example, we are sometimes advised to hold our **goals** lightly – to visualize them, and then to 'forget' about them at a conscious level. The same can apply to asking a question. As Sanaya Roman (1986) puts it, we get a question answered by asking it and then letting it go. This seems to be another instance of the principle that whatever we resist persists. Letting go hands the 'problem' over to the **subconscious** or **Higher Self**.

Leverage

The devices by which we influence ourselves or others to take the **action** that gets results.

PD tutors recognize that one of the major challenges many of us face when we want to **change** or move forward in our lives is getting started. This is often the case, even when we are clear about how we wish to develop. Leverage is linked to motivation but is often used in a more specific sense to describe particular steps or mechanisms that initiate change. The metaphor of the lever suggests a modest force to achieve a substantial 'lift'. Leverage in PD terms suggests small actions that can eventually lead to big results or to a good return for an investment of effort.

One of the principles of leverage is that of early rewards. Take a step that will be rewarding, preferably in an obvious and tangible way, very soon after. That will then serve as an incentive to sustain the change process. Another principle is to take small, manageable steps. If it is a big problem or a major change, then it should be eaten like the elephant, one bite at a time. A third principle is to begin with whatever gives us most pain. If we are finding it difficult to take any action, then it may be that we are not experiencing enough pain, or rather that we associate pain more with changing than we do with staying as we are. If this is the case, then we may find it helpful to induce pain by, for example, visualizing the longer-term consequences of not changing, or promising ourselves that we will punish ourselves if we do not fulfil our promise to change. Anthony Robbins deals in depth with leverage through pain and pleasure in *Awaken the Giant Within* (1992) and *Personal Power* (1993).

Whether we should use pain as well as pleasure to achieve leverage is a matter of debate. Some PD tutors believe that linking pain to desired change is contaminating – it sets up the wrong associations. They sometimes link it to *restrictive* motivation, when we try to get ourselves to take action out of fear or a feeling of obligation. However, the crucial factor may be whether or not our **subconscious** or some other, deeper aspect of ourselves subscribes to the application of fear. If we are proposing to change in line with our self-image, our **beliefs**, **values** and standards, then the pain we are using for leverage may be already there, within us. We are simply focusing upon it and making it more intense. There are all kinds of other devices for producing leverage, two of the simplest being **Acting 'As If'** and 'just doing it' – taking any relevant action that will loosen the dead grip of inertia.

Life skills

The skills we require to be self-empowered individuals, capable of facing **challenges** and changes with **competence** and confidence. Related terms include 'people skills', 'personal and social' skills, 'personal effectiveness', **'personal power'** and 'self-efficacy'.

Life skills are variously defined and categorized. Some are clearly of a higher order than others in that they are more directly related to **self-efficacy** and self-empowered living. These would almost certainly include assertiveness, **decision-making**, conflict management and **rapport**-establishing skills. Generic life skills would include listening, flexibility and **adaptability**.

One classification by two of Britain's best known authorities on life skills groups them into four very broad groups: 'Me and you' skills (those we need to relate effectively to another); 'Me and others' skills (those I need to relate effectively to others in general); 'Me' skills (those I need to manage and grow); and 'Me and specific situations' (those I need for education, work, home, leisure and life in the community). This constitutes a teaching program for school students (Hopson and Scally, 1981).

Locus of Control

This is where we perceive the control centre of our lives to be located. If we are an 'internal' then we percieve it to be within us. We are likely to be self-directed, to attribute little to fate or environment, to believe that we can control our destiny and accept personal accountability for who we are and what we do. If we are an 'external' then we will perceive it to lie outside ourselves. We believe that we are largely at the mercy of fate, other people and other forces beyond our control. We are other-directed and we accept little personal accountability.

PD is overwhelmingly 'on the side' of internals. Much PD literature is about converting externals to internals, or about reinforcing the beliefs and practices of the already committed. For example, many of the **beliefs** we are invited to **challenge** are about the Locus of Control. Clearly, an internal Locus of Control is central to the concepts of self-empowerment, **self-efficacy** and **personal power**.

The literature on Locus of Control is substantial. Research evidence generally validates the assumptions and contentions of PD tutors. For example, we know that internals enjoy more academic success, tend to be more competent (as well as more willing) helpers, and more effective managers of stress.

(See **Responsibility**.)

Mastery

In relation to a skill or activity, mastery is the ability to produce excellent results time and time again. Mastery is characterized by a capacity to reproduce successful performances effortlessly and more-or-less at will. It is also identified with unconscious competence. We often don't recognize that we are master performers; neither can we say what precisely we do to achieve our results.

AS **NLP**ers remind us, we are all masters. The areas concerned might include driving a car, cooking a meal, programming a video recorder, spelling 'correctly' and comforting a friend. PD courses designed to boost the **self-esteem** of the participants will often take them through a skills audit to encourage them to appreciate the number of taken-for-granted areas over which they have mastery. This is an antidote to the negative programming which highlights the evidence to suggest we are lamentable journeymen rather than master craftsmen (eg, the three words we've misspelled rather than the 300 we've mastered).

Mastery often includes physical skills, but in PD, especially in NLP, the emphasis is upon internal states, mental strategies and patterns, beliefs etc. Mental syntax – the sequence in which we perform thinking operations – is a particularly important factor. **Modelling** is the key strategy for developing and enhancing mastery.

In PD generally, 'mastery' is a relative term. Very rarely is a skill considered beyond improvement. There are contexts, however, in which mastery is an either/or matter – we've either achieved mastery or we haven't. The assessment of a student's learning is sometimes based on the mastery of criteria principle. Often, though, the criteria relate to threshold competencies

rather than to levels of excellence beyond the minimum level.
(See **Excellence**.)

Meditation

The discipline of turning our attention from the world outside
ourselves to the world within.

'It is about learning to become more receptive and attentive to
whatsoever you are' (Claxton, 1984). Meditation almost always
involves stilling our minds so that we are no longer aware of the
normal chatter and clutter of images. Getting into this tranquil
state usually requires us to concentrate upon one particular idea
or stimulus – a candle, a mantra, our breathing etc. Once we are
in this state of clear tranquillity, we may experience insights, but
they cannot be willed.

Many authorities on meditation insist that the process itself
has to be experienced to be understood; it cannot be captured in
words. The nearest we can get to defining it by external reference is through the use of symbols for, like meditation, symbols
link the conscious and unconscious minds.

Various forms of meditation are recognized and practised.
Key distinctions include *passive* versus *dynamic* meditation. The
former involves giving over our mind to the **Higher Self** or
using it as we use the mind in receptive visualization. Dynamic
meditation is the form we use for working on ourselves to bring
about **change**. It is akin to programmed **visualization**. Another
distinction is between meditation in which we clear our minds
of content and meditation where we allow ourselves to be aware
of the images which float through our conscious mind.

There is a substantial body of literature on meditation. Some
of it is obscure, but there are also some highly accessible 'manuals' and handbooks on the subject (eg, Fontana, 1991; 1992), and
plenty of people who teach it. There is no question that meditation occupies a massively important place in many of the
world's spiritual and philosophical traditions. But what is its
place currently within the world of PD generally?

It is probably true to say that few of us nowadays still regard
meditation as an esoteric practice for hippies and spiritual odd-
balls – and a good thing too! Meditation has become more (if not

entirely) 'mainstream'. Perhaps the main reason for this has to do with its perceived practical benefits. As someone has put it: it's a preparation for living, not an escape from it. Its most obvious benefits are calming and relaxing the mind and body. Practised by itself or as part of a method of mind control (eg, the Silva method), meditation can be a highly effective technique for reducing stress. The purist might not like this very much, for tranquillity without illumination is hardly meditation. But the effect in practice has been to turn meditation from a mystical minority art to a respectably down-to-earth technique for 'ordinary' people and purposes.

Practised by itself or in combination with visualization, dynamic meditation and transcendental meditation (TM) can be used for **healing** and health-enhancing purposes. The scientific evidence for this is overwhelming. We know, for example, that meditation can reduce cholesterol, help the immune system to function properly and benefit some people with Aids, cancer, heart conditions and asthma. Jane Alexander (1996) reports that meditators tend to visit their doctors less frequently and spend 70 per cent less time in hospital.

Emphasizing the medical benefits of meditation confers upon it a kind of scientific respectability. Seeing meditation as 'scientific' rather than 'mystical' has come about also with the 'discovery' of different brain wave rhythms and, in particular, with the association of meditation with the alpha state, which is also the state for **accelerated learning** (AL). Exponents of TM and AL make similar claims for their alpha-based activities: improved learning, memory and performance, quicker reaction times and enhanced sensory acuity. One of the newer primers on meditation, Harold Kampf's *The Speed Technique to Alpha Meditation and Visualisation* (1995), suggests in its title both that meditation is brain-based and adaptable to a culture which expects quick results.

Currently, then, an interest in meditation is consistent with a general interest in mental states and processes, and how we can use them to enhance performance and development. The view at the leading edges of the AL and NLP worlds is that we have only begun to explore and utilize the potential range of both our mental states and mental powers. As Colin Wilson put it in *Religion and Rebel* (1957), we have a whole keyboard of mental states but most of us stick to three or four notes. For the majority of us, meditation is not one of them, but it's becoming increasingly less likely that this has much to do with its being perceived as weird and mysterious. Indeed, it's not improbable that meditation will come to be regarded as just one (very special) state of consciousness to which each of us can and should have access. It might be seen as a training ground for the power and importance of **focus** – a process central both to meditation and to the most popular personal development books and programs of our time.

This does not mean that meditation has or will necessarily become demystified and secularized totally. We may be using it increasingly as a technique for everyday purposes, but it is still regarded as the principal vehicle for spiritual development. Kampf quotes Joel Goldsmith's assertion that 'without meditation it is difficult if not almost impossible to make spiritual progress, because spiritual attainment is accomplished in the mind.' Meditation is still widely seen as the main route to our Higher Self, to transcendence, **enlightenment** and, even, our awareness of oneness with the Whole. For as long as spiritual development is a primary concern for many people, meditation will play an instrumental role in it.

More debatable, perhaps, is the idea that meditation is a tool for *personal* growth. Many advocates of meditation describe it as such, and some assert that meditation is not so much a technique as a process of experiencing who we already are. It's often suggested that meditation can make us more accepting of both ourselves and others, that it enhances our **creativity** and sense of peace and **well-being**. It also opens up our awareness.

Authorities on meditation also say, however, that meditation at higher levels can bring about a partial dissolution of the personality or ego. Many meditators have professed to feeling their body as well as their consciousness melting away or spreading out into some Universal Life Force. One book on enlightenment and meditation, *Beyond the Personality*, declares this with its title. One thesis of the book is that when we attain through meditation the emptiness of mind that permits us to understand the true nature of reality, then we are 'no longer preoccupied with compulsive satisfaction of needs and desires' (ITC, 1987). Similarly, Kampf says that in meditation 'one finds that one goes beyond the need for purely personal gain and development.'

These views seem to fit uncomfortably with the thrust of popular PD programs, in which the emphasis is very much upon developing our individual personalities – enhancing our **personal power**, for example. Most PD programs are packed with content – ideas and strategies for using, controlling and improving our minds. The virtues of silence and stillness are sometimes extolled (see Holland, 1993), but we're more often told to talk positively to ourselves than not to talk to ourselves at all. To put it crudely: PD programs tend to fill our minds; meditation is designed to empty them. PD activities generally promote mental motion; meditation teaches stillness, on the supposition that it is the perpetual motion of our minds that blurs our normal perceptions of reality.

Finally, meditation and PD programs tend to differ in regard to intentions and expectations. Meditation is a humble discipline. With practice, patience and commitment, it can yield outcomes that many of us find of great value. But virtually every teacher of meditation teaches us to approach it without specific expectations of what it might or should deliver. Goal-setting and meditation can seem uneasy bedfellows, and yet goal-setting for the self is at the heart of most PD programs.

It would seem, then, that meditation stands in rather complex relationship to the world of popular, mainstream PD. Its perceived practical benefits, its demystification and its consonance with technologies for developing the mind bring it within the compass of this world. But some aspects of meditation resist easy alignment with the assumptions and approaches of PD generally.

Mental Maps

These are our personal models of reality, our perceptions of 'the way things are out there'. They are built up from our experiences, particularly referent experiences, and our neurological make-up, including our **beliefs** and **values**. Collectively, our mental maps add up to our map of reality or our model of the world. We share aspects of these with other people, but no two people have identical maps.

Mental maps are relevant to personal development in a number of respects. Development itself can be construed as a process of developing and changing our mental maps: enriching old maps and finding 'better' or different ones. Changes to dominant mental maps are sometimes called paradigm shifts, and PD tutors may seek to bring these about in us. An example would be moving us from an external to an internal Locus of Control model, or from a 'no-win' to a 'no-lose' model of **decision-making**. Shifts can occur when we become converts to a particular approach or pathway to personal growth such as a mind-body discipline, a therapy, a religious or even a personal change technology such as **NLP**.

For personal development to occur, it's important for us to be around people with different mental maps from our own. They enable us to see our blindspots and to see things differently.

Appreciating that other people do not necessarily share our mental maps is one of the fundamental keys to effective inter-personal communication. Similarly, being able to get into someone else's mental maps is an invaluable skill. It's basic to the improvement of relationships and conflict management, and figures prominently in some PD programs – Abe Wagner's *Say It Straight or You'll Show It Crooked* audio program, for example. And it's virtually identical with the fifth of Steven Covey's seven habits of highly effective people (see Covey, 1992).

The essential skill is patient, empathic listening. We give our partners our total attention to show that our first priority is to understand their definitions of the situation. It sounds easy and obvious, but many of us are more often concerned with putting across our definition – which may seem to us the only or obvious one. Trying to make sense of someone else's mental map before seeking to present ours to them is both profoundly simple and effective. It's supremely logical, in that we cannot understand the other if *we* are doing the talking. It also enables the other to have their say and then to be in a psychologically more receptive state of mind to extend the courtesy.

How precisely can we listen our way into someone else's mental maps? Since we betray our maps naturally, as it were, sensitivity to key words and images is crucial. We can also pick up body language cues or clues – physiological indicators of interest or boredom, for example. And we can ask questions to tease out the relevant maps and show interest at the same time.

The exciting news is that in the last 20 years or so we have begun to understand and label some of the more common mental maps. NLP, in particular has enabled us to acquire a kind of 'mapping literacy'.

NLP tells us that we map partly in terms of dominant modalities - that some of us will prefer to represent (or re-present) reality in visual terms, others in auditory terms and still others in kinaesthetic terms. These preferences will be reflected in the language we use. But modalities are not the only 'filters' we use to 'frame' reality (to use other favoured NLP terms). We also 'sort' (and delete) information on the basis of what is important to us. These are often called *Frames*, and some of the entries in this book identify a few of these. For example, there is the '**Outcomes** Frame', where we define the situation in terms of the outcomes we want rather than the problems it presents. There is also the '**Ecology** Frame' where we define the situation in terms of how it impacts upon other aspects of the system or our lives, rather than upon the thing itself. (For example, we will frame a decision to accept a new job in terms of its implications for our family life, our leisure, our long-term goals etc.)

Frames which indicate habitual sorting tendencies are sometimes called *metaprograms*. These are our key distinctions for responding to reality, the major principles by which our mental maps are constructed. Identifying our metaprograms can significantly enhance our **self-awareness**. Identifying the metaprograms of others can help us to establish **rapport** and communicate much more effectively with them.

NLPers recognize a number of common metaprograms. One relates to whether we prefer to map reality in terms of similarities or in terms of differences. In NLP language, do we tend to 'match' or to 'mismatch'? In a discussion situation, for example, do we tend to focus upon ideas which match our own or ideas that differ from them? Another metaprogram concerns our referencing tendencies. We can be 'externally' referenced, in which case we tend to rely upon other people for fulfilment, validation etc, or 'internally' referenced, in which case we are likely to be independent and to look within for satisfaction or otherwise. A third metaprogram is 'sorting by self' (being oriented principally to our own needs and interests) or 'sorting by others' (defining situations in terms of other people's needs and interests).

Clearly, these are only tendencies, and many of us will sort on both principles on different occasions. Recognizing our tendencies can also enable us to make changes where they might be helpful to us.

The practical applications of metaprograms have only begun to be appreciated, but they are certainly massive. For example, they might make a substantial contribution to job selection procedures. It's obvious that for certain kinds of roles and positions a sorter by others might be preferable to a sorter by self, or a matcher preferable to a mismatcher – but clearly not for all roles. Professional helpers (counsellors, therapists, etc) might also benefit significantly from being 'metaprogram literate' as well as sensitive to the efforts of mental maps in general (which many certainly are already).

Mental Rehearsal (MR)

The process of going through or practising in our mind the performance we intend (shortly) to do for real.

MR is a subset of the practices known collectively as *mental rehearsal skills* (or *exercises*). They include **visualization, affirmations** and controlled **self-talk**, including the use of 'power' language (ie, words with strong biochemical or physiological effects). Some forms of **writing** and problem-solving skills are also included.

We all 'go through' in our minds how we think we are likely to perform in certain forthcoming situations. This is not always the same thing as effective MR, which can take many forms, but often involves **modelling** either ourselves performing the relevant skill(s) well or someone else whom we've seen doing the same thing. It's mainly a matter of recalling the precise actions in sequence – getting the mental syntax right, as NLPers would put it. The process often involves two stages. Step one is viewing the excellent performance in our mind's eye in a disassociated state. Step two is performing **as if** we were the model (ie, in an associated state). The same process can be done by proxy, as it were. That is, we model a performance we visualize rather than recall (see **Ideal Model**).

(See **Instant Preplay; Instant Replay**.)

Mentoring

One of the helping, empowering relationships which contribute to personal development.

It has been described as 'one of the broadest methods of encouraging human growth' (Shea, 1992), and can contribute to the development of all manner of things: **values, competences,** character, knowledge relevant to performing effectively in a role or organization, insights into experience, careers etc. Mentoring is not nannying or directing. Rather, it is usually thought of as a nurturing, caring and influencing process by which one person (the mentor) helps another (the protégé) to exploit **opportunities** to grow and acquire insights, skills and knowledge.

An effective mentor will have the experience, expertise and personal skills to be useful to the development of her/his protégé in lots of ways, one of which involves defining and realizing **goals**. There is currently much emphasis on this function. For example, Lessem (1987) calls 'dream realization' the most crucial development role of the mentor. With reference to mentors for young adults, he says that the mentor 'fosters your development by believing in you, sharing the youthful "dream" and giving it his blessing.'

A major theme of mentoring literature is the extent to which mentoring can be highly developmental for the *mentor*. Mentors can pick up ideas, gain insights into their practices and **attitudes**, and develop a range of skills with value beyond the mentoring relationship. These include respectful and active listening, confrontation, and skills which empower and encourage protégés to take **risks**, reflect on experiences, plan learning opportunities etc. The best mentors seem often themselves to be committed to lifelong self-development.

The current growth in mentoring and interest in it can be explained in a number of ways. Within modern organizations, it reflects the move to flatter structures with fewer managers, more self-directed individuals and teams and the need to find creative, cost-effective ways to accelerate learning. For some observers, 'mentoring in the community is one response to the fragmentation of our society' (Hamilton, 1994). Fewer accessible family 'elders' being available to mentor and develop more junior members may be one explanation for the growth of mentoring in residential care settings, schools and other places. It may even help to explain the enormous popularity of PD tutors, who arguably serve a similar function for large numbers of unknown individuals to that served by family, tribal and community 'elders' in less complex and less fragmented societies. (See **Coaching; Counselling**.)

Meta Model

A model which specifies both the standard ways in which we delete, distort and generalize meanings through the language we use, and the standard responses by which we can challenge these forms of imprecision in others and ourselves. It was outlined originally by the founders of NLP (Bandler and Grinder, 1975).

The Meta Model borrows from linguistics (specifically, from transformational grammar) the idea that when we use language to represent an experience we may be uttering only a partial and incomplete version of it. This version has transformed the full version that lies at a deeper level. For example, 'The plate got smashed' is a transformed form of *'something or someone smashed the plate'*, but the agent (what or who did the smashing) is deleted and the utterance is rendered in the passive. What we actually say (the *surface structure* utterance) differs from what we could say if we represented our experience in the complete *deep structure* form. Always to use the full version would make communication very cumbersome, so we use shortened, altered forms for the sake of simplicity, economy and clarity (or deliberate unclarity at times). Unfortunately, these transformational operations can have a variety of negative effects upon us and our communication. They can lead to pain and misunderstanding, lock us into unchecked assumptions about the way things are, disconnect us from the fullness of experience and put a stop on personal change.

Transformations occur in regular patterns known as the Meta Model violations. A number of NLP books provide readable descriptions of these (eg, Lewis and Pucelik, 1990; O'Connor and Seymour, 1993). The Meta Model itself is a set of standard questions to recover or direct attention to whatever information has been deleted, distorted or generalized in the Meta Model violation. These are called the Meta Model responses. Being able to recognize and respond to violations is a powerful tool for improving communication and effecting personal change. We can apply the Model to our own **self-talk** as well as to the talk of others.

Meta Model responses can have a number of benefits. They can help to clarify the meaning of utterances. They can help us to identify the boundaries we've placed on our perceptions, give us insights into our **beliefs** and ways of organizing experiences, and show us that we have more **choices** than we might have realized in terms of how we behave, feel and perceive the world. They can also help us to avoid the pain that comes from misunderstanding and assumed limitations. For example, we might have a belief that loving someone means being able to know what they are thinking. If this remains buried and unexamined it might cause us and others pain. But almost certainly it will surface in our utterances, allowing someone else to identify and so challenge it.

Mind-reading is, in fact, one of the recognized Meta Model violations, and a standard response to it is: 'How do you know?'. 'If you loved me, you would know what I thought' is an example of another Metal Model violation called a *complex equivalence*, to which a response is: 'How does *this* (knowing your thoughts) mean *that* (I love you)?'

A final example will illustrate the violation of the *modal operator of possibility*. We may say, 'I can't' ('I can't change', 'I can't do anything else') because we *perceive* a limitation, not because we *are* limited by the situation or by our ability. A response to this might be: 'What stops you?' or 'What would happen if you did?'. This opens up the possibility of our awareness being expanded so that we see other possibilities represented linguistically in 'I won't, 'I choose not to' etc. (See **Deletion**.)

Mind Map ®

A device for recording information in the same way that the brain appears to store it.

The human brain does not store information in lines and

columns, but rather in branching or dendritic networks based on pattern and association. As Dryden and Vos (1994) point out, the more we work with rather than against the brain's method of working, the easier we will find it to learn.

A mind map can be built up by noting the main theme of the map in the centre of a sheet of paper. We then allocate a branch to each sub-theme, and branch off from here with single words for each concept etc. We can enhance the mind map as a learning tool by incorporating pictures and symbols and generally enhancing its visual impact.

Mind maps can be used to preview, review and record notes on books read and topics studied. It can serve as a tool for linking information in new, creative ways. Not surprisingly, it is a favoured tool with the advocates of **accelerated learning**, including Nancy Margulies (1991) and the originator of the mind map concept, Tony Buzan (1993). (Mind map ® is a registered trademark of Tony Buzan.)

Mission Statement

Either a succinct statement of our life's **purpose** or a statement translating that purpose into our life's **goals**. The latter would be *the*, or at least, *a* goal described at the highest possible level. There is a third possibility, recognized by some PD tutors, that the purpose of life is to find and pursue our mission.

Mission statements are brief. The advice generally given is to make them no longer than a paragraph, but often they consist of one or two sentences, and can be as short as a motto. (One old soldier said that his company commander had used the motto 'forward regardless' which had served as his own mission statement for 60 years.) This mission statement can be enlarged upon and translated into more specific goals or **vision** statements.

Whereas a purpose is generally regarded as unending, a mission can be completed. It is possible, then, to have more than one mission, consecutively rather than concurrently, and thus to have serial mission statements. For example, we may believe that our purpose in life is to be of service to others, but that may take different forms at different times in our lives.

Mission statements are invariably written down, though they

may be rendered in other media also. To be meaningful they need to be memorable, and since their purpose is to keep us focused on our life's purpose, PD tutors often advise us to print and leave our mission statement where we will see it on a regular basis – on our walls, our office desk, in our purse or wallet etc.

Modelling

Learning how to do something very well by replicating the strategies and behaviours of someone who is exceptionally good at doing it. Modelling in PD terms has also been defined as 'a process of accelerating what we have all learned early in life – the skill of imitation' (Porter, 1993).

Modelling by imitation is a natural and very powerful way of acquiring new skills. It's the way in which young children learn many things. Adults also learn by imitation, mostly informally but sometimes formally – in apprenticeships, for example, and in 'sitting-by-Nellie' training – though our models are not always excellent.

One way to model is to identify an excellent performer in the relevant skill area and then to use **Acting 'As If'** and **visualization** techniques to help you act and feel like this person. Athletes sometimes use this approach. It is also possible to model a master in one field and then imagine you are that person in your own field. Some sports people have modelled themselves on Margaret Thatcher, for example.

Modelling has been developed by NLP into one of the major technologies of personal **excellence**. NLPers believe that if one person can do something well, then virtually anybody can – with the right modelling. This assumption, together with the precision by which excellence is codified and the attention to internal as well as external patterns, has made the contribution of NLP to the ancient art of modelling of inestimable value.

NLPers seek models of excellence in every area of human activity, including education, therapy, business and interpersonal relationships. An NLP modelling project involves identifying excellent performers and then asking them to do whatever it is they do particularly well. By observing, listening to and questioning them, the NLP modellers will elicit their strategies (both conscious and, as far as possible, unconscious, internal and external), focusing upon language, non-verbal behaviours, physiology, **beliefs**, **values** and thought patterns and programs. By taking away each of the elicited elements, one at a time, it is possible for the modellers to determine whether or not particular elements are crucial to excellent performance. Crucial elements are left in, and those that seem to be unnecessary are left out, thus simplifying the model.

If not a science, modelling the NLP way is at least a process of detection driven by curiosity and informed by an acute sense of what to look for. The most basic modelling question is 'How do you do that?' but NLPers use many other how/what/when questions. 'Why' questions are rarely considered useful for modelling purposes. Because of what they are looking for in eliciting strategies and behaviours, NLPers 'notice' things that have never been built systematically into, say, apprenticeship models – eye movements, for example, or a specific belief that underpins a set of behaviours.

Some examples of modelling may have a certain transfer value. For example, the strategies an athlete uses to psych himself up before an event may be useful to, say, business people preparing for an important meeting. Generally, however, models are situation-specific, the recognition of which is another NLP contribution to the field of personal excellence.

From a PD viewpoint, modelling stands in an interesting relationship to the concept of experience. It acknowledges that experience is not a sufficient nor even, for some things, a necessary condition for excellent performance. If we model a second rate performer, all the experience in the world may not make us excellent. If we know precisely what to do, then we may achieve excellence at the first attempt. Also, other people's experience may be more valuable than our own if we can model it and avoid the waste of time and effort of trial-and-error and reinventing the wheel methods. However, we can certainly model ourselves as well as other people by, for example, working out what we did to get an excellent result at a task performed in the past and then reproducing the behaviours so as to use the skill more widely and at will.

It is important to note that modelling other people does not mean trying to become them. We are actually modelling strategies rather than particular individuals. This is where sensitivity, judgement and flexibility come in, for modelling is an art as well as a science. Excellent modelling is rarely a matter of slavish copying, and it is unfortunate that modelling has also been called 'success cloning'. Finally, it is worth noting that PD literature itself offers many models of excellence for all manner of activities, though some are not as precise and multimodal as NLP models. For example, there are models for decision-making, for meditating, for overcoming fears and for self-assessment. (See **Ideal Model**.)

Music

Music can make significant contributions to **healing** and to personal development. There is considerable evidence now to show that music can expand memory, improve concentration, speed up the learning process and reduce stress.

The idea that music can have beneficial effects on both the mind and the body is far from new. In recent decades this ancient truth has been tested, refined and applied in systematic ways for therapeutic and, in particular, learning purposes. What we know now is that different kinds of music can be used for different purposes – for example, visualizing, changing our state and writing at speed. We know that music with a slow, steady beat helps people with heart trouble and hypertension. Baroque music is especially well regarded for learning purposes. Its characteristic rhythms are like a slow human pulse, and it has, as Diana Beaver (1995) observes, the symmetry and harmony of music written 'to free the soul from earthly matters'. Baroque and some other kinds of music put the listener in a relaxed and yet alert and receptive state of mind. We know now that it is associated with the alpha brain-wave state which gives access to deeper levels of the mind than we get in the 'normal' beta state.

What makes music particularly powerful for learning purposes is that it requires no special attention or concentration. Compared to, say, **meditation**, it is effortless – and fast. According to Colin Rose (1985), 'music can do in minutes what weeks of meditative practice strive towards.' And yet, music (with the appropriate patterns) can get us to **focus** within and perhaps even carry us 'inward to the Higher Self', as the Borysenkos (1995) suggest. The calming effects of chanting are well-recognized. The use of music to explore, unblock and express feelings is also well-known and central to music therapy.

Techniques for using music to enhance performance are now taught to athletes and other performers. One of these involves finding a song or piece of music which has a quality associated with the skill the performer wants to improve. This could be patience or power, for example. The performer would listen to the song and then 'hear' it internally when rehearsing his performance. It might be appropriate to play it during or just prior to an actual performance but, at this stage, a song with a different quality might be more fitting.

(See **Accelerated Learning**.)

Musturbation

A term coined by Ellis (1975, 1987) to refer to irrational beliefs linked to 'should' or 'must' type thinking.

Musturbation is akin to **cognitive distortion**. Examples of musturbatory thinking include 'I must be liked by every significant person in my life' and 'I must be perfect at everything'.

The rigid thinking implied by musturbation is inimical to personal development. It is associated with high levels of anxiety and negative **self-talk**. Musturbation appears to be achievement-orientated, but the 'goals' are unrealistic and the absence of **choice** reveals the mentality of a victim rather than of an agent.

Negative Thinking

Our thinking is negative in content when we allow it to dwell upon what we *don't* want or what is *wrong* with a situation rather than what is right with it. Our thinking is negative in its effects when it limits and disables us. This happens, for example, when it puts us in a depressed and unresourceful state, when it distracts us from our goals at the time or when it drains the energy we could have used more productively elsewhere.

Apparently, the majority of us spend much more time thinking negatively than positively. Lee Milteer (1990) estimates that 80 per cent of our thoughts are negative on a *good* day! A major thrust of self-help books is to reduce our negative thinking. The assumption is that we both can and should gain access to strategies that enable us to identify, challenge and positively redirect our negative thinking states and patterns. This is another way of saying that negative thinking is a choice, not a necessity.

None of us is positive all the time, but some of us are habitually and obsessively negative. We allow negative thoughts to arise spontaneously, or to be activated by all manner of 'events', and for those thoughts to bear little relationship to the reality of the situation. Cognitive psychologists call these 'negative automatic thoughts'.

Negative thinking tends to have disruptive and adverse effects on performance. This is why sports psychologists place heavy emphasis upon mental training and positive preparation programs for the athletes they work with. Negative thinking can be verbal 'put-down' **self-talk** and negative self-labelling for example ('I'm stupid!' 'I'm hopeless at anything practical'). It can also take the form of images, including pessimistic fantasies about how a situation is likely to turn out. Negative thinking also produces negative moods and states, though negative physiology (eg, slouching in a depressed way) can also play its part.

There are many reasons for negative thinking and many strategies and techniques for dealing with it. At a fundamental level, we may need to 'upgrade' our self-concept and sense of self-worth, for if we have a comparatively low and unfavourable view of ourselves, then it will be difficult to shift from negative to positive thinking on a consistent basis (see **Self-Esteem**). Negative beliefs about ourselves, the world, life and other people can also lock us firmly into negative thinking patterns. External locus of control beliefs are likely to lead to negative thinking. We are also likely to think negatively if we believe that, say, people are generally 'bad', life is cruel to us, and there's little we can do to improve ourselves. Having a 'scarcity' as opposed to an 'abundancy' mentality is also associated with negative thinking, particularly fears based upon beliefs that there is insufficient money, talent and love to 'go round'.

Most strategies for dealing with negative thinking work on thinking itself. Those used in cognitive therapy tend to focus on content. For example, therapists might help their clients to put their fears into perspective, to distance themselves from them, to encourage them to see that even the worst that could happen would not be dire, and to question the evidence that supports the negative thoughts (ie, reality testing).

Techniques deriving from **NLP** and the mental training programs developed for athletes can train us to turn negatives into positives by controlling our brains. The simplest technique is simply to command our brains to stop thinking negatively (see **Pattern Interrupt**).

More elaborate or imaginative techniques include those using **visualization**. For example, Kassorla (1984) suggests imagining a tiny vacuum cleaner moving across the forehead sucking up the negative thoughts and images. We can also re-edit the mental 'films' that re-play old, negative experiences, so that they have positive effects upon us.

Doing something about negative thinking patterns depends in the first instance upon recognizing them. If they have become habitual, then this is not always easy. It's another good reason for becoming more self-aware. How we explain negative thinking patterns depends partly on our theoretical perspective. For example, from a psychosynthetic point of view, negative thinking seems sometimes to involve conflicts between sub-personalities. This is certainly one way of explaining self-sabotage. One sub-personality is determined to act positively, but another undermines its efforts. From the perspective of Gestalt therapy, much of our negative thinking may be explained in terms of the ways in which our contact or engagement with others can be interrupted. For example, if we become negative, upset or angry with certain people or situations, then it may be because we are *projecting* a 'quality' *we* have (but cannot or do not wish to see in ourselves) onto them. Another example is the negative thinking and feeling that comes from swallowing the demands and expectations of others without truly assimilating them. This process of *introjection* happens, for example, when we play a role which we haven't really become. The negative consciousness emerges from our sense of the mismatch between what we are and what we are doing.

A quite different strategy involves becoming more aware of how we can use our physiology to drive away negative states (see **Body Awareness**). A final strategy concerns becoming more aware of the 'messages' that are coming to us from our environment. The specific advice sometimes offered here is to stay away from predominantly negative sources of information (eg, newspapers) and people who depress us with their negative talk (see **GIGO**).

(See **ABC Theory; Attribution Theory; Cognitive Distortions.**)

Neuro-Linguistic Programming (NLP)

The study and practice of human **excellence**.

NLP practitioners (NLPers) study the mental processes, the language and the body language of people who do certain things exceptionally well. They then model or copy whatever seem to be the key processes and behaviours to get the same results themselves, or to help others to get them.

NLP's unique and substantial contribution to personal development lies in its focus upon *subjective* experience. Before NLP (it 'began' in the 1970s), books on achievement, **success** and personal **change** told us in general terms what we had to do and think in order to achieve results. But they didn't tell us specifically what we had to do inside our heads to optimize our chances of getting excellent, lasting results. NLP isn't generally prescriptive and it does not assume that we all think in the same ways. But it does give us access to information about what other people do neurologically and with language to achieve successful outcomes.

In some ways, NLPers seek to do for subjective experience what linguists do for language. They identify the content of our mental processes; the modalities (visual, auditory, kinaesthetic, etc) by which we prefer to process sense impressions and the images we make with our inner senses. NLPers also seek to identify patterns in our thinking, since the sequence of our mental processes can be as crucial for effective performance as the syntax of words for the meaning of a sentence. NLPers also show us how we can manipulate the specific attributes (or submodalities) of our thought images (their size, colour and speed, for example) in order to achieve the effects we want. And in NLP, images are coded in much the same way that languages have grammatical terms for different parts of speech. For example, *Vi* is the code for a visual image internally generated (ie, visualized) and *Ae* stands for an auditory image (a sound) that has an external source.

Another way of defining NLP is as a 'science' of human communication, since most NLP skills are communication skills of one kind or another, and since NLP acknowledges the powerful effects of language on perception, mental processing and feelings. NLP is concerned with how we communicate with ourselves, with other people and with reality generally.

One of the fundamental ideas in NLP is that the map is not the territory. We don't experience reality directly and neutrally, reality 'as it is', but always through the maps by which we try to represent it and make sense of it. These maps include language and our **mental maps** of reality about 'the way things are'. If I say 'X is a problem for me', I am not 'telling it as it is' but rather assigning a particular meaning to a situation that I have perceived in a certain way. I might have said 'X is an opportunity for me'. Neither version is right or wrong, but each has a particular set of effects on my thinking and feeling. NLP draws our attention to the 'filters' and 'frames' (favoured NLP words) through which we perceive the world, and shows us how we can create **choices** in the way we perceive things. For example, we can change key **beliefs**, change the frame through which we perceive (**reframing**), see something from the position of some-one other than ourselves and alter the mental images in our mind's eye. In NLP, experience is never given or fixed forever; we can always manipulate it from within.

NLP is above all about how we communicate with ourselves. This includes how we manage our thinking, our memories and our states (see **State Management**). These processes are seen as the key to achieving successful results in just about every aspect of our lives. Managing aspects of our physiology is also impor-tant because of the links between physiology and neurology. For example, different eye movements are linked to thinking in dif-ferent modalities, and our posture can significantly influence our state of mind. NLP practitioners are expert at reading aspects of our body language in order to gain access to what we are doing internally. They are also adept at fixing and then trig-gering at will certain desirable states through the techniques of anchoring (see **Anchor**).

NLP is concerned also with inter-personal communication. Some of the main presuppositions of NLP ('There is no failure, only feedback' and 'The meaning of the communication is the response it gets') are directly relevant to this area. Appreciating the implications of the map/territory distinction, and that dif-ferent people have different ways of thinking and managing mental processes, are very important NLP ideas in the area of person-to-person interaction. Another major area of interest is **rapport** and the skills of establishing and maintaining it.

As a phenomenon, NLP is remarkable. In spite of an unpromisingly technical title and the fact that it is riddled with jargon, it has undoubtedly been one of the major success stories in the world of PD – arguably, *the* success story of the present time. And the story is clearly far from over. There are now a great many books on NLP, and many organizations worldwide offering training in it. It has been applied to counselling, psy-chotherapy, human relationships, teaching, training, selling, business generally, sport and to a number of other areas, and the list is growing. Most people who 'get into' NLP seem to become enthusiasts (excellent enthusiasts, of course!) if not evangelists. How can we account for its appeal?

The brief answer is that 'it works'. At least, NLPers would say that it offers them practical, highly specific ways to achieve rapid, sometimes radical and often lasting results. Many professionals have experienced it as a frustration-buster. At one time they weren't able to give their clients the really effective help they knew they needed. NLP techniques now enable them to do this.

Some people are attracted to NLP because it offers highly pragmatic tools and yet it has a compelling theoretical base. Its credentials are sound also because much of it is based upon evidence that comes under scrutiny whenever the relevant strategies are used. The NLP approach is: if the model doesn't work, then you change it. In this sense, NLP is rigorous enough to be deemed the 'science' that some NLP advocates claim it is.

NLP requires no special equipment, only our brains and bodies. And yet, it is a high-tech approach to PD in that it construes the mind-body systems to be a set of technologies comparable to those we find in the real world, if vastly more sophisticated and dynamic. NLP teaches us to treat the brain in the same way as we treat the technologies we have in our homes and offices. What we do with our submodalities parallels what we do with the controls of, say, our video machine and TV sets: alter the volume, the colour and contrast, switch channels, pause, re-wind etc. In an age of high-speed high-tech computer graphics, **programming** our minds by creating and manipulating images is unlikely to seem a strange thing to do; only a few decades back, it may well have done.

It is almost certainly no accident that NLP has grown up in a period of rapid technological and socio-cultural change. We demand, it would seem, personal change technologies that deliver equally rapid results and yet are themselves capable of evolving rapidly. NLP attracts curious, enterprising, accelerated learners who ensure that it remains dynamic. Certainly, NLP is forever developing, and it would be surprising if it were not barely recognizable in its present form in ten years time.

Opportunities

Personal growth is partly a matter of seeking, seizing and creating opportunities for development. Optimizing these opportunities is a theme of PD literature.

One way of achieving this is to set **goals**, for once we have a goal we open ourselves up to 'see' opportunities and possibilities that we couldn't have 'seen' before. But spotting or making opportunities depends also upon something even more fundamental than goals: having positive mental **attitudes** (PMAs).

Frequently, opportunities are 'disguised' as problems or situations that on the face of it seem unpromising. What we 'see' when we confront them depends upon our perception and perspective. PMAs will help us to see opportunities where other people might see only problems. There are techniques we can use to make this process conscious and systematic. For example, we can pose a question to ourselves, such as: 'What opportunities are there in this situation to help me to achieve my goals?' There is also the well-known SWOT Analysis technique, which in part involves trying to turn Weaknesses into Strengths and Threats into Opportunities. Collaborating with the inevitable ('making the most of a bad situation') is also a process of defining or positively re-defining a situation to exploit the opportunities latent within it.

Helping others to see and develop opportunities where they could see none before is a major objective of many forms of PD tutoring. For example, career consultants can sometimes help their clients to see development opportunities coming out of redundancy. It's also a major function of counselling to assist clients to be more aware of and more capable of managing opportunities for their own development.

Outcomes

The specific results we want from an experience, situation or change in our lives.

'Outcomes' is a favoured term with **NLPers**. It means much the same as **goals**, but tends to be applied to a wider range of situations. NLPers are more likely to talk about the outcomes than the goals of, say, communicative interactions. A concern for outcomes is consonant with being future- and **solution-centred**.

In NLP terms, an outcome is worth having only if it is 'well-formed'. Leslie Cameron-Bandler (1985) states five conditions for a well-formed outcome. First, it must be stated positively, not as a 'don't want' statement. If something not wanted is removed, then it usually has to be replaced with something that is wanted. 'I don't want to watch television every evening' must be replaced with something such as, 'I want to play squash two evenings a week'. Second, a well-formed outcome can be stated in sensory-based terms. That is, we ought to be able to say how we will feel or behave as a result of the change – what evidence will be available to our senses to show that the outcome has been successful. Third, the situation or context for the outcome can be stated precisely. For example: 'I am going to feel more relaxed in weekly staff meetings'. The fourth condition is that the outcome is under the control of the doer. At least, the doer must be able to initiate and sustain the outcome. An outcome that depends upon the behaviour of others or upon circumstances is not well-formed. The fifth condition is that the outcome must enable 'positive by-products' to be preserved. That's another way of saying that it must be able to stand up to an **ecology** check. It's clearly no good putting one thing right if the effect of this is to have an adverse effect upon some other feature of the situation. Another frequently discussed criterion of well-formedness is that the outcome is of the 'right' size: big enough to motivate but small enough to be achievable.

Formulating well-formed outcomes is not always easy. Many of us do not know precisely what we want and/or how to express this in outcome terms. Therapists, counsellors and other professional helpers have the job of assisting their clients with outcome formulations, and have to be skilled in eliciting the necessary information. NLP has almost certainly helped to sharpen and clarify thinking about the precise kinds of questions to ask (or refrain from asking) others or ourselves in a host of different kinds of situations.

From some perspectives, outcome orientation is not necessarily either healthy or helpful. It can breed anxiety, indecision and a reluctance to take any life path unless the outcomes can be fully foreseen and delineated. Having a somewhat cavalier or, at least, a curious attitude towards the outcomes that may flow from making a particular decision, rather than needing to 'fix' the outcomes before the decision is even made, may be a legitimate alternative viewpoint to the outcomes approach as far as some situations are concerned. It's a viewpoint that places a premium on the values of adventure. The idea that *any* path we take in life is strewn with opportunities, so that we do not need to be overly concerned about which one we choose, is key to the strategy for confronting the fear of choosing presented by Susan Jeffers (1991).

Outdoor Development

Opportunities for finding and developing our strengths through predominantly outdoor activities. In a human resource management context, outdoor development is **outcomes**-led, planned for systematically and almost invariably team-based.

The advocates of outdoor development argue that it has distinct advantages for team-building and other development exercises over more traditional, 'classroom'-based activities. Participants can get fully and holistically involved, with feelings and emotions being as important as intellectual activity, and the impact is long-lasting. People who have outdoor development experiences rarely forget them.

Outdoor development tends to be misunderstood. Very frequently, the emphasis is not upon physical endurance, strength or commando-like skills, and participants tend to learn most from exercises that are not physically challenging.

Pattern Interrupt (PI)

A term frequently used for the process of stopping our minds from playing **negative thinking** or self-defeating programs. We identify the pattern and then, when we catch ourselves about to indulge in it, we interfere with it before it can do damage. PI has many equivalent terms, including *thought stoppage* (Sutherland, 1993).

The simplest PI is a standard command to the mind such as 'cancel this program'. It's better to have a positive alternative to run in its place, so a command such as 'change channels' or 'run x program' may be preferable. The 'x program' might be a permanent stand-by, such as a piece of special place **visualization**.

Some authorities suggest not just interrupting but permanently breaking negative patterns, including negative memories. One technique (to switch the image once more) is 'scratching the record', by which we mentally lacerate our negative thinking record until it is unplayable. We can also break unwanted **anchors** and patterns of **association**. This can involve uncoupling the links in one pattern (eg, smoking + good feelings) and establishing a new coupling (eg, smoking + feeling of nausea).

Peak Performance

A performance in which we feel 'fully functioning' in some area(s) of experience or expertise. A demonstration of excellence.

Abraham Maslow (1962) developed the concept of a 'peak experience' as part of his theory of self-**actualization**. He defined it as 'an episode, or a spurt in which the powers of the person come together in a particularly efficient and intensely enjoyable way ....' It is a 'more of' experience in every positive sense. We feel more integrated, more spontaneous and expressive, more creative, more humorous and more truly ourselves. The effects of peak experiences are also beneficial, leaving us less anxious and more in touch with our feelings.

In his later writings, Maslow (1970) distinguished between 'peak experiences' and 'plateau experiences'. The former are intense and put our being in a state of excitement, whereas 'plateau experiences' offer more sustained, serene and quietly enjoyable states of being. The latter are easier to access.

Some PD authorities have suggested that peak states may be comparable to the transcendent state obtainable through quality **meditation**. At the higher levels, both are characterized by 'pure awareness' rather than by perception of specific objects or events (see Bloomfield *et al*, 1976).

The term 'peak performance' can be applied to any kind of performance, including, most obviously, sporting performances. (Maslow himself studied peak experiences in a wide range of groups, including engineers, students, social scientists and politicians.) It implies the happy convergence of all the relevant skills and states. In the case of sporting and many other kinds of performance, these will include physical skills and physiological states (eg, ability to relax), technical skills (eg, **focus, mental rehearsal**). A peak performance occurs when we are able to 'get it all together'. At the deepest level, this may even include our **values**, which O'Connor and Prior (1995) believe determine our peak performances. Clearly, the concepts of **congruence, alignment** and **inner team** are relevant here.

Peak performances tend both to look and feel 'effortless'. They rarely occur when we try 'too hard' or too consciously. However, the apparent effortlessness is usually the result of mental (or mind/body) training and preparation, which might have included techniques such as **modelling, visualization**, focusing, goal-setting and techniques to interrupt **negative thinking**. Preparation would almost certainly have included **mental rehearsal**.

A somewhat more technical definition of 'peak experience', applied particularly in sports contexts, is 'an altered state of consciousness associated with performing at an automatic level,

without having to think about the things you are doing'
(Nideffer, 1992). This is generally thought of as difficult to create
at will, and when athletes have one they say it feels as if time
slows down, that balls look bigger and that they feel certain that
their shots will hit their target.

Getting what Maltz (1960) calls 'the Winning Feeling' that
accompanies peak performance would not nowadays be considered as spontaneous or 'mysterious' as it might once have
appeared. **NLP**ers would say it's a matter of knowing how to
manage our states and knowing which strategies work. In theory, peak performance ought to be almost entirely a matter of
choice. However, the concept of a peak *performer*, which some
PD tutors work with, seems illogical. If we perform consistently
at a peak level, then that presumably is our plateau performance: it just happens to be a plateau of **excellence**.

Personal Development Plan (PDP)

A plan that identifies the personal strengths and needs of
individuals and specifies the goals for their development.
Personal Development Plans (PDPs) can be fairly comprehensive, covering aspects of educational, professional and **career
development**, as well as of more personal aspects of **development**.

The PDP process tends to be a variant of the Plan-Do-Review
model, though the plan stage tends to be preceded by a **self-
audit** or, more typically, by facilitated self-exploration. This is
likely to highlight a range of personal strengths, needs, qualities,
interests and aspirations. On the basis of this, the plan is likely
to be constructed, and typically specifies both long-term 'macro'
goals (eg, becoming self-employed) and short-term, 'micro'
goals (eg, doing a course in book-keeping). The latter tend to be
specified in SMART terms: (Specific, Measurable, Achievable,
Relevant, Time-bound or Trackable).

Personal development planning, as it is currently practised,
tends to be a shared activity, involving the individual concerned
together with a tutor, mentor, 'learning manager' or facilitator.
The shared nature of the activity may reflect a preferred model
of learning (that two heads are better than one), but it certainly

reflects also the organizational context in which the activity invariably takes place. Most frequently, the organizations are places of work, schools and colleges. 'Outsiders' may be involved (eg, members of a careers service) as external service providers (see Dawes, 1995). Sometimes, the planning process is a three-way activity (eg, individual, line manager and external facilitator).

Not surprisingly, the ownership of PDPs is an issue. Few, if any, are purely personal documents, and as Tony Watts (1991) notes of PDPs (or the very similar Individual Action Plans) in school settings, they can be viewed as devices for managing people rather than for people to manage their own development and learning. A related issue is the extent to which PDPs should be linked to institutional and business development plans. The benefits of linking individuals to institutional development are sometimes lauded (Dawes, 1995), but this may again compromise the personal nature of and **commitment** to the PDP.

When the PDPing process is clearly centred on the individual, then the planning *process* can be as important, if not more important, to the development of the individual than the final plan. Much depends on the quality of the 'owner's' commitment to and active participation in the various activities involved, which include analysing, reflecting, reviewing, formulating and other processes, not just planning.

PDPs have a growing number of advocates who argue that PDPs can:

- encourage and increase **self-awareness** and **self-acceptance**;
- encourage reflection upon experience;
- encourage a view of life as rich in **choices**, and promote the skills of **decision-making**;
- identify areas for growth;
- open the mind to **opportunities** for growth;
- promote self-**responsibility** and a sense of ownership for personal, educational and career development;
- improve the ability to prioritize;
- where relevant, ensure coherent progression – for example, from one course of study to another at a higher level;
- encourage greater personal flexibility – with regard to management style, for example.

In some contexts, PDPs can cover home, family and relation-ships, as well as personal and career development. This is the case, for example, with development programs pitched at peo-ple in mid-life considering a major change of direction. But few PDPs are truly comprehensive, whole person or internally co-ordinated; that is, the effects and implications of one area of development on others are rarely identified (see **Ecology**). Very few PDPs deal with development at the deepest, most private areas of feeling and the self. There is much scope for develop-ment here, though ownership and confidentiality would cer-tainly be issues to sort out.
(See **Action Plan; Contracting; Goals; Holistic Development; Mission Statement; Values.**)

Personal Power

The power that each of us has over our own life and ourself.

Specific definitions vary somewhat according to perspective and context. Personal Power in the context of a course on assertiveness skills, for example, may have a different emphasis from the use of the term in the context of spiritual **enlighten-ment**. Nonetheless, there is a lot of agreement about the nature, sources and applications of personal power. Most PD tutors would concur with the following statements.

- Personal power is inborn. It is not given to us by other people.
- We never lose all our personal power until we die, but we do sometimes allow other people to take some of it away from us.
- In reality, no one *feels* powerful all the time. The level of per-sonal power we perceive fluctuates according to a number of factors, including the state we are in. Theoretically, it is possi-ble for us to regulate all or most of these factors.
- In a PD context, 'power' has almost entirely positive conno-tations. It has nothing to do with controlling and manipulat-ing other people. Indeed, if we feel the need to dominate oth-ers then we are almost certainly experiencing a perceived lack of true *personal* power. The fact that 'power' appears in the

titles of dozens of PD books, (eg, *The Power of Positive Thinking, Unlimited Power, Awaken Your Inner Power, Personal Power, Personal Power Through Awareness*) indicates its positive associations as well as its importance.

- We can both *misuse* and *abuse* our personal power. According to Gaudry and Spielberger (1995), we misuse it when we give it away and we abuse it when we use it to control and manipulate other people.
- We each have within us the power and the resources we may need to meet and develop through the changes and challenges of life.
- It is never too late to recover power we have given away or to use and develop latent power.
- Our individual power is 'completed' or enhanced if we access universal energies, though these may be channelled through us – by the **Higher Self**, for example. (The concept of 'universal energies' is not within every PD tutor's frame of reference; to others it is vitally important.)
- Personal power implies an internal **locus of control** and an acceptance of personal **responsibility**. We believe that we can **change** aspects of ourselves and our lives in the directions we wish. We acknowledge that we always have **choices**.
- We have power over our thinking, perceptions, responses and language. We can substitute **positive thinking** for **negative thinking**. We can bring about perceptual shifts. For example, in a conflict situation we can, as Gerald Jampolsky and Jack Keeler (1979) suggest, shift from seeing others as attacking us to seeing them as fearful. We can use the language of power rather than the language of negativity and helplessness ('I won't 'rather than 'I can't', 'an opportunity' rather than 'a problem').
- We have a secure sense of self, and a high level of self-acceptance. As Jeffers (1991) observes, power and love go together, and love is distorted by a perceived lack of power.
- Liking ourselves, we can like and value others.
- We are assertive when we choose to be.
- We feel whole, congruent and aligned. There are no significant or long-term wars raging within us. Our **inner team** is working well as a team. The interconnectedness of mind, body and spirit is recognized, 'exploited' and enjoyed.

Vitality is experienced in all aspects of our being.

- Our personal power is not drained or significantly distracted by unforgiveness or the blame we attach to others. We are prepared to let go of past attachments to guilt, fear etc (see **Letting Go**).
- We are committed to developing our **self-awareness**.
- We understand the true bases of personal security, appreciating that these lie within us, and not in, say, exerting control over other people.
- We can derive personal power legitimately by proxy from others, as when we engage in **modelling** others or visualizing ourselves as them.
- We know our life's **purpose**. A purpose or a **vision** generates passion which magnifies personal power.
- We live in the moment, knowing that the present time, not the past or the future, is the site at which we can exert our power (see **Here and Now**).

Developments in the last two decades, particularly in **NLP** and **Accelerated Learning,** have provided us with the tools and technologies for making significantly better use of our personal powers, particularly in relation to self-communication.

Self-empowerment is the exercise of personal power. It is a relative term, in that we can behave in a *more* or *less* empowered way.

(See **Self-Efficacy**.)

Positive Thinking

Our thinking is positive when we focus it upon the things and resources we have or want rather than upon those we don't have or want. When we think positively, we see possibilities rather than limitations and what's right about a situation rather than what's wrong. We are likely to be **solution-centred** rather than problem-centred. Positive thinking is characterized also by its effects. Its champions tell us that positive thinkers tend to be happier, more self-confident and decisive, less fearful or doubt-ridden and more likely to achieve '**success**' than are negative thinkers.

Positive thinking has also been defined in process terms. Vera Peiffer (1989), who devotes an entire book to its power and applications, defines it as 'making use of the suggestibility of your subconscious mind in a positive way'.

'Positive thinking' is the best known phrase in PD. As a 'philosophy', it was popularized initially by a highly influential group of North American writers especially active between the 1930s and 1950s, including Napoleon Hill, Clement Stone, Norman Vincent Peale and Dale Carnegie. In best-sellers such as *Think and Grow Rich, Success Through a Positive Mental Attitude, The Power of Positive Thinking* and *How to Win Friends and Influence People,* they emphasized the importance for personal growth and achievement of thinking only positive thoughts, strangling negative thoughts before they could become what David Schwartz (1959) called 'mental monsters', getting the best by expecting the best and displaying abundant **faith**. Scores of subsequent PD writers have preached the positive thinking philosophy, and its essential validity continues to be affirmed. If anything, research evidence and our more sophisticated models of mind-body relationships have reinforced our beliefs in the importance of maintaining a positive **focus**. We know, for example, that teachers who think positively promote higher standards of achievement and **self-esteem** in their students. We know also that the emotions generated by thinking positively have beneficial biochemical effects, including the release of the body's own 'feel good' peptide molecules (endorphins).

While the emphasis upon 'the positive' remains as strong as ever, the phrase 'positive thinking' has fallen somewhat into disrepute in the last decade or so. A minor reason for this is the fact that in its original packaging it tended to be linked closely with faith in God. The religious connotations were especially strong in the books of NV Peale. A much more important factor is the crude way in which the positive thinking message has been delivered by some PD tutors. Positive thinking may be necessary for happy development, but, like love in the Beatles' song, it's not all you need. If we want to achieve great things, then simply psyching ourselves up to think positively won't deliver the goods. To believe otherwise is psychologically naive and reductionistic. To be told that we can lift ourselves from the ghetto to become self-made millionaires can also seem socio-

economically naive, if not downright offensive. Thinking positively can seem like blatant reality denial; not so much selective
perception (picking out the positive aspects of a situation) as
perceptual blindness (wilfully ignoring painful realities). In
some situations it may be better for us to confront our fears or
difficulties rather than trying to smother them with a blanket of
generalized positive thinking. First-rate self-help specialists
have always made it clear that positive thinking is not a panacea
for all development needs; Maxwell Maltz in *Psycho-Cybernetics*
(1960), for example. On the one hand, Maltz relates stories of the
remarkable transformative power of shifting from a negative to
a positive frame of mind. On the other, he makes the point that
'Positive Thinking cannot be used as a patch or crutch to the
same old self-image'. That is, we cannot change our habits or
external circumstances by positive thinking if our self-concept is
not up to accomplishing these things.

Contemporary quality PD tutors tend to distance themselves
from the crude positive thinking message by making their own
distinctions. For example, Stephen Covey (1992) distinguishes
'positive thinking' from 'proactivity'. The latter, he says,
involves facing up to both reality and our power to choose a
positive response to the situation. By implication, positive thinking falls short of this. Similarly, Patrick Fanning (1994) distinguishes positive thinking from a technique he calls 'positive
imaging'. His comment that his own technique is 'not as greedy,
or success-orientated as positive thinking' points to another reason why 'positive thinking' has lost favour: its associations with,
for example, go-getting, get rich types pumped up by empty
motivational hype.

The prevailing view of positive thinking seems to be that it is
a necessary but an insufficient basis for development and success. It helps with motivation, but motivation is not in itself
enough. There must be appropriate, effective action. We need
specific strategies and tools that work. NLP and other modern
technologies of personal change have made these available, thus
greatly improving the chances of turning the rhetoric of positive
thinking into a reality.

Potential (personal)

Our inherent, but as yet not fully used or realized, powers and capacities.

The idea that our potential is a slumbering force which we need to arouse, is reflected in the titles of a number of self-improvement books (eg, *Awaken the Giant Within, Awaken the Genius, Awaken Your Inner Power*).

In one way or another, virtually every writer in the PD field reiterates the point made by William James in *Varieties of Religious Experience* (1929), that 'most people live . . . in a very restricted circle of their potential being'. That is, we tap only a fragment of our potential. An associated truism is that we have consistently under-estimated human potential. The ascendant view is that our potential is truly vast, perhaps as virtually limitless as the capacity of the human brain. Most PD writers acknowledge that *everyone* has major untapped resources and that there are many ways to release them. This helps account for the highly positive, even ebullient, tone of PD literature in general. However, the shadow side of this is the extent of unused human potential. For Egan (1994), this is a more serious, because more widespread, social problem even than emotional disorders.

Why do so many of us realize so little of our potential? There are, perhaps, three sets of factors to explain this, the first of which concerns our needs. The humanist psychologist and key figure in the human potential movement, Abraham Maslow, suggests that our individual potential is realized through the progressive satisfaction of needs and desires. His view is that we do not actualize our full potential, or anything approaching it, until we have satisfied more basic (deficiency) needs, including fundamental survival needs (food, shelter) and higher level needs such as friendship and self-expression. To put it crudely, if we devote ourselves to, say, improving our material comforts, socializing or expressing ourselves through work and leisure interests, then it is unlikely that we will get in touch with, let alone develop, other aspects of our being. We will remain, to use a word used by Covey (1992) in relation to potential, relatively 'embryonic'.

This is not the only way of construing the concept of potential. Emphasis can be placed on the process of releasing what is already available to us (the resources of the Higher Self, for example) rather than a process of developing some aspect of ourself that is currently embryonic. This fits well with the view within psychosynthesis, and many related approaches to personal development, that we already have within us everything we need. The potential for growth lies in finding appropriate ways to access, assemble and synthesize our faculties.

The second set of factors which hold us back from becoming or being all of which we are capable are negative personal factors. The most commonly discussed are fear, including the fears both of failing and succeeding, and disabling self-**beliefs**. The latter might include beliefs that we have little or no talent, that we cannot change the 'way we are', and that we already know all that we are. A strong ego, one which is blind to the possibility that there are many aspects of our being not 'contained' within the conscious concept of who we are, is a major obstacle to fulfilment of potential. Many PD programs are designed to have us **challenge** the beliefs which block our **development**, to raise our **self-awareness** and to give us the strategies to overcome the fears that prevent us from 'trying out' new aspects of ourselves. They also give us 'permission' to concentrate on the realization of our own potential rather than see this as selfish and neglectful of our duty towards others.

The third set of factors relates to know-how. Having vast potential is one thing, but even if we want to access it, we can do so effectively only if we know the strategies that work. Only some twenty years ago, Bloomfield et al (1976), commented that the search was still on for 'an effective program to unfold man's untapped resources'. Most PD tutors would today contend that we now have available a range of powerful tools and technologies for tapping potential. These include 'old' technologies made more accessible (eg, **meditation**) or developed and applied in new ways (eg, **visualization**) and mainly new technologies, such as many features of **accelerated learning** and **NLP**. The latter, for example, offers techniques for bridging the left and right brains and for accessing parts of the brain of which we may not have made much use.

How do we know the extent of our personal potential? The truth is that we probably cannot know, but since it seems difficult to overestimate many aspects of it, erring on the side of caution is rarely advocated in PD programs. We can glimpse our potential in **peak experiences** and through the silence of meditation that gives access to new levels of awareness. We can also attempt to visualize our potential, perhaps through a vision statement or by making use of the **'what-if' frame**. Indeed, Syer and Connolly (1991) believe that visualizing our potential is the first step to achieving it. Relevant here is Napoleon Hill's oft-quoted assertion that 'whatever the mind of man can conceive and believe, it can achieve' (Hill, 1966). The idea that many of the limitations we perceive about ourselves are self-imposed, and that our potential is close to what we believe it to be, is generally in the ascendent. This may not mean that everyone is a genius without (necessarily!) knowing it, but the view of Porter (1993) that with the appropriate methods we can each, 'attain a sense of genius in our own right', seems more in tune with the possibility thinking of current PD than does the more deterministic view of Hodgkinson (1993) that 'some of us will always be daisies, while others will be exotic orchids!'

Programming (Personal)

Programs are procedures or instructions for our minds. Programming is the process for installing them. More generally, programming or conditioning (the terms tend to be used interchangeably) is any process that influences us or predisposes us to respond in certain ways to certain actions or situations. It covers 'the shaping of our attitudes and behaviours by outside influences' (Corey, 1986).

Since the mind has to have something to run on, software to direct its operations, programming is necessary and unavoidable. Hence, a major theme in PD is that we should be the gatekeepers of the process (see **GIGO**). If we don't take charge of it, then others will. Besides, the results that we can get by installing the right programs – effective, empowering programs – are enormous.

Most PD courses have a deprogramming element where we are invited to identify and challenge the more influential programs by which we operate. They may include core **beliefs,** behaviour patterns that reflect early conditioning and a host of views and expressions which may have seeped so deeply into us that we need techniques to recover them. Their effects can be profound. For example, as children some of us may have been programmed to please other people before pleasing ourselves. If we are still operating this program, it's possible that we may have become so desensitized to our own needs and feelings that we are almost strangers to ourselves. Other programs may have impacted significantly on our **self-esteem** or the way we relate to other people. If we were programmed to be wary of strangers, for example, we may still be wary of strangers we encounter today – especially if they bear the adult equivalent of sweets. (No wonder salespeople are often given a hard time!)

PD coaches are optimistic about deprogramming. As Colin Turner (1994) puts it, 'any conditioning created in the mind of the individual can be reversed or re-created.' Practising counsellors and psychotherapists are not always as sanguine!

Deprogramming is usually a precondition for successful reprogramming, the process of *deliberately* installing new programs. Most self-improvement books and courses are mainly about reprogramming. The emphasis may be on **success**, achieving our full human **potential**, better relationships or more effective learning. It may be pitched at the 'executive program' levels of really key **values** and beliefs, about choice, for example, or at a general end-result – the state of **congruence**, for example. At 'lower' levels, programs vary in range of application, specificity and technicality. For example, there are various step-by-step programs for personal change which can be applied to all manner of situations. Similarly, there are programs for getting motivated, interrupting an unwanted thought pattern or achieving a 'probable future' which are also wide in application. An example of the latter would be the three word sequence: desire, imagination, expectancy. We arouse and associate the emotions of desire with a vivid image of the object of desire and then expect this to materialize (see Edwards, 1991).

There are also programs for producing very specific results. These would include the **NLP** programs for 'mending' phobias and poor spelling, as well as for the NLP techniques themselves – elicitation, reframing, anchoring etc (see **Anchor**). NLP has significantly advanced our understanding of programs. For example, we now appreciate that sequence is as critical to the coding of subjective experience as it is to the meaning of language structures and to more technical programs, such as those that operate machines. That is, the order in which we think something or take the steps that lead to a result can be critical.

Many of the techniques most discussed in PD literature are (re-) programming techniques and most of these involve talking to the **subconscious**. Positive **self-talk** is one such technique. Another is 'programmed visualization', where 'you create what you want to see and hear and feel in great detail and manipulate it according to a predetermined script' (Fanning, 1994).

While the emphasis in PD is on self-programming, the contribution that skilled others can make (counsellors, hypnotherapists, NLP practitioners etc) is acknowledged, with the effect that 'programming' and 'conditioning' have lost some of their less pleasant connotations (manipulative brainwashing etc). However, programming techniques – particularly those which work directly on brain processes – can be highly powerful and need to be used with caution. Wholesale deprogramming can be particularly hazardous. (Consider the potential effects of eliminating any sense of wariness of strangers.) Skilled and ethical professionals working with NLP and hypnotism acknowledge this. Steve and Connirae Andreas (1989) assure us that 'any time we change someone's brain program we [ie, they] are very careful to preserve any benefits of the old program as we add more.'

Psychometric Tests

Psychological 'tests' used for job selection, occupational assessment and a range of other purposes.

One type is 'real' tests in that they measure attainment, ability and aptitude – what we can do. The type of psychometric test of more direct relevance to personal development is a personality inventory rather than a test. Typically, participants have to answer a number of questions about themselves to which there are personally appropriate rather than right or wrong answers. From these responses, assessments can be made about a person's personality, beliefs, values, interests etc. These assessments can be used to determine potential for promotion, assist

career development, enhance **self-awareness**, target training and indicate whether a person is well-matched to the requirements of a team or job.

Psychometric tests are big business. There are several thousand on the market, and as many as 75% of organizations in the UK make use of them.

Purpose

This is one of the central concepts in PD and concerns the *why* of what we do rather then the *what* or *how*. It is almost axiomatic in the PD world that knowing *why* is more fundamental than knowing *how*, though 'how' questions are crucial when we are in a position to act.

Most PD tutors would accept that *one* purpose, if not *the* purpose, of life is to discover our own life's purpose. The key word here is 'discover', for there is widespread but not complete agreement that our life's purpose is not something we decide and define in the same way that we do with our **goals**. Some PD tutors clarify the concept of purpose by contrasting it with 'goals'. Colin Turner (1994) talks of choosing our goals but discovering our purpose. The view of psychosynthesis is that our life's purpose is a kind of 'ideal pattern' that is within us but emerges and unfolds over time, and we have to be sensitive to apprehend it (see Ferrucci, 1990). Dina Glouberman (1995) distinguishes between '*setting* goals' and '*sensing* goals' but sensing might also be applied to the purposes behind the specific goals we set. 'Sensing' also implies a more than cognitive process. It implies a mind-body or whole-being apprehension. 'When you have a purpose', write the authors of *Think to Win*, 'you can connect with some deeper more central part of yourself' (Syer and Connolly 1991).

At the highest level, purpose is whatever gives meaning to our lives and to the growth and **development** we experience. Unlike a goal, our life's purpose is not an end in itself. Indeed, if we can see where it ends, then it is probably not our over-arching purpose. Also, purpose drives our action, but it is not itself an action. As John Kalench (1990) puts it: 'Purpose isn't something you *do*. Purpose is something you *be*.' When we express our purpose, then, it is likely to be in the continuous present tense rather than in the future tense that we use for goals.

How do we know that we are in touch with our 'true' life's purpose? Most PD tutors recognize that this is something we sense rather than simply know intellectually. The major indicator is an enduring sense of passion, as well as perhaps more occasional feelings of intense joy that we are fulfilling our purpose. Purpose gives us passion and passion gives us power: the power to go forward even when times are hard, the power to say 'no' to possible life paths, etc.

PD literature offers various suggestions for discovering and clarifying our life's purpose. One way is to ask ourselves **questions** which may point the way. For example, we can ask ourselves whom we most respect, and why, or what seems most to motivate us and give us joy. These questions offer a route to our deepest **values** to which our purpose must inevitably be aligned. Another route is through connecting with the Higher Self. This may involve 'inviting' the Higher Self or unconscious to proffer images or symbols which may help us to see our purpose.

With regard to questions about the purpose of life generally, some PD tutors address these directly, but 'answers' are implicit in most PD books. Living life to the full and realizing (in both senses) our vast **potential** are two of the more common responses. 'Spiritually'-inclined literature tends to emphasize seeking the truth about ourselves and life generally, and living in tune with the whole living world. The theme throughout, though, is that knowing our specific purpose makes it possible for our personal development to be focused rather than entirely a matter of serendipity or chance.

At the other extreme from 'the' purpose is the value of having clear purposes for many of the things we do in our lives. For example, we learn something more effectively if we have a purpose for learning it. Where PD authorities differ is on the question of our knowing and being able fully to determine our intentions. One view is that we have full control of our intentions. A quite different view is that we are subject to unconscious intentions, motivations and programs, so that determining our purpose is rarely an entirely conscious process. Clearly, one purpose of personal development is to become more aware of these inconspicuous influences.

Questions

Posing questions to ourselves can be a powerful tool for learning, **development** and the achievement of **success**.

Good teachers have always known the value of questions and questioning. Effective teachers ask a lot of questions, the majority of which are challenging open-ended questions (to which there can be no simple 'yes' or 'no' answers) and probing questions that give students **opportunities** to show what they really know and understand. Unfortunately, teachers know the answers to most of the questions they pose, and they tend to suppose their students do (or should!) as well. For personal development purposes, the most productive questions are generally those which stimulate fresh ideas and insights rather than address the familiar.

Whenever we ask a question, we engage the mind. We can get it to work positively and productively on our behalf by, for example, identifying the issues around a problem, generating solutions and options, making discoveries and seeing a situation from a different angle, if not re-defining it altogether. But we can also ask questions that keep us mentally or emotionally blocked or in a rut or which disable and depress us by, for example, encouraging the mind to wallow in self pity ('Why me?').

The implication of this is that there are questions and questions. We can be highly self-questioning and yet not stimulate our personal growth. The 'wrong' questions can lock us into the status quo or even entrench our feelings of being helpless and hopeless. Questions are powerful things. They **focus** our attention and direct our thinking and feeling, so we need to be very careful what questions we ask ourselves and how precisely we formulate them. Even a slight change of wording can make a huge difference. For example, in difficult circumstances we might ask, 'How can I survive in this situation?' This is probably a much better question than 'How did I get into this mess?' because it focuses attention on strategy and **action** rather than upon possibly fruitless analysis. But we might have asked, 'How can I *prosper* in this situation?' which opens the mind to a whole new set of possibilities.

Different approaches to PD tend to prefer different questions. For example, some PD tutors working from a Gestalt perspective make regular use of the 'What's so?' question to focus upon awareness of the present situation. NLPers have a number of 'favourite' questions including the **'what if?' frame**, which opens awareness to **choices** and possibilities, and the who, why, how, what, where, when series which correspond to our neurological levels. 'Who?' questions focus upon our identity, 'why?' upon our **beliefs** and **values**, 'how?' upon our capabilities, 'what?' upon our behaviour, and 'where?' and 'when?' upon relevant aspects of the environment we inhabit. Personal **change** can be effected (or blocked) at all these levels, but the first two levels are the more fundamental. It clearly matters at which levels we pitch our questions, and being clear about the distinctions between them. For example, if I want to improve my golf swing, it would probably be better to ask, 'What do I need to *do* to improve my golf swing?' (behaviour level), rather than 'Why am I pretty useless with a golf club?' (capability) or, worse still, 'Why am I such a lousy sportsperson?' (identity). By contrast, if I sense a lack of motivation to improve my game of golf, then 'who?' and 'why?' questions may be more helpful. It may be, for example, that I don't really see myself as a golfer (identity) or that golf has low priority in my life (values).

As a questioning art, NLP has done much to emphasize the value of asking questions, particularly to elicit the strategies and modalities we use when performing a task or getting into a particular situation. As Richard Bandler (1985) says: 'If you ask a lot of weird questions, and if you're persistent, you can find out how anyone does anything.'

Rapport

A relationship of mutual trust, understanding and responsiveness. If other people feel that we are seeking to understand their points of view, that we are putting them at ease and 'talking their language', then it's probable that we have established rapport with them.

The ability to establish and maintain rapport is considered by PD authorities to be a pre-requisite for effective communication. Without it, the chances of achieving successful **outcomes** in any situation where we are relating to others are slim indeed. Some activities, such as selling, negotiating, teaching and **counselling**, probably couldn't take place without it. **NLP** has helped us to understand the precise processes and skills involved in rapport.

When people are in rapport, their body language seems to match and synchronize. That is, they seem unconsciously to adopt similar postures, gestures and eye movements. They may speak at more or less the same pace and express themselves through similar tones of voice. Even their breathing patterns may be similar. If one person makes a movement, then the other person may mirror this movement.

NLP shows us how to create rapport with others in a more conscious way. This may involve **modelling** 'experts' at rapport or ourselves when we do it naturally well. NLP adds another ingredient for excellent rapport: matching the language patterns of the other. This means listening to them to see if they betray a preference for a particular modality. For example, if they use a lot of words that suggest they have a visual preference (eg, 'I see', 'Set the scene', 'the big picture'), then we can use visual words to strengthen rapport.

Matching and mirroring has to be done sensitively and as naturally as possible. Mimicry is clearly crude and disrespectful, and will not establish rapport. Mismatching can also be a useful skill, particularly to close an exchange.

Once rapport has been established, it is possible to use it for influence purposes – to take the conversation in a particular direction, for example, or to elicit a certain response from the other person. An invaluable skill here is *pacing*, an NLP term that means showing respect for the other person by getting into his or her state or map of the world. We can pace actual behaviours or the **beliefs** and **values** which underpin them. For example, if someone is sad about the loss of something, then we can reflect back that sadness and talk about loss.

Rapport and pacing enable *leading*, the skill of 'encouraging' someone to change their behaviour by changing our behaviour. For example, if we have shown through rapport that we understand their sadness, then we can smile and begin to lead them into a smiling state as well.

Reference Experiences

The experiences to which we can or do refer in order to support a state, a belief, a decision or some other act of mind.

In theory, everything we've ever done, seen or experienced in some sense is available to us for reference purposes. This includes our own experiences and the experiences of other people that we have heard, seen or read about. In reality, experiences are only useful to us as references if we can recall them and appreciate their referential potential. In other words, what matters is not just our knowledge of the experience itself but how we make sense of, organize and utilize the experience. It's what we might call the perceived 'transfer value' of an experience. Can we transfer it from the context in which it has been experienced and stored in the memory to the context where it can serve a useful purpose?

Anthony Robbins (1992), who discusses references in depth, says that the more references we have and the higher their quality, the better. Although he is right, what ultimately counts is the use we make of the references we have. I may be able to recall only one or two experiences which bear testimony to, say, my ability to perform effectively under intense pressure, but if I draw upon these experiences at any time I need to feel strengthened, confident, resourceful etc, then I am optimizing their transfer value. Clearly, it's fruitless having hundreds of potential reference experiences if we don't perceive them or use them as such - at least, on a conscious level.

Personal development can be construed in terms of expanding both our reference experiences and our frames of reference (or paradigms) for making sense of them. When we deliberately seek out experiences which take us outside our **comfort zones**, we are in effect setting out to expand our fund of empowering references. At some level, our mind is telling us that if we dare to do the thing that frightens us most, then there is nothing we won't dare to do. We can use references, then, to give ourselves 'permission' to tackle with confidence a challenging task, to bolster a belief or an idea, or to support a change of state.

Reframing

The process of redefining an event, experience or statement by placing it within a different frame of reference.

The assumption behind reframing is that meaning is not inherent in things or situations but rather is assigned to them. It's we who do the assigning, so if we can view the thing or situation from a different point of view, or put it into a different context, then we can probably give it a different meaning.

In PD contexts reframing is generally valued as a technique for performing a kind of perceptual alchemy that leaves us feeling more positive. For example, we can reframe threats as **opportunities** or find a context in which a seemingly negative experience (eg, becoming ill) can appear to have positive effects (eg, enforced rest or learning through suffering). But reframing need not be used to see the good in everything or to pretend the negative doesn't exist. In itself it is a 'neutral' technique, though it testifies to the fact that there are always alternatives – alternative versions, choices and perspectives. Appreciating this point can be liberating and empowering in itself. It tells us that we do not have to get stuck in the first frame we put round an experience.

Asking ourselves questions such as, 'What else could this

mean?' is one way to trigger a reframe. Sometimes adopting a different viewpoint can be helpful, as can changing a belief that keeps us fixed to a frame. For example, if we change an 'I'm too old' belief, then we can reframe 'There's no point applying for this job', to 'I've got all the experience they could need'. Re-editing in our head the 'film' of an event that didn't go as well as we'd hoped is another reframing device.

This might involve inventing a different ending and then experiencing the positive emotions associated with it. All the time our conscious mind knows what we are up to, then we are not deceiving ourselves, and we can enjoy the benefits of **imprinting** this more empowering version onto our **subconscious**.

Reframing is by no means peculiar to **NLP**, though it is a technique much used and refined by NLPers. The six-step reframe is one of the standard NLP strategies for effecting personal change. It's particularly useful for finding alternatives to unwanted behaviours which ought to fit into our **inner team**. In brief, the steps of the reframe are:

- Identify the behaviour to be changed.
- 'Talk' with the part within responsible for the behaviour.
- 'Talk' again to this part to show you are aware that the behaviour is separate from the intention. Seek the co-operation of the part in trying for an alternative, better behaviour to achieve the same end.
- Ask your creative part to generate these better alternatives.
- Ask the original part if it will use the alternative(s) in the coming weeks.
- By way of an ecological check, ask your other parts whether any of them object to the new behaviour(s). If there is an objection, then you can either re-establish communication with that part or request the creative part to come up with more possibilities (see **Ecology**).

To the uninitiated, six-step reframing can seem bizarre, but it is now much used for personal development purposes and helps to ensure that we don't inadvertently jettison behaviour which serves our interests.

Responsibility (Personal)

The belief that each of us is responsible for our actions and **choices**, and even for our **emotions**, is pervasive in PD programs. It implies an internal **locus of control**, and is at the heart of many other key concepts, including **self-efficacy** and goal-setting.

The personal responsibility message frightens many of us. Assuming responsibility for our actions can seem a burden too hard to bear, and so we give ourselves all kinds of 'reasons' why we cannot or need not take responsibility. We play the victim, 'blame' conditions or fate or past-**programming**, believe that other people 'make' us do and feel things, allow 'experts' to be responsible for us, etc. This list of excuses, though *we* may see them as valid reasons, is endless. One of the challenges for PD tutors is to get us to acknowledge personal responsibility. It's not even valid to say that we 'accept' it, for that implies that someone or something else is offering it to us. The most we can do is to decline to acknowledge it.

And yet, PD literature presents personal responsibility as liberating rather than alarming or oppressive. To be responsible means to be in control, to have **personal power** to exercise. We can, for example, choose how we respond in any situation. As we are often reminded in the literature, 'responsibility' equals 'response-ability'. Only we can know what our feelings are. And only we can judge how best to respond. The power to respond is always ours, and we do not have to be at the mercy of anyone or anything outside ourselves.

It can also be liberating to realize that we are no more responsible for how other people feel than they are for how we feel. We can contribute to and influence the feelings of others, but since we cannot own or determine these feelings we cannot take responsibility for them. On one level, it may be frightening to think that we are responsible for our health and ill-health. Handing over our physical well-being to 'experts' can be comforting. But as PD tutors on **healing** remind us, the responsibility is ultimately ours, and the price we pay for surrendering responsibility is helplessness.

What acknowledging personal responsibility is *not* about is being dutiful. We may feel that we have responsibilities to oth-

ers, and it is certainly our responsibility to accept the consequences of behaving or not behaving in line with these. But the
emphasis in a PD sense is not on moral obligations. Indeed,
from some points of view, Gestalt therapy included, it would be
personally irresponsible of us to ignore our own needs. The PD
emphasis on personal responsibility is sometimes thought to be
selfish, but in fact the ego is most active when it is trying to
dump its responsibility on others.

If exercising personal responsibility means not blaming others, it also means not blaming ourselves. PD tutors frequently
urge us not to 'beat up on ourselves'. Playing victim to our own
persecutor is not to be truly responsible. From a PD perspective,
the proper exercise of responsibility involves acknowledgement
of the situation, an attempt to learn from and even grow
through whatever we feel we may have done wrong, and to try
to understand its significance, perhaps on more than one level.

This last point is interesting and important, for there are those
within the PD world who take what might be considered an
extreme view of self-responsibility. The 'those' would include
psychospiritualists, PD tutors who emphasize the metaphysics
and power of human consciousness. This view is that each of us
is personally responsible in some way and at some level for
everything that happens to us as well as for everything we make
happen. At some subtle level of our being we are responsible for
(ie, we attract, we resonate with) even the accidents which
appear to befall us. This theory can be linked to the doctrine of
karma or to a more Western view of a multi-layered psyche
inhabiting a multi-dimensional reality. If we equate 'person'
with 'ego' or the conscious self, as do many PD tutors, then the
notion of total responsibility is likely to seem absurd, if not
repugnant. But it could be argued that this view of things is simply the Law of Attraction taken to its logical conclusion. If we
draw to ourselves that which we focus upon with the conscious
mind, why should our unconscious fears, obsessions, impulses
etc, not have similar effects?

Another area of interest is personal responsibility in relation
to other people. One theme is the importance of not trying to
assume responsibility for others, even in helping and development contexts. Therapists and helpers need to check that they
do not make invalid assumptions about what Egan calls the

client's 'psychological fragility'. We all need to resist what in transactional analysis is called 'rescuing' – doing for others what they are capable of doing for themselves, which only serves as a put-down, even if we don't intend it to be.

Much has also been written about personal responsibility in the context of intimate relationships and of personal development through them. A point often made is that we have to be responsible both for our pain in difficult relationships, even if we feel that the pain is being inflicted upon us, and for managing that pain. The steps one might take include reinforcing the behaviours we want from our partners rather than being angry at the behaviours we don't want, seeking alternative means of deriving the support etc we want if our partner does not provide it, and asking for what we want in a calm but assertive manner.

(See **Decision-Making.**)

Reticular Activating System (RAS)

This is a network-like structure of brain cells that serves an important gatekeeper function.

By monitoring the sensory data we receive from the world around us, and screening out data that does not seem to be of immediate value to us, the RAS ensures that we do not become overwhelmed with information. This is important because we can attend to only a limited number of things at one time, though the overall capacity of our brain is vast.

What counts as information of 'immediate value' is obviously critical. The way to ensure that information is perceived as relevant to us is to set a goal. As soon as we've done this, our RAS is activated to 'notice' whatever may be relevant to it. Almost by magic, it would seem at times, we begin to 'see' things – people, information, resources, possibilities – that we probably never even noticed before and still wouldn't notice had the goal not been set. Hence, the RAS is an absolutely key piece of brain hardware as far as personal development is concerned, if only indirectly.

(See **Goals.**)

Risks

Actions that we choose to make in the knowledge that we cannot know or determine their **outcomes**. From a PD perspective, risks are generally considered to be good things. If we don't take them, then we are unlikely to grow, at least in certain directions. Taking risks can enhance our **self-esteem** and **personal power**, and expand our **comfort zones**. The more risks we take, the more we are willing to take, and the bigger they become. Most PD tutors encourage us to take risks – Susan Jeffers (1991) suggests one a day – and help to prepare us for confident risk-taking. Gail Sheehy (1981) identified the willingness to take risks as characteristic of pathfinders who approach personal **change** without anger, fear or defensiveness.

Risk-taking may illustrate the idea that there is 'no gain without pain', but the thinking behind the advocacy of risk-taking is not just about growth through suffering. The key elements are the *volitional* nature of risk-taking, the fact that of necessity it has to be a personal act of choice – and our awareness of not being able to control the consequences. If we experience personal development through the risks that we take, then it has little, if anything, to do with whether our risk brought us the outcomes we wanted. **Attitude** is considered critical here, for if we rail against the outcomes, then we probably betray the fact that we believed at some level that we were in control of the outcome. This attitude limits the scope for growth.

For PD tutors generally, a risk pays off if we receive **feedback** from its consequences. We haven't necessarily failed if these aren't what we hoped for, but in any case, we may not always know precisely what the consequences are beyond the immediate and obvious ones. What is certain is that taking risks provides us with **references**. With sufficient quality references we can support empowering beliefs and tackle challenges.

Although risks are a matter of choice, there is sometimes no apparent option but to take them if we want the possibility of development or some other positive result. Therapy often involves risks. For example, we must sometimes risk the unpleasant emotional consequences of making and sustaining contact with unwanted emotions. As Latner (1986) says, we may have to make them part of conscious living if therapy is to work.

However, this risk has to be taken voluntarily, and PD tutors contend that we should be the principal beneficiaries of its consequences. Rusk and Read (1986), for example, say that if we are going to risk a change, then it ought to be something that is going to satisfy a need in us.

Some risks are undoubtedly bad for us (and possibly for other people as well). How can we tell a bad risk from one which might enhance our **well-being** or **development**? Jeffers' view is that a good risk is empowering because it rests on love and integrity (of ourselves and/or others). A bad risk lacks these elements. Another variable is ego involvement. From this point of view, what really counts is our attitude towards the action, not the action itself. If we are motivated to risk climbing a challenging mountain, by the glory that 'success' might bring, then the risk may be a bad one in the sense that it won't hold **potential** for our **development**. Choosing to climb the mountain to stretch and test our inner resources makes it a good decision.

(See **Challenge; Decision-Making; Failure**.)

Self-Acceptance

Self-acceptance is a prerequisite for significant personal development. Greater self-acceptance may also be an outcome of other areas of self-development, including **self-awareness**. There are 'mild' definitions of self-acceptance, which include feeling OK and feeling comfortable with oneself. 'Stronger' versions include having a 'high regard for yourself' (Johnson, 1981) and even a kind of self-love (Rusk and Read, 1986).

Self-acceptance is generally regarded as an indicator of psychological health, and the very opposite of self-centred absorption with the self. People who do not accept themselves, who are cynical or critical about their strengths, who cannot accept praise without feeling guilty, who do not see themselves as likeable, capable or worthy to others are much more likely to be inward-centred. They are much more likely to dissipate the energies that could have gone into growth or building positive relationships in worrying self-rejection and internal turbulence. It's for these reasons that self-acceptance or being yourself is seen by so many experts in personal change to be the first step to the mastery of our lives. Free from serious hang-ups, self-accepting people are able to throw themselves into all kinds of activities with potential for self-expression and growth. Self-accepting people are also much more likely to accept other people and do the kinds of things (eg, self-disclosing) conducive to gaining acceptance from others.

For many psychologists and psychotherapists, 'Love yourself' is a more fundamental injunction even than 'Know yourself'. It is also an essential part of any program for healing and developing 'damaged' adults, including the *transactional analysis* process of self-reparenting (see James, 1981). It's worth noting that for some experts self-acceptance is something you either have or you don't have. As Rusk and Read put it, 'you can't gradually get into loving yourself.'

Self-Audit

An inventory of our skills, strengths, achievements, weaknesses and development needs. In carrying out a full self-audit we might also take stock of core **beliefs** and **values**, and do some biographical analysis to pick out whatever patterns may be relevant (eg, career trends or decision-making patterns).

A self-audit is recommended in most books on career management and life planning. A systematic approach to personal development planning requires it. As Bridget Wright (1991) contends, it 'provides the firm foundation upon which to build [our] option choices.' If we cannot know exactly where we are going without a **vision**, then we cannot know exactly where we are starting from without a broad self-audit. Knowing how to do it, which questions to ask, how to tease out aspects of ourselves outside conscious awareness are difficult matters, and there are many books to assist with the process (eg, Hopson and Scally, 1991).

A *skills self-assessment* is similar to a self-audit but concentrates on the skills we have in relation to those we require for successful performance or goal achievements in a particular field. Examples include sporting performances, management development in an occupational role and specific tasks, such as giving a presentation and appraising a subordinate.

There are ready-made checklists of skills that can help with self-assessments. Those for technical skills are inevitably subject-specific, but physical and mental skills tend to be more general. The most thorough and useful approaches to skill assessment involve our rating ourselves (on a 1–10 scale, say) in terms both of our current ability and the importance of the skill as we perceive it to be. The skills we focus upon for development are likely to be those in which our current rating falls some way short of its importance.

In self-assessments, any comparisons we make should almost always be between our own performance levels (past, present and desired) rather than between our performance and someone else's. The assumption here is that if we are in competition with anyone, then, from a personal development perspective, that has to be with ourselves. Besides, what often matters is our individual skills *profile* rather than isolated skills, so comparing our performance with someone else's performance in just one skill may be misleading. They may *need* to do X better than we can because they cannot do Y as well.

Another recommendation is that we share our own self-assessment with a trusted other, who may be a manager, a coach or simply a colleague or friend. Someone else may have a different estimation of our skills. Areas where we don't agree can lead to fruitful discussion. For example, if our trusted other thinks we have over-rated our performance in one skill area, then this might indicate a blind spot.

Self-Awareness

The ability to attend to, monitor and examine our behaviour and our inner world of thoughts and feelings is a peculiarly human capacity and probably the single most important facility for personal development. Self-awareness can operate on many timescales. We can apprehend the contents of our mind at one moment in time and be sensitive to very specific feelings and responses. We can also develop a more general, ongoing awareness that we do not have a single unitary self but rather many selves or many aspects of the one self. This may be a slow process taking years to unfold.

The spotlight of self-awareness can be turned on all kinds of things. The interests of PD tutors influence the matters to which they direct the awareness of their 'students' or clients. To cognitive psychologists it may be 'automatic thinking' – the thoughts that immediately come into our head when a particular event occurs. To psychosynthesis tutors it might be awareness of multiple sub-personalities. To all those interested in change it might be becoming more aware of the key **values** and **beliefs** that impact upon the actions we take, and of our **habits** and fixed behaviour patterns. To those interested in what we might call our intrapersonal sensitivity, it might be awareness of our emotional flow – of the feelings we are experiencing in any situation and, more importantly, what are we doing with those feelings (changing? displacing? projecting? acknowledging? etc).

Developing self-awareness (in both senses of 'developing') is important for many reasons. At the broadest level, it is generally accepted that we cannot really know ourselves if we do not really know our minds. This can mean knowing the contents of the less conscious aspects of our mind as well as of the conscious aspects. (This is an argument for **meditation** and it is a result of **enlightenment**). More often it means knowing rather than just identifying with the ego through which so much of our experience is lived. Gill Edwards (1991) puts it strongly: 'When we observe the Ego . . . we discover our Self.' It means also becoming aware that the ego is but part of a much more expansive self, and that this larger self includes the 'shadow' aspects we usually deny, suppress or fail to acknowledge. Some contemporary thinkers in the PD field believe that the integration of the ego within the larger self is the principal project both for individuals *and* for humanity generally, and for this, 'awareness of self as both spirit and body is imperative' (Hall, 1993).

From the perspective of psychosynthesis, personal development is in part a matter of getting to know rather than being dominated by our sub-personalities – identifying with them, disidentifying with them and getting them to communicate with one another. Self-awareness has a major role to play here, which Ferrucci (1982) says is one of liberation as well as integration.

Self-awareness can also help to integrate the internal with the external. If we are fully in touch with our needs and longings, then we are more likely to see and seize **opportunities** for meeting these in the world outside us.

A high level of self-awareness is associated also with a high level of self-control. For example, it makes it possible for us to identify and counter self-defeating thinking patterns and, more generally, to regulate the communication we have with ourselves. If we are very self-aware then we are also likely to accept **responsibility** for our actions and our lives, if only because we have a much clearer idea of the kinds of people we are and are capable of becoming. For instance, if I discover through self-examination that I have an inner strength that I have not previously acknowledged, then I am likely to approach difficult situations with a greater sense of fortitude or power. Even if I discover a 'weakness', by acknowledging it I am less likely either to feel a victim to it or to encourage its persistence by declaring war upon it. Self-awareness can also make us conscious of the **comfort zones** we may need to go beyond in order to develop.

Clearly, self-awareness enables us to learn from and evaluate our experiences and, as Covey (1992) points out, the experiences of others. In recent years, a specific form of this capacity, *metacognition*, the ability to 'think about thinking' and 'see ourself and others as problem-solvers', has received much attention by cognitive psychologists interested in learning development (Gardner, 1991).

Self-awareness is particularly vital for establishing successful relationships with other people. As Stephanie Dowrick (1992) elegantly captures it: 'we cannot know other people better than we know ourselves.' We can only understand what other people may be feeling and thinking if we know our own thoughts and feelings. This applies to working relationships as well as to personal ones – especially in an age when team work is becoming increasingly common. As Thoroughgood (1994) observes: 'An unaware person cannot work well in a team'.

Given that personal development depends upon (and promotes) self-awareness, it is significant that many of us lack it to any high level. One reason for this is the generally low status attached to introspection and reflection in most Western cultures. The societal values of doing, achieving and getting are almost everywhere accorded more time, resources and importance than the values of knowing oneself and, to a lesser extent, knowing other people. The situation may be changing as more and more people seek to understand who they are and make use of literature and other means to achieve this. But even for many 'truth-seekers', the pressures of day-to-day living, many of which give prominence to the ego, mean often that self-awareness is largely confined to small parcels of time (eg, meditation sessions) reserved for the purpose.

Another reason that self-awareness is not a major pursuit for many people is that it is often considered selfish and egocentric. Introspection, if it is excessive and unconcerned with personal growth, can be psychologically unhealthy. But self-knowledge is not the same thing as self-absorption. Indeed, it is very nearly the opposite, certainly in its effects. People who know themselves, and who accept what they know, are much less likely to be selfish and much more likely to focus their energies on others. As Dowrick puts it, self-awareness leads towards 'that lovely, desirable capacity to take yourself, rather than others, for granted.'

From a development perspective, self-awareness is not so much an acquired capacity as a natural capacity programmed out of us by our upbringing and, for some, acquired again through conscious efforts. At the heart of this theory is the idea that as we grow up we learn to modify our behaviour to gain the approval of others. We learn, for example, not to display (and feel) anger if anger gets us disapproving messages. Over time, we so edit, deny and distort our thoughts and feelings that increasingly we become disconnected from them. We become strangers to ourselves, no longer in touch with exactly what it is we do think and feel. If this is so, then expressing what we feel is a secondary problem; the primary problem is *knowing* what we feel.

For people disconnected from their inner lives, connecting again can be uncomfortable or even painful. Egan (1994) calls it the 'fear of disorganization', the disorganization or disequilibrium a person may experience when, through self-disclosure, they begin to find out 'unpleasant things' about themselves. But, as Egan goes on to note, disequilibrium may be the price of growth, since we tend to grow at times of crisis.
(See **Actualization; Emotions; Disidentification; Self-Acceptance.**)

Self-Efficacy (SE)

Our **beliefs** about the extent to which we can influence what happens in our lives. More specifically, SE refers to our judgement about whether we can perform a particular task or bring about a successful outcome. For Albert Bandura (1977), SE implies beliefs about successful accomplishment, but other authorities (eg, Mager, 1992) confine SE to expectations about performance ('I can do it') rather than actual outcomes ('I know I can do it successfully').

The essential point about SE is this: if we have high SE, then we will probably attempt a task and succeed at it. If we think we can't pull it off, then we probably won't even try. Our perceived SE, then, affects our willingness to perform an action, our **commitment** to it, and our persistence, including our recovery from setbacks and 'failure'. High SE correlates with the belief that **failure** is an inevitable part of learning.

Our level of SE also affects our aspirations (eg, the careers we choose), the **goals** we set, the effort we put into achieving them, whether we visualize **success** or failure scenarios, whether we use **self-talk** to enhance or limit ourselves, our resilience in the face of difficulties, our **focus** (on strengths or on weaknesses) and our proneness to anxiety, depression and stress.

Fortunately, SE can be strengthened most powerfully through performance **mastery** ie, learning how to do something well, then doing it well. According to Lemme (1995), it is acceptable, even desirable, to overestimate our SE. 'Over' confidence leads us to try harder which improves the chances of success which enhances SE. This is consistent with the 'aim high', 'you can achieve whatever you believe you can', messages which permeate popular self-help books.

However, SE doesn't automatically increase when we demonstrate a skill or perform well. Nor is practice alone enough to strengthen it. What matters is interpreting success as 'down to us'. That is, we need to change on the inside. We need to believe that performance mastery results from our skills, not from external factors, such as luck, the 'right' conditions, help from others, etc. Others can help us to attribute success to our personal capabilities through the feedback they give. *Encouragement* and *persuasive comments* can also enhance our SE.

Two other factors benefit SE. One is **modelling** other people who are doing what we are considering doing and doing it well. This works effectively provided we perceive the models as people like ourselves. The other factor is *physiological feedback*. We are more likely to try a task if we associate it with pleasure rather than with fear or anxiety. Our interpretation of the physiological effects of effort is also crucial. If the performance of a task exhausts us, we may assume that it's because we lack the capacity. Our SE will be higher if we can be persuaded that it's because the task is intrinsically demanding or because we haven't yet learned how to do it without getting exhausted.

As an area of study and applied research, SE is burgeoning. It is certainly making an impact on personal development within **counselling**, health care and some training contexts, but its implications for personal development generally are massive. Like its semantic cousin 'agency', 'self-efficacy' is not in wide currency in popular PD books and programs. Nonetheless, it relates directly or otherwise to many terms and concepts which are (eg, 'proactivity', **personal power**, personal **responsibility**, **will**, **locus of control** and **decision-making**), and the idea of self-efficacy is central to PD programs, most of which are based on the premise that we can shape our own destinies and make things happen. Metaphors describing us as the 'creators' and 'architects' of our lives abound, and the following assumptions are widespread in PD.

- We are not fixed forever. We can act upon ourselves as well as upon the world. There are few things we *have* to be.
- The power to make things happen is natural to us. Some PD tutors would contend that we don't so much develop SE as recover it. That is, we come into this world as confident agents, but upbringing and **programming** can lead us to believe that we are ineffectual and helpless. We also possess the means, the physiological and neurological equipment, to be efficacious. It's just that we don't fully believe it or we don't know how to use it to full effect. This is where PD tutors can help.
- If things are to happen, then we must make them happen. Others can sometimes support us, but they cannot be our agents on a consistent basis. We must take full responsibility for our lives and destiny.
- Decisions rather than conditions determine our destiny. Choice plays a bigger part than chance in personal development. Sociologists may debate the respective power of agency and social structure, but PD tutors are clearly on the side of agency. That is, they are confident that individuals can act independently of social and environmental constraints. Recognition that we always have **choices**, regardless of circumstances, is fundamental to this capacity and our exercise of it.

- If we are not self-determining by design, then we shall be so by default. Some psychologists believe that we are autonomous beings who choose the actions we take. This is called *agent causation*. Others believe that our actions result largely from some contents of our mind of which we are not generally aware (eg, repressed memories and early life experiences). This is called *psychic determinism*. PD tutors do not always make their assumptions explicit, but the majority responsible for popular self-help books and programs would probably contend that we not only choose our behaviours, but we also have the capacity to choose and control the mental programs which produce them. For example, we *choose* what we believe and don't believe, which in turn will lead us to behave in certain ways and, cumulatively, to be certain kinds of people leading certain kinds of lives. If we don't actively *choose* our mental programs, then we shall still be influenced by the **beliefs** we hold; we just won't control the process.

Self-Esteem

The value we place on ourselves. More accurately, it's the value we place on specific aspects of ourselves, since we can have high self-esteem in some areas of our lives, but low self-esteem in others. We can feel confident about our abilities in the work context, for example, but lack confidence about our abilities on the sports field. Or our self-esteem can be high as a swimmer, but low as a runner.

Sometimes self-esteem is defined in terms of the relationship between our self-image (how we 'see' ourselves) and our **ideal self** (how we'd like to see ourselves). Our self-esteem is our evaluation of the discrepancy between these two things. If we can accept this discrepancy without necessarily feeling self-satisfied, than our self-esteem will be comparatively high.

There is general agreement that high self-esteem is crucial to our **well-being** and our capacity for personal development. Turner (1994) says that it 'directly determines' how effective we are in every area of our lives. For Johnson and Swindley (1995), 'an investment in building [our] self-esteem is nothing less than an investment in life itself.' Virtually every PD tutor who devotes time to self-esteem says that high self-esteem correlates with a willingness to respond to **challenges** and seek out **opportunities** for development and success. We've got to feel that we are likeable, capable and worthwhile people before we can risk doing things that hold the promise of development. (see **Risks**).

If our self-esteem is low, then we'll probably be self-protective. We'll resist **change** and run ourselves and others down when we feel seriously threatened by it. We'll probably reject praise and we won't recognize our own achievements. We'll find it difficult to open ourselves to major learning experiences. Because we blame and complain a lot, others will find us difficult to work with.

If our self-esteem is relatively high, we'll want to try new ventures and we won't see risk as seriously risky. We won't put ourselves down with excessive negative **self-talk** and, feeling worthy, we will attract respect and compliments from others. We'll work on our personal development because we'll see ourselves as worthy of it, and we will almost certainly help to enhance the self-esteem of others. We may or may not be 'high performing', but we'll certainly consider ourselves capable of achieving success - however we might define it.

For most PD tutors, our level of self-esteem is mainly a matter of choice. We can choose low self-esteem, but we have also to accept its consequences. The assumption that underpins this thinking is that after our early years, when significant adults shaped our self-esteem, the value we place on ourselves is determined more by our thoughts and internal images than by the way others behave towards us. (The literature on building self-esteem in children has a different emphasis, since it is directed at adult influencers such as teachers and parents.) Our self-esteem can be low, even when others behave positively towards us. In any case, we cannot take responsibility for their behaviour. To enhance our self-esteem, then, we have to work mainly on changing inside. Changing for the better what we think and say to ourselves, and see in our minds, will change our level of self-regard and attract the high regard of others.

There are many other techniques for developing self-esteem, including the following.

- Identify and then target the areas in which self-esteem particularly needs building. (Where and when do you have low self-regard?)
- Audit strengths and weaknesses, but particularly the former (see **Self-Audit**).
- Work on changing **beliefs** which link your feeling of self-worth to your job, social status or possessions.
- Work on living the belief that there are very few 'have tos' in life. Live on a 'choose to, want to' basis.
- Accept the praise and compliments you receive from others.
- Don't generalize negative feedback or 'failure'. Don't reprocess 'you have failed' (a comment about behaviour) as 'you are a failure' (a comment about identity).
- See whether it is possible to reframe situations in which you feel low self-esteem. Instead of defining a situation as 'I'm the odd one out', assign to it a different meaning – 'I'm glad I have a different set of interests', for instance.
- Work on changing 'I'm too . . .' beliefs (eg, 'I'm too quiet', 'I'm too old').
- Have a fund of positive **reference experiences** on which you can call. For example, visualize flicking through a photograph album which captures the occasions when you have felt confident and worthy.
- Use the **NLP** anchoring technique to trigger at will a state associated with high self-esteem.
- See yourself liking yourself – smiling at your reflection in a mirror, or smiling as you sink into a warm bath.
- Replay in slow motion past situations where your self-esteem slumped, and track the negative commentary from your inner critic.
- See yourself moving incrementally towards success, but not experiencing it straight away. For some people, struggling towards success is easier to picture than enjoying it without a struggle.
- Use the **'As If'** technique – ie, act as if you are already feeling high self-esteem in a situation where you want this to be the case.
- Model the behaviour of high self-esteem people. Make a study of the body language of confident people.

- Break daunting situations down into psychologically more manageable parts. At a party of strangers, for example, set a goal of talking to one person. You don't have to talk to everyone to maintain a level of self-esteem.
- Accept that some situations cannot be changed and that some people may not like you or respect you as much as you should like.
- Above all, constantly use positive affirmations and self-talk to encourage yourself and to counter what Fanning (1994) calls the 'pathological critic'. You can also use phrases which acknowledge that you are not and need not try to be perfect. At the appropriate times, such phrases as, 'I don't know . . .', 'I need help here . . .', 'I was wrong . . .', 'I forgive myself . . .' and 'I forgive you . . .' can also be very valuable.

Self Help

This is the idea that each of us can and should administer to our own **healing** and **development** needs. In much of the world today, self-help is more than a concept. It's the DIY philosophy that legitimates a multi-million dollar industry that services self-helpers with computer software, books, audio and video programs, seminars and all number of other support resources. It is also a movement – a social landscape dotted with countless **self-help groups** and self-improvement organizations.

The self-help philosophy is based on the premise that each of us has the resources within us to effect beneficial personal **change**. We may even have at some level access to the answers we are seeking. We certainly have potential **self-efficacy**, the capacity to make things happen in our lives. These **beliefs** support the 'can' of the above definition. The 'should' is the view that we must accept individual **responsibility** for the actions we take, or don't take, and the consequences of them. This can include taking responsibility for our 'side' of a relationship – ie, taking unilateral **action** to improve it (see McKay *et al*, 1994).

The ideology of self-help is too involved to discuss here, but we need at least to acknowledge that it is biased in certain directions. Most obviously, it plays up the role of the individual in personal promotion, and highlights his or her more innate resources – cognitive capacities especially. Just as obviously, it plays down the influencing factors which are most socially and economically variable, including the individual's access to material and external resources, such as education and training **opportunities**. We can all help ourselves, but we are not all as well placed to do so.

Some of us are scared by the concept of self-help, particularly if we understand it to mean, 'going it alone'. Self-help books and tutors combat this in two ways. First, they emphasize the merits of being in control of our lives. One of these is economy of both time and money. Paul Lisnek (1995) uses a service station analogy to make this point. At one time, we had to wait for an attendant to fill our car with petrol (gas). Now we can do it ourselves. In life, too, we 'pull into the service lane' whenever we want to be in control of our lives. We can also save on time and money by not handing our problems over to expensive professionals to 'solve'. Some PD tutors also stress the emotional pay-offs of the DIY approach – excitement, the joy of accomplishment etc.

Second, self-help authorities point out that self-help does not necessarily mean unsupported help. Self-help means using the resources of the self *for* the self, but it also means being resourceful - finding and using resources outside ourselves to service our needs. Self-help also implies referring without necessarily deferring to other people's expertise. Certainly, no self-help book or program has all the answers, and we have to take responsibility for separating the wheat from the chaff. Above all, no self-help book can 'do it' for us. Taking the appropriate action is what self-help is really all about.

For the self-helper, there are plenty of books to turn to. Some deal with personal change generally, others focus upon particular areas (eg, building confidence, improving relationships) or are based on a specific methodology or technology (eg, Gestalt, **NLP**).

Self-help books vary significantly in approach and quality. In terms of approach, Rusk and Read (1986) distinguish between two general categories. There are 'nice friend' books, heavy on platitudes, quotations and inspiration, but light on lasting effects. And there are the 'recipe' or how-to books. Their quality is variable. The better manuals tend to address personal change at a variety of levels (**values**, skills, behaviours etc) and to be informed by quality research in relevant areas such as cognitive psychology and psycholinguistics. They also acknowledge individual differences. Prescriptions and strategies, where they are presented, are adaptable enough to have wide application. The highest quality self-help books are not over-laden with either general exhortations at the one extreme nor simplistic 'tips' at the other. They also present systematic programs for change rather than a series of disconnected points, and make original contributions to the subject. A lot of self-help books, it has to be said, repackage familiar themes and examples.

Clearly, many of us find self-help materials motivating, interesting, and of real, practical value. However, there is plenty of anecdotal evidence to suggest that while they preach the virtues of independence (or interdependence), some of us seem almost dependent upon them. Attending seminars, reading books and listening to tapes on taking action for personal development may be substitutes for actually taking action ourselves! Which is why Rusk and Read suggest that self-help books should self-destruct after use!

Self-Help Groups

Groups in which members usually meet face-to-face to help both themselves and other members to improve their lives in certain common directions.

Some self-help groups deal with addictions (Alcoholics Anonymous is the most famous example) or are set up by and for people with specific clinical conditions (HIV, for instance). There are also consciousness-training groups (men's groups, for example) and groups of people with common interests, such as Gestalt, **transactional analysis** or some other kind of therapy. These tend to be led by 'experts' and to attract dedicated self-developers, so the term 'self-improvement' might be better than self-help.

In some countries, including Britain and, in particular, the USA, self-help groups have burgeoned in the last two decades. Liz Hodgkinson (1993) says that they are 'among the most important strands of the personal growth movement'. One estimate of the number of small groups in the USA with a broadly spiritual orientation was put at 3 million in 1992 (cited in Egan, 1994). The fact that the self-help group movement has its own publications, including, in the USA, the *Self-Help Reporter*, also attests to its having come of age.

Why do many of us turn to self-help groups in preference to professionals such as psychotherapists? One explanation is cost effectiveness, with the emphasis on cost and, some suggest, on effectiveness as well. Another is that professional support might not always be available.

In an article providing advice on setting up a self-help group Val Fallon (1992) suggests that self-help groups meet three requirements. First, they put us in contact with people in the 'same boat' as ourselves. Second, they help us to feel empowered so that we do not have to rely on professional help in order to change our lives. And third, we can enjoy the support of others in a group without a hierarchy.

We can add to this that self-help groups tend to offer their members a lot of understanding with very little judgement. The environment is one of sharing experiences rather than of debating theory, and members often feel secure enough to make honest disclosures. At the same time, the emphasis tends also to be on action in bite-sized steps. Peer pressure as well as group support can assist this.

There is evidence (see Kaminer, 1992) that for some people the group itself can become the focus of concern, and that group processes can be substituted for individual action to effect genuine personal change.

Self-Talk

What we say to ourselves when we are awake, or 'the verbal aspect of thinking' (Nelson-Jones, 1989). It can be vocalized, but is often internal.

A dignified alternative term for self-talk is *inner dialogue*, suggesting more than one 'participant' in the intra-personal communication process. In the literature, the participants are variously defined as conscious self and subconscious self, self and **Higher Self**, self-as-process ('I') and self-as-object ('Me'), and even as right brain and left brain.

Most PD tutors recognize and emphasize the central role of self-talk in influencing our feelings and behaviour and aspects of ourselves that are more enduring. It plays a part in virtually every personal development process, including the shaping of our self-concept, our **beliefs** and the making and breaking of **habits**. And yet most of us appear to do little to control our self-talk or use it to serve our interests. Much of it is negative, undirected 'mind babble'. We allow it to put us down, limit our thinking, sap our energy and block out the quiet voice of the Higher Self.

The message PD specialists drive home is that we must control our self-talk otherwise it will control us. The good news is that it can be used to support and affirm the positive aspects of our self-concept, to energize us and, in its crafted, deliberated forms (ie, **affirmations**), to program our **subconscious** in line with our development requirements. We can also learn to quieten or even stop the chatter in order to listen more intently, either to others or to the quiet voices of wisdom within ourselves. One of the aims of cognitive therapy is to help those of us with emotional disorders to modify the self-talk or the 'negative automatic thoughts' which express emotional distress. These thoughts occur more spontaneously and far more frequently in the distressed, but none of us is free of them completely.

There is evidence, especially from sports psychology, to demonstrate the efficacy of self-talk for improving performance. Studies have shown that different types of self-talk interventions, including statements relevant to the task ('accelerate along this straight'), 'mood' statements and words (eg, 'drive', 'go for it') and positive self-affirmations ('I enjoy feeling so strong') can all enhance actual performance (see Rushall *et al*, 1988; Cox, 1994).

Self-talk is the basis of inside-out as opposed to outside-in **change**. Rather than trying to change our behaviour directly, we use self-talk to program our subconscious to bring about the changes we want. Self-talk which evokes the 'right' mental images and emotions can be especially effective. Self-talking ourselves into enjoying our meals, for example, may be more effective as a strategy than trying to force ourselves to eat more slowly. PD tutors suggest many techniques to enhance the quality of our self-talk. Self-talking in the present tense so that our statements have maximum strength ('I enjoy eating' is stronger than 'I could enjoy eating if I ate more slowly') is a major technique. Others include prefacing statements with 'I choose', emphasizing the process ('I enjoy running') rather than the outcome ('I must beat four minutes'), and using 'I' rather than 'you' statements.

Because of the intimacy of language and thought, the language in which we do our self-talking is crucial. Much has been written on the psycholinguistics of self-talk. We know, for example, that we should avoid words that the subconscious will interpret as negatives (eg, 'I'm hopeless', 'I can't', 'I'm not to blame'). Some leading PD tutors have invented their own names or systems for language which shifts negative into positives. Robbins calls his 'Transformational Vocabulary' ™. Jeffers calls hers 'Pain-to-Pleasure' vocabulary.

From a psychospiritual viewpoint, *inner dialogue* may have a more specific meaning than self-talk, one much closer to **intuition**: a reception in the conscious mind of 'messages' from a Higher Self. Assagioli (1990) termed it 'vertical telepathy'. It might be thought of as the spirit in communion with the mind, over which it has dominion when the mind is still enough for this process to occur. The psychosynthetic technique of having a dialogue with one of our subpersonalities, such as the Wise Old Person, is also a special case, one which links talk with guided imagery. In this case, self-talk may serve as a therapy as well as a tutorial.

Solution-Centred

This means focusing upon finding solutions to problems rather than dwelling on the problems themselves. Anthony Robbins suggests we spend 90 per cent of our time on solutions and only 10 per cent on problems, and PD tutors generally advocate a solution-centred approach to life. They regard it as characteristic of **positive-thinking**, self-responsible and personally effective people. Gillen (1995) cites it as a feature of 'effective influencers'.

There are some obvious reasons why it can be productive and

developmental to focus upon solutions. One is that it prevents us from getting stuck in unproductive or even counterproductive states, such as anxiety, worry and annoyance. It also allows us to bring into play our capacities for divergent and creative thought, and to make use of the numerous techniques for problem solving (see Juniper, 1989). Dwelling on the problem can also entrench us in analysing it and speculating on why it occurred. Some diagnosis can be helpful and we clearly need to define the problem as precisely as possible before we start searching for solutions. But frequently 'how' and 'what' questions (eg, 'What do I *want* to feel like?' or 'How can I ensure this problem never recurs?') are actually more helpful in taking us forward. The **NLP** techniques for helping people to solve their problems are very largely responses to specific 'how' and 'what' questions. In fact, one of the best known NLP books is actually called *Solutions* (Cameron-Bandler, 1985).

Another good reason for being solution-oriented is that it encourages us to define the outcome we want, ie, to be goal-directed. This primes our **reticular activating system** to 'spot' possible solutions. It is particularly powerful when we assume that our problem is soluble. Indeed, PD tutors encourage us not only to seek solutions but also to work on the assumption that there are solutions to all or most problems. Not all problems *are* soluble, but keeping our minds, eyes and ears open ensures that we optimize the possibilities of finding solutions where they do exist.

State Management

The ability to get into and out of states at will. In particular, the capacity to get ourselves into supportive, resourceful and empowering states on a consistent basis.

The concept of state is central to **NLP** and psychotechnological approaches to PD. At one level it refers to the vast number of neurological processes that go on inside us to make us feel in a certain way at any one time. The emphasis is upon how we feel, but 'state' sums up all the aspects of an experience and includes our thoughts, internal pictures, **emotions** and all manner of bodily states and patterns, including our breathing patterns, muscle tone, posture and expressions. There is widespread agreement that we can manage and control this 'internal environment' and that it's this, rather than the external environment, that determines how we feel and behave.

Many PD tutors make the point that successful people are effective at positive state management. The key word here is 'positive', for 'getting into a state' is not a problem for many of us. Indeed, some of us are highly competent at getting ourselves into negative, unsupportive states, such as depression and anxiety. All we need to do is to **focus** upon unpleasant experiences for long enough, or to overwhelm ourselves with the thoughts of, say, all the household jobs that we still haven't tackled. We can achieve similar effects in more physical ways. For example, we can assume the slumped posture of the depressive, or we can eat a huge meal until we feel, literally, 'fed up'.

Alternatively, we can use exactly the same techniques to switch from an unsupportive to a resourceful state. That is, we can either think ourselves into feeling resourceful or change our physiology to achieve the same end. How we think about things, represent them internally, picture them, define them, and so forth, makes a huge difference to our state of mind and therefore to our feelings and physiognomy. This is part of the reason why focus is such an important concept and why we have to be careful about our operating **beliefs** and the **questions** we ask ourselves. Selecting 'good' things to think about, recalling happy experiences, defining situations positively – these are the general strategies for entering positive states. Resourceful states can also be achieved more economically with the right **anchors**, but for much of the time, the quickest way to change our state is to change what we are doing with our body. Something as simple as standing up straight or smiling can radically influence our neurological processes and, with these changes, how we feel generally.

For NLPers, state is largely a matter of choice. We can choose to feel confident, resourceful, excited, eager for action, productive etc, or we can choose to feel one of the negative states. We can choose, proactively, to determine our state or we can allow ourselves to react to external factors – other people, the weather, events etc.

The state we are in is enormously important for it influences what we do and how well we do it. We can perform the same task on two occasions, with startlingly different results, simply because we felt resourceful on one occasion and unresourceful on the other. Being able to influence another person's state can also be extremely useful. If we feel, for example, that a partner is treating us 'badly', then we might do better to help effect a change in his or her state than to try to change his or her behaviour directly.

Finally, goals and outcomes need also to be thought about in state terms. Many of us fail to do this, and so end up achieving what we thought we wanted, only to feel somehow disappointed.

Subconscious (The)

The part of our mind that strives to bring about or maintain in reality whatever is presented to it by the conscious mind. This includes our **goals**, matters about which we **worry**, the images we have of ourselves and the problems we want to solve. In short, our subconscious seeks to ensure that we reap in life whatever we sow in our minds.

It would be difficult to exaggerate the part that the subconscious is assumed to play. In the self-help world, it is a far more important concept than the unconscious. Some books are devoted entirely to it (eg, Murphy, 1988), and many others lean heavily upon it. It underpins the theory of goal-setting, **success programming**, and the impact of **beliefs** and **attitudes** on personal development. Huge claims are made for its powers and functions. Joseph Murphy asserts confidently that it 'controls all the vital processes of your body and knows the answers to all problems.' Ron Holland (1993) tells us that 'it never makes a mistake' and creates a plan for anything we see with our 'mind's eye'. It's conceived as the workshop in which our futures are made. Most PD tutors would agree with Jack Black (1994) when he says that the future has to exist in the subconscious before it can become a reality.

There is widespread agreement about the operations and requirements of the subconscious, which include the following.

- The subconscious is fed 'information' by the conscious mind, ie, the reasoning part of the mind that works on the materials of present awareness. Our subconscious is both tireless and omnivorous. It works on anything the conscious mind sends it. It is impersonal, obedient and accepting. It makes no judgements about what might or might not be in our own best interests. Hence, our conscious mind must be a vigilant and responsible gatekeeper. It must *not* feed or program our subconscious with thoughts, desires and images that it does not want to bring about in reality (see **GIGO**).
- The operations of the subconscious benefit from repetition and **imprinting**. It prefers to receive messages which are precise, specific, intense, vivid and repeated so that they can cut deep. Visual images are good; multi-sensory images may be better. PD tutors give advice on enhancing the impression we can make on the subconscious. For example: use words which evoke strong images and **emotions**; find and study photographs of whatever you want to acquire; obtain an object associated with the situation you want to bring about (eg, a seat cover for the car you are goal-setting to own).
- The subconscious does not discriminate between the real and the vividly imagined. For example, it cannot tell whether I'm really self-confident or just 'pretending' to be – provided I 'pretend' in precise, compelling words and pictures. In this respect, the subconscious is easily duped, which is extremely useful for personal change and goal achievement purposes.
- The subconscious has access to a vast storehouse of information, and it can perform any number of operations. This makes it an efficient problem-solver. It prefers problems to be expressed clearly and precisely, and it likes to have time to 'get on with it' without too much conscious interference. It benefits from conditions of silence and stillness, though it often presents the conscious mind with solutions when the latter is busy on matters of its own. It won't be disciplined into finding solutions or providing them at the convenience of our conscious mind. It tends to transmit its messages when we least expect it.

The creative, problem-solving capacities of the subconscious are sometimes explained with reference to Gestalt therapy and/or the concept of cognitive dissonance. When our conscious mind formulates a goal or a problem to be solved, it automatically establishes a new Gestalt or pattern. To begin with, this is not in harmony with the way things currently are. The subconscious makes use of the tension inherent in this situation by becoming creative in finding ways to 'restore' or bring about the new pattern. That is, it seeks endlessly to match the world without to the world within – which is why PD tutors make so much fuss about what we allow into the world within.

In all PD models of the mind, the conscious is linked to the subconscious. However, in some models the subconscious is one component, in others it is divided into the subconscious proper and the creative subconscious. Some PD tutors call it a 'mind'. Maltz (1960) says it's not a mind at all but a 'goal-striving, servomechanism', comprising the brain and nervous system, which the mind uses and directs. Some PD tutors imply that the subconscious is itself a vast repository of information. Others see it as a transit camp for the information stored permanently in the unconscious. These differences in terminology and modelling cause some confusion and difficulty in making comparisons, but they do not distract from the fundamental messages about the enormous power and significance of the function known as the subconscious.

Success

Success generally implies the achievement of whatever it is we set out to do, become or bring about, though for some PD tutors, success is as much about attempting as achieving. As Susan Jeffers (1991) puts it: 'You're not a failure if you don't make it; you're a success if you try.'

This highlights one of the themes of 'success' literature: that each of us must decide what counts for us as success and set criteria to enable us to know when we have succeeded. The point is often made that if *we* don't determine our success criteria (or rules), then others will do it for us. These 'others' might include self-help books on success, the implicit message of many being that 'success' means mega-achievement and mega-prosperity. Titles like *The Magic of Thinking Big* and *How to Think Like a*

Millionaire seem to imply this. At the same time, one piece of advice offered by some PD tutors is not to set success criteria too high – that is, not to make it extremely difficult for us to succeed. This is a matter of influencing our own perception rather than of having low expectations. Jeffers' own no-lose model of decision-making is a good example. If we have a go at something, and choose path A rather than path B, then provided we acquire new learning experiences there is no way in which we can lose. Similarly, if success for us means doubling our income rather than increasing it ten-fold, then our chances of succeeding may be many times better.

The literature on success is considerable. Much of it is based on values which include individual freedom, material wealth, and 'external' achievements in such realms of work and relationships. Some of it is empirical and based on the serious study of primary sources (ie, people who have achieved success), but a great deal of it is more anecdotal, derivative and based as much on secondary sources (ie, other books on success) as upon original field research or properly tested theories. Many of the principles of the literature on success published in the last 50 years can be traced to early mid-century classics such as Napoleon Hill's *Think and Grow Rich* (1937) and Dale Carnegie's *How to Win Friends and Influence People* (1938).

In recent years, success thinking and literature has developed in two directions. First, under the impact of **NLP**, **accelerated learning** and related psychotechnologies, success thinking has been sharpened up at the micro-level, as it were, in that far greater attention has been given to how we can run our minds and bodies to achieve successful **outcomes**. An earlier generation of books told us that we had to think positively; the new generation of books tell us how to do this in practice. Second, books on success are increasingly reflecting the principles and messages of holistic, mind/body/spirit-based approaches to personal development. For example, it is not unusual now to find a book on success dealing also with getting in touch with our Higher Self or emphasizing **self-awareness** as much as self-**mastery**.

Many of the entries in this book figure in success philosophies and programs. These defy easy summary, but generally contain the following messages and themes.

- Success is a natural state. We are born to develop our **potential** and so we are born to succeed.
- Success is no more difficult to achieve than **failure**, which in any case is always a contributory factor to success.
- We can program ourselves for success. We need to focus consistently on being successful (not on failing) and to make success consciousness habitual or second nature to us.
- Success rarely depends significantly upon natural talent, or even acquired technical competence. Success has much more to do with attitude than with aptitude.

Many PD tutors proffer systems or formulae for success. Hill and Stone's famous course on *PMA, The Science of Success* was based on 12 principles (see Hill and Stone, 1960). Brian Tracy discusses six requirements for success in his *The Psychology of Achievement* (1994) audio-cassette program, and Jack Black (1994) identifies four characteristics for successful living. Six of the more commonly suggested success secrets are the following:

- Know precisely what you want to achieve ('definiteness of purpose').
- Maintain positive **attitudes** and retain only empowering **beliefs**.
- Maintain high levels of health and energy.
- Align action with purpose.
- Learn from 'failure'.
- Develop good relationships with other people.

Team (context)

Small groups of people who interact effectively together for shared purposes afford personal development **opportunities** for individual group members. Indeed, a lot of our learning and growth almost certainly requires a group or team context.

Most books on personal development have what might be called an atomistic perspective: they address individuals as independent entities. This is legitimate in many respects, most obviously because no one else can 'do' our developing for us. Real development always happens on the inside, irrespective of what may happen on the outside. But this does not mean that personal development has to be a solitary affair, nor that other people cannot contribute substantially to it. Much intentional personal development certainly has a group context which is considered important if not essential. Examples include **self-help groups** and improvement groups and courses on specific 'pathways' to development in which the group dynamic is intrinsic to the process (eg, **transactional analysis**, Gestalt, Reiki). The same is true of 'planned' learning within organizations. As David Casey (1993) says in regard to management education at all levels, 'there is no more effective forum to advance self-awareness than the small learning group.'

For many of us today, it is the small, often self-directed work team that has become the major vehicle for personal as well as professional development. There is also a welter of training material on team processes, including the facilitation of learning within them. Teams have become popular (even unavoidable) for all manner of reasons. The pace and complexity of change requires flexible modes of organization which enable and promote equally rapid learning. Teams fit the bill, are generally regarded now as learning organizations in their own right, and have many characteristics conducive to the development of their members. Participation in effective teams can be motivating, rewarding and fun. A team's collective resources is greater than the resources of any individual, so members can learn from each other and complement each other's skills and expertise. If the culture is right (candid, open, respectful) then ideas can be challenged and growth can come from this. To contribute effectively to dynamic work teams, individual members have to be on steep learning curves and to commit to **continuous development**. Nowadays, teams are rarely easy options.

The trend towards self-directed teams (subject to minimal external control or management) is in many respects consistent with the **values** dominant in the PD world. These include taking **responsibility** for **action** and its consequences, efficiency, autonomy, goal-setting and planning, **risk**-taking and **failure** as **feedback**. Where the emphasis seems to differ is in regard to the social nature of learning. The team premise is that 'learning is a social activity motivated by the wish to belong to social learning groups' (Abbott, 1994). The implicit message of much self-improvement literature is that personal development is above all *intra*personal and can be effected by individuals working on themselves and, in the first instance, for themselves.

Time

Time is an extremely important dimension, both in personal development processes and in approaches to them. Experiencing significant personal **change** often entails fresh insights into or a re-evaluation of our personal histories and how we account for them. Similarly, PD programs are invariably based on models of time, and beliefs about the interrelationships of past, present and future. Most seek to influence our own views of these relationships.

PD tutors differ in terms of their primary orientation to time in relation to our lives. Some emphasize our earliest influences, including the therapists who seek 'answers' to some of the things that trouble us as adults by reference to our experience of birth (*rebirthing therapists*) and our earlier existence(s) (*past-life therapy*). For other PD tutors, including *Gestalt therapists*, our awareness in the **here and now** is paramount, including our experience in the now of unresolved feelings. By contrast, the majority of PD tutors who present programs for success and the realization of our potential are distinctly future-orientated, stressing the importance of having a **vision**, setting **goals** and planning.

In spite of these differences in focus and emphasis, there are a number of beliefs about time which enjoy widespread support. Chief among these is the belief that the linear model of time with which most of us operate for much of the time is neither valid nor helpful. Rather, it is narrowing and constraining in that it encourages us to think in categorical terms. We see the past as frozen and immutable and the future as untouchable and unknowable. We can do little to control or influence either.

A great many PD tutors would wish us to subscribe to a much more plastic, dynamic and creative model of time, one which was healthy, empowering and liberating in its effects upon us. Central to this model would be the idea that we are able to interact creatively with both the past and the future, as well as the present.

Creative interaction with the past means first acknowledging that it is not dead and buried. We may not be able to alter the facts of the past, but we can endlessly negotiate the meanings we assign to them. Personal development can mean coming to a quite new (and probably revivifying) interpretation of our past. It can also mean more actively 'creating' it: re-writing past experiences, installing new 'memories' and deleting others (see **Change Personal History**).

Some of us may feel uncomfortable 'tampering' with the past, particularly if we feel that this somehow involves cheating ourselves. But PD tutors from approaches as different as metaphysics and **NLP** put forward arguments for creative memory management, one of which is that the past offers us resources for the present. At the least creative level, we can identify positive past experiences and use them to make us more resourceful in the present. More imaginatively, we can put them to similar uses by making them impact upon past events in our lives. A similar idea is 'returning' as an adult to offer support to ourselves as a child. The reverse is equally possible: bringing our child self into the present to energize our adult self. We can also imagine our possible past selves and histories, and extract from these qualities and achievements to enhance us in the now. Perhaps we can even learn from mistakes we never gave ourselves permission to make.

Even if we do not interact creatively with the past, we need to examine our legacies and histories in order to ensure that we have not been saddled with, say, disabling **beliefs** or self-defeating patterns of behaviour. If we have, then we need to change them.

This links with a view that is very prominent in popular PD programmes: the view that the past does not determine the future – provided we have some awareness of the past. Most PD tutors today do not subscribe to the psychic determinism of Freud and traditional psychoanalytical theory. We are not assumed to be the victims of early childhood experiences or unconscious repression. Rather, the assumption is that we can choose not to repeat past 'mistakes' or to continue with beliefs and behaviours which have disabled us in the past. In short, our futures are decided by present decisions not by past conditions. This belief is neatly captured in expressions such as 'The past does not equal the future' and 'There are no facts about the future'.

The view that present thoughts determine future realities, that we become tomorrow what we think about today, is very widespread in mainstream PD today. It's part of the rationale for **affirmations**: present tense descriptions of a reality yet to be fully realized. Without this conviction in the determining powers of present thoughts, affirmations would be lies rather than statements that tell the truth in advance.

The belief that some degree of future orientation is healthy and necessary for growth is also widely held. This includes having a clear commitment to a preferred future. Visualizing ourselves in the future can be a powerful way to motivate ourselves in the present. We can also interact creatively with the future as we can with the past. For example, we can visualize or call upon our future selves to guide, support, energize and enlighten us in the present.

Can we be *too* future oriented? Some PD tutors believe we can and that we need to balance future expectations and present needs. One frequent piece of advice is to plan for the future and then relax and trust in our future self to make things happen.

Another view is that our **vision** of the future must be very strong, but that it is essential to remain aware of present reality, if only to ensure that we retain the drive to push towards the vision.

If we live in what Dina Glouberman (1995), calls 'a present that makes sense to us', then it is very probable that it makes sense to us because we 'have' a future that makes sense to us. Our present is informed by our future. In this context, the view advanced by some writers, including Gill Edwards (1991), that the future creates the present, may seem less bizarre than it may at first appear. Our future is the 'effect' we seek; our present is the 'cause', the way we have chosen to achieve the effect. A powerful vision, for example, will exert a pull on the present that may seem almost determining in its effects.

Coming to an understanding that time might not be linear, that our normal separation of past, present and future may be just one possible configuration, or even an illusion, is often associated with becoming generally more aware. A model of time centred on the eternal present is common among those on the path to **enlightenment**. The integrating forces are usually taken to be **karma** and the expanding consciousness of the mind, but what allows us to shed our illusions is our decreasing concern for our personal needs and wants. To the enlightened mind, the linear conception of time reflects our preoccupation, in an unenlightened state, with the fears and hopes of the personality or ego. With higher consciousness leading to a diminished concern for the personality we are freed from forever looking backwards and forwards and so experiencing time as linear.

We do not have to be enlightened to appreciate that past, present and future can coexist simultaneously. Any approach to personal development that emphasizes the experience of living through the present moment (eg, Gestalt) or depends on the powers of the imagination and the mind (eg, **visualization**, NLP) will inevitably present an alternative to rigidly linear conceptions of time.

Timelines (Personal)

These are the 'lines' by which past and future are connected in our mental maps of time.

In actual fact, these models may not be simply or even mainly linear. For example, time may be represented as an area rather than as a line, and past and present may not have a single, continuous line running between them.

Work on timelines falls within **NLP**. The focus is upon our subjective experience of time, how we represent and codify time internally, and the many variations in the ways we do so. How we represent time can be very revealing. It can, for example, show the extent to which we 'look forward' to things or whether we have a preoccupation with either the past or the future.

Although there is no one 'right' way to map time, some ways appear to be limiting and problematic for some individuals. Timeline therapists invite clients with time-related difficulties to try out alternative and possibly more empowering ways of mapping time. This may be nothing seemingly more radical than, say, putting the past to their left rather than to their right. (Most of us do, in fact, see the past in the personal space to our left.) Such changes can bring about significant and even profound personal and personality changes. However, there are often 'good' reasons for having a particular, individual way of representing time, and expert therapists are careful always to take clients through ecological checks to ensure that no part of them is uncomfortable with a re-organized timeline (see **Ecology**). The way we map time ought to be in our best interests; we may need to consult with our **intuition**, **Higher Self** or subpersonality team to be certain that it is.

The most significant variable in our timelines appears to be location: where we 'see' past and present and whether our 'now' is placed just outside our body or inside it. If we sense 'now' just in front of us and see our past and our future running in a U-shape or V-shape away from us, then we are experiencing 'through time'. If, however, we sense the past behind us and the future going out in front of us, but focus firmly in the now (within us) then we are said, to be 'in time'. Those of us who have a 'through time' model are likely to be more effective time managers (planners, time-keepers etc). But having an 'in-time' model can be good for some things: enjoying the here and now, for instance, or giving people time and attention.

Another variable is colour. We may see either or both past and present in colour or in black and white. Or we may see one in colour and the other in monochrome. A third variable is clarity. Is past or present clearer, more in-focus? Or are they equally well-defined or equally fuzzy? Does fuzziness indicate uncertainty? Other variables include movement (still image or movie film?) and line arrangement (single line? branching network? fanning arrangement? etc).

We can experiment with all of these variables, either by ourselves or with the assistance of an expert timeline therapist. Altering a variable (eg, making the future literally brighter) may or may not have an effect upon us, and this may or not be beneficial. If we make a change that doesn't feel right, then we can simply revert to the original arrangement. Timeline work offers the possibility of altering our orientation to time in any way that meets our development needs. This may involve helping us to build a future about which we feel more motivated, or even making changes to our map of the past to benefit our future development. It can also help us to stay more effectively and happily in the here and now, if that's what we need.

Transactional Analysis

Transactional Analysis (TA) is a set of concepts and techniques for making sense of our personalities and for promoting our personal development. It can illuminate patterns in our lives and interpersonal relationships, including those between our thinking, feeling and behaviour.

Eric Berne (1958), the founder of TA, was optimistic about our potential for personal growth. He believed that virtually all of us have the drive and the neurological capability to develop into autonomous and psychologically healthy individuals. He was less optimistic about what many of us actually *do* with this **potential**, and some of the key concepts of TA shed light on the ways in which we limit it.

One of the central TA concepts is *scripting*. This is the preconscious process by which we decide our general lifeplan.

Significant script decisions tend to be taken in response to early childhood experiences and parental programming.

For example, on the basis of an early experience we might conclude that trusting other people brings only pain. Our evidence may be flimsy and our reasoning immature, but the conclusion might exert a lasting and largely unconscious influence on the way we play out our lives. As Nelson-Jones (1995) observes, scripts can give us 'an illusion of personal autonomy' when in reality we are carrying out our script directives.

The **beliefs** underpinnning our scripts can also limit our autonomy if we strive to maintain them when the evidence before us should put them in doubt. These might include the 'I'll be OK, if . . .' beliefs (or myths) known as drivers. 'I'll be OK if . . . I'm strong; I'm perfect; I try hard; I please others; I hurry up'. Drivers offer strategies for surviving, but since we can never do them enough, never realize them in full, they carry the implicit message 'You're not good enough'.

Scripts are acted out on a moment-to-moment basis through communicative exchanges. The smallest recognisable unit of exchange is the *transaction*, which put simply means: 'You do something to me and I do something back'. Through our transactions with others we seek to give and receive units of recognition known famously in TA as *strokes*. A patterned and predictable series of transactions, particularly one in which we manoeuvre ourselves or put down others in order to get the strokes we want, is called a *game*. Games can be psychologically damaging and, because they are habitual, they too can limit our scope for behaving autonomously. One of the two books that have done most to popularise TA is Berne's *Games People Play* (1964). (The other is Thomas A. Harris's *I'm OK, You're OK* (1970)).

To understand fully these and the many othe concepts of TA, we need to be familiar with the central TA theory of *ego states*. Ego states are ways of being, each with its distinctive pattern of feelings, behaviour and thinking. The three main categories are those of Adult, Parent and Child. We are in the Adult ego state when we operate in the **here and now** and process information-in a rational way. When our behaviour is a relic of our behaviour in childhood we are in the Child ego state. When we replay behaviours we have learned or copied from parent figures – or when we catch ourselves repeating to our own children the phrases our parents used with us – then we are in the Parent ego state. Our Parent state can be Nurturing (caring, sensitive, etc) or Controlling (rule-imposing, criticizing, etc). Similarly, our Child ego state can be Natural (curious, fun-loving, impulsive, etc) or Adaptive, as when we behave in line with other people's expectations in order to gain their approval.

Transactions are distinguished and analyzed in terms of the relationships between the ego state addressed and the ego state that responds. A transaction engaging two Adult ego states is *complementary*, as is a Controlling Parent-Adaptive Child transaction. But a Controlling Parent who gets an Adult response would be in a *crossed* transaction. Transactions in which there are hidden psychological agendas are described as *ulterior*.

There is no 'best' ego state to be in, although in the early days of TA the Adult ego state was sometimes presented as such, and the Child ego state is much valued in some contemporary PD programs (see **Child [within]**). What matters is our ability to choose which ego state to operate in at any one time, and our ability to maintain our ego states as reasonably well-defined and bounded modes of being. Psychological and communication problems occur when the Adult is involuntarily contaminated by aspects of the Parent or Child.

How is personal development construed from a TA perspective? Principally, as the process of becoming an autonomous, adaptive and integrated Adult who is also capable of releasing Child and Parent states at will. In the ideal condition, ego states do not conflict or block each other. The Adult's rationality, for example, does not stop the Child from expressing itself. The Adult is not locked into a script; operates predominantly in the here and now while recognizing the influence, if any, of archaic influences.

Personal development in TA terms also means growing rich in the three capacities Berne associated with autonomy: *awareness*, shown by fresh perceptions in the here and now; *spontaneity*, including the expression of feeling free from the constraints of parental programming; and *intimacy*, the capcity for high quality relationships free from games and over-adaptions to parental influences.

Personal development is also a trajectory towards the *life posi-*

tion of 'I'm OK, You're OK'. In TA terms, a life position is a general attitude related to a general existential position. It's our dominant psychological portal onto the world. Being able to recognize that a position of mututal respect yields the greatest psychological satisfaction, and being able to choose it in preference to one of the 'non-OK' positions, are capacities of the autonomous individual. (The non-OK positions are: 'I'm OK, You're not OK'; 'You're OK, I'm not OK'; and 'I'm not OK, You're not OK'.)

Though no longer modish, TA enjoys enduring appeal. Most serious self-improvers will know at least something about it, and it is in the toolkits of a wide range of PD professionals, including psychotherapists, counsellors, management consultants and trainers.

TA is arguably the most accessible of the psychotherapies. In its simplified forms (Transactional Analysts know how rich and subtle it can be in practice), TA concepts are specific and high in recognition value. Encounters with TA typically lead to **'Aha!' experiences** and expressions, such as: 'Now I understand why I . . .'.

TA also lends itself to self-application and a DIY approach to personal(ity) development. As Julie Hay (1992) observes, when we realise that we can make sense of our actions and the response of others to them, we give ourselves 'licence to continue the process of self-development'. TA includes specific techniques for ministering to unmet needs of the Child within. The process is called *self-reparenting*.

TA fits in well with current thinking in mainstream personal development programs. Many of the terms discussed in this book, among them, **adaptability**, **commitment**, the **actualisation** of **potential**, (personal) **responsibility** and **self-awareness**, are key concepts in TA. TA also provides a theoretical framework for concepts which are not peculiarly TA in origin. **Self-talk**, for example. Negative self-talk can be explained as the voice of the Controlling Parent in another ego state. Positive self-talk the systematic use of **affirmations** can be thought of as tools to shape the self-image in the Adult ego state.

Although TA acknowledges the power of early inflences, it offers thinking tools for personal change, and is more sanguine about the possibilities for self-initiated change than are some of the other psychotherapies. Because the goals we set using TA can be very specific, achieving them can be relatively quick and effective. This also aligns it to the thinking behind popular programs for personal development.

Finally, TA cross-fertilizes with other major PD technologies, including **NLP** and Gestalt Psychology. TA and NLP share an emphasis upon the power of (unexamined) beliefs to negate or sabotage overt behaviours. The concept of *drivers* can be found in a number of NLP books and audio programs including Alder (1994) and Faulkner and McDonald (1994).

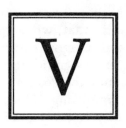

Values

Anything we hold dear or believe to be intrinsically desirable for us is a value.

Within a PD context, our values are enormously important. They lie at the heart of personal identity, so much so that Hopson and Scally (1991) call them 'a mirror image of who we are at any moment'. They drive our lives in that they provide the 'philosophy' by which we live and determine what we want and don't want. Without a clear set of values, we have no criteria for making life decisions, and no principles and priorities upon which to base our personal **vision** and **goal**s. The metaphors attached to values in PD literature (magnets, maps, compasses etc) point to their direction-determining effects.

As far as **development** is concerned, our values can be problematic in a number of ways. The main problem for many of us is that we have never made our key values explicit. We're not always sure what they are or how comparatively important for us they are. A problem resulting from this can be misalignment. Some of us allow our lives to be blighted because we do not get our values consistent with our **beliefs** and behaviour. For example, we may have 'family relationships' as a top value and yet devote huge chunks of our lives to **career development**. 'Happiness' may in theory be our top value and yet in practice we do not hold the belief or do the things that give us happiness (see **Alignment**).

One of the reasons for misalignment is that we acquire and change our values at different times in our lives. The same applies to beliefs and goals. The trouble arises when they do not change in tandem. So our lives can be driven by obsolete or vestigial values – those drip-fed into us when we are children, perhaps. As adults we may have goals to become rich based on the appropriate values; but these may be mixed with negative values regarding wealth that we acquired when young. Conversely, we may have pursued career goals long after our value hierarchy underwent a significant re-organization, so that the old values underpinning the goals are no longer there.

A linked problem is conflicting values. One part of us may enjoy the values of security, comfort and familiarity, and yet we may also value risk-taking and adventure. Conflicting values pull us in different directions and bedevil decision-making, unless we adopt a 'can't lose' approach, accepting that moving in the direction of any one set of values will bring us good things. (This works only if we can desist from speculating too much about what life might have been like had we chosen to be more in line with a different set of values.)

Some of us appear to suffer from what has been called 'horizontal values' (ie, everything seems to be of equal value to us), but for most of us the problem is that we just haven't clarified our hierarchy of values. We can suffer also from confusion between *ends* values, the things or states we want to achieve or be in (eg, freedom, having a family) and *means* values or, more accurately perhaps, *evaluative beliefs*. For some of us, being wealthy may be important in itself, an end value, but for many of us it will be only a means to an end. So we may have the evaluative belief that owning a yacht will help us to experience freedom.

A quite different values problem which can impact significantly upon our relationships with others and our interpersonal development results from believing that *our* values are right and other people's are wrong. For example, if we place great importance upon being punctual then we may take a very dim view of people with apparently different time values. As Hare (1988) points out, this can create a win/lose approach to situations, with unfortunate consequences.

Given the range of difficulties surrounding values, it is not surprising that some PD specialists place major emphasis upon our excavating, clarifying, ranking and sorting our values. Many of the better PD programmes, including those for adults reviewing their lives generally (eg, Hopson and Scally, 1991; Smith, 1992), suggest a range of appropriate exercises to assist with these processes.

The training and development of occupational and other

groups (eg, social workers, psychotherapists, doctors) tends also to involve a process of clarifying personal values which need to be considered in relation to the values both of their professions and of their clients.

If personal development is partly both about and dependent upon educating our values, then it must involve becoming more sensitive to the tell-tale signs that all is not right with our value system or the way it is operating in practice. One tell-tale sign is a feeling of disappointment or relative emptiness on achieving a goal. It tells us that the goal is not rooted in a key value. Having real problems in making life decisions (eg, about changing jobs, partners and lifestyles) can also indicate a need to think through value priorities.

Finally, there are values which underpin PD itself. Shakti Gawain (1995) distinguishes between three sets of values (she calls them 'aspects of life') which she says tend to be lived in the sequence have-do-be, but should be lived in the reverse sequence (be-do-have) if we want to experience happiness. That is, we need to decide who we are, then do whatever we need to do to have the things we want. This may be so, but it is true also that some PD tutors place much more emphasis upon 'being' than do others. In other words the value hierarchies which underpin personal development programs are not entirely uniform within the PD world generally, though many of the entries in this book indicate that many values are consensual (eg, personal **responsibility**, and **development** itself).

Vision

Our personal vision is the inspirational mental image of the future we strongly desire for ourselves. It may exist only as a picture or set of pictures in our head, but if we have delineated it seriously, then it probably exists in a more palpable form. It might consist of real pictures or a written statement or exist in some mixed media format. What matters is that the vision takes a form that works for us, which is likely to mean that it is congruent with our preferred modalities.

In what might be called the teleological hierarchy or order of things, a vision tends to be placed 'below' **purpose** and mission and 'above' goals. That is, our vision translates our life's purpose into images specific enough to focus our development upon, and it puts flesh on the bones of our **mission statement**.

When we take our vision and cut it up into specific statements of things we want to be or achieve, then we arrive at our major **goals**. When we 'chunk down' still further we formulate shorter term and still more specific **goals**, which may not link to the vision obviously or directly, but should be aligned to it (see **Alignment**).

For many PD tutors, a personal vision is a fundamental requirement for optimum personal development. It clarifies what we really want in and from life, and ensures that our lives have meaning and purpose. If it is a 'true to ourselves' vision, then it will embody and synthesize all that's most important to us, including our **values** and primary personal qualities. It provides the basis for deleting everything that is not really important to us: the quality of a vision lies in what it leaves out as well as in what it includes (see **Deletion**).

A powerful vision inspires, motivates and both focuses and releases our energies. Its attainment provides one of our major **challenges** in life, and we can't rise to a challenge unless we have one. If the vision is strong enough to permeate the **subconscious**, then in theory it ought to release in us the creative energies needed to achieve it. The more keenly we feel the discrepancy between the reality we want to bring about (the vision) and the reality we currently experience, the greater our drive and creativity to 'close the gap'. A powerful vision is one with the capacity to make us feel 'keenly'. In itself it will be a source of pleasure, but its contrast with the current situation ought also to link it with pain.

Does this mean that our vision should be 'far out'? By implication, it is bound to be discrepant with at least some aspects of our **current reality**, but 'distance' is not itself the issue. What matters is that it is both worthy of us and motivating. A *compromise vision* ('It's not what I really want, but at least it's realistic') is unlikely to meet either criteria. A vision that our subconscious cannot 'buy into', because it is so outrageously different from anything we know or can imagine for ourselves, may also fail to motivate us. The rule of thumb is to delineate a vision that is sufficiently 'far out' to motivate and to fulfil our **potential** but sufficiently 'close in' to be credible to our subconscious.

Keeping one eye on the present situation is important. It ensures that we don't lose contact with the world in which we have to operate at the moment. At the same time, it reminds us constantly of what we want to move away from, thus fuelling the **dissatisfaction** that drives us towards the vision. Nonetheless, our vision has still to be brighter, clearer and more compelling than present reality – not occasionally but more or less continuously. Sustaining a dominant vision is probably one of life's greatest challenges for those of us with a serious commitment to our personal growth and improvement. Assisting us in this task is one of the major challenges for PD tutors.

Visualization

In PD terms, visualization is using the imagination as a tool for **self-help** and personal **change**.

Lee Milteer (1990) refers to the imagination as the 'workshop of the mind'. This encapsulates the idea of using the mind in a conscious and deliberate way to create mental pictures or, more accurately, multi-sensory mental representations that might help us to improve ourselves or our lives in some way. These representations can be of people, scenes, performances, ideas, symbolic objects and other things. Because they don't have to be visual – entirely or even at all – some writers prefer alternative terms. In an excellent book on the subject, Dina Glouberman (1995) uses the term 'imagework'. As she notes, it is an exact description of the process of working with images.

Visualization is a natural process. We can all do it, and virtually everyone does. But it is also a set of techniques that can be developed. It has many possible uses, but in a PD context the emphasis is upon using it to effect personal change or to deal more effectively with aspects of our lives. It rarely if ever replaces other techniques, and frequently works most effectively in conjunction with others, especially **affirmation**. A general benefit of developing positive visualization is that it can displace negative visualization (rehearsing mistakes, re-playing worries etc), at which many of us are unfortunately rather good.

Books and programs on visualization tend to include guidelines for how to do it well. Suggestions include: doing it only when we are relaxed (though visualization can help to make us more relaxed) so that we send consistent messages to our muscles; closing our eyes and engaging as many of the senses as we can or choose; doing it normally in an associated state (ie, from 'inside') so that we feel strongly; and practising the skill regularly.

There are many theories of visualization (see Fanning, 1994), and explanations of why we 'need' images when we have the resources of language at our disposal. Images clearly have different qualities from language. Glouberman rightly points out that they are more metaphoric, holistic, personal and concrete than their verbal 'equivalents'. We could add that visual images are also much more powerful at arousal than language, partly because of their immediacy of impact and because they can naturally resemble whatever they represent. And add to this the fact that our earliest memories are pre-linguistic, which in part may explain why images can serve as a bridge between our unconscious and conscious minds.

Visualization in which the conscious mind opens itself to communication from the unconscious mind (or **Higher Self**) is sometimes called *receptive* visualization. It is particularly valuable for helping us to clarify our feelings, work out what we really want and explore resistance in our lives. When the conscious mind is the active source of communication, visualization is *creative* or *programmed*. Here we 'make up' images, singly or in sequence, rather than wait for them to emerge. Programmed visualization is especially useful for helping us to accomplish **goals**, improve performance, speed up **healing** processes and work with the images we have invited into our conscious mind.

Since it is virtually impossible to isolate the reception from the construction of images in the conscious mind, it is fairly certain that visualization is typically a mix of receptive and programmed forms. This is usually called *guided* visualization (or imagery). Examples include going to a 'mental sanctuary' to relieve stress or solve problems (often called Quiet Place visualization) and visualization to contact the Wise Old Person within you, perhaps the personification of your Higher Self, who can help you with particular problems.

Visualization and guided imagery techniques are used and recommended by all manner of PD tutors, including stress

counsellors, therapists and healers of most kinds, psychosynthetic specialists, sports psychologists, self-improvement coaches and experts on self-presentation. Among the scores of uses to
which visualization can be put, the following stand out in PD
contexts:

- Coping effectively with situations that provoke anxiety or
  challenge (eg, **mental rehearsal** of dealing with one such situation or seeing ourselves literally 'let off steam' to relax);
- Improving our performance in sporting or other skill-inten-
  sive activities (eg, mental rehearsal of playing a winning vol-
  ley in tennis);
- Attaining a goal (eg, visualizing ourselves getting married to
  our ideal mate);
- Performing in a role (eg, visualizing ourselves as a caring,
  effective parent);
- 'Looking back' on a successfully managed task (eg, visualizing having solved a problem we are currently facing);
- Understanding other people better (eg, imagining what it
  would be like to live in the shoes of another person);
- Understanding ourselves better (eg, visualizing the shadow
  sides of ourselves or trying to 'read' a symbol presented by
  our unconscious);
- Creating a generally positive state of mind (eg, visualizing
  favourite places, people and pastimes or all the many things
  for which we feel grateful).

Well-Being

This is an accumulative, deep and enduring sense of equanimity and good feeling, particularly about ourselves. Well-being is different from states such as resourcefulness, stress or equanimity itself in that it persists over time and in spite of the daily fluctuations in our states. That is, we can enjoy a sense of well-being even if we experience periods of frustration and unhappiness.

Well-being is associated with many of the concepts discussed in this book, including **self-acceptance**, **centredness**, **congruence**, **healing** and **positive thinking**. In the PD world, it is a more central concept in programs with a holistic perspective than in programs based more on, say, applied cognitive psychology. Clearly, well-being also implies a heavy emphasis upon the values of *being* as well as of *doing* and *getting*.

One of the major pieces of research into well-being was conducted and reported upon by Gail Sheehy in her substantial book *Pathfinders* (1982). She identified ten hallmarks of well-being, some of which may seem surprising. For example, Sheehy discovered that people with high levels of well-being had generally experienced one or more major transitions in their lives, and that they had managed these effectively or creatively. This may come as a surprise to those of us who assume that a life with no great changes is more likely to lead to well-being.

Other hallmarks include the following:

- A sense that life has direction and meaning;
- Achievement of at least some long-term goals of importance;
- A positive attitude towards failure, and feeling only rarely cheated or disappointed by life;
- A sense of pleasure at the personal growth and development experienced;

- Mutual love with a partner;
- Many friends;
- A cheerful disposition;
- Not being sensitive to criticism;
- Having no major fears.

In addition, high well-being people tend to be energetic, to plan ahead but not to spend much time on self-reflection.

'What-If' Frame

An **NLP** technique or frame of reference for generating possibilities and opportunities.

Asking ourselves 'what-if?' **questions** in relation to areas of our lives that we should like to **change** stimulates our imagination and shifts the focus of our perception and thinking. We open our minds to possibilities we might not previously have considered.

The 'what-if?' frame is consistent with the NLP principle that it's good to have **choices**. In technical terms, it seems to work well because it engages both 'sides' of the brain.

There is no end of 'what-if?' questions we can address to ourselves. One of the most powerful general 'what-if?' questions is a version of: 'What if you knew you could not fail? What then would you be willing to do?'

Will (The)

The part of us that directs energy to bring about specified ends.

Although the concept of will is closely linked with other key concepts in contemporary PD, such as **goal**-setting and **self-efficacy**, some PD tutors scarcely refer to it. A probable reason for this is that it brings to mind stern 'Victorian' values – harsh discipline, self-restraint and self-denial. Other PD tutors, especially within psychosynthesis, contend that 'the will' has been misused and misunderstood. Properly understood, it is 'a prime factor in the process of growth and the manifestation of potential' (Hardy, 1987) and 'the key to human freedom and personal power' (Ferrucci, 1990). It enables us to be autonomous, to act freely in accordance with our nature, or entirely on the basis of our own self-awareness, as Covey (1992) reminds us, rather than be dictated to by external forces. It is also our causing agent and thus the basis of **self-efficacy**.

In *The Act of Will* (1974), Roberto Assagioli presents the will as a 'skilful', psychologically 'intelligent' power that can synthesize our multiple parts. Its effect is to ensure action (which is vital for **development**) but it is pre-eminently a course-setter – a decider at the highest level. Ferrucci calls it our 'mega-agent'. Problems arise for us when we allow one of our subpersonalities to be our sole agent and impose itself on all the others. Muriel James (1981) says that will is 'determination to act in spite of self-doubt', but ignoring or suppressing messages of resistance from other parts of our mind or body can lead to pain and disorder.

Using the will to impose or discipline can also be psychologically inept. There is now widespread agreement that trying to *will* a new behaviour doesn't work if we haven't changed on the inside. If we are holding onto old **beliefs** or emotional positions, then we are likely to sabotage our willed behaviour. Willing ourselves to manage our time better won't work if we cling onto beliefs such as 'I am a disorganized person' or 'I must do everything perfectly'. Willing ourselves to be a more loving partner is unlikely to work for long if we have not also dealt with old resentments.

Forcing ourselves to act differently also deprives us of more powerful and yet more gentle ways of changing. Once we have got a goal, for example, it is much more effective to talk to ourselves in appropriate affirmations, and to ask the creative function of our subconscious to find the 'hows' to accomplish it, than it is to use force of will. And if we want to change our state, then simply changing our **focus** is much more productive than using our will as a stick (see **State Management**). As Maltz (1960) observed, feelings can be 'wooed' but not commanded into changing. That is, we don't change a 'bad' feeling by conscious effort but by thinking about something that gives us a good feeling. It's another illustration of the principle that whatever we resist persists. The least effective way to drive out negative thoughts is to concentrate attention on them.

Authorities on the healing powers of the mind (Bernie Siegel, Norman Cousins and others) tell us that people who survive 'terminal' illnesses don't will themselves not to die. Rather, they make up their minds to live life to the full. That is, they allow their will as their mega-agent to direct and organize their creative energies (Maltz reminds us on this point that Jesus told us to drive out evil with good, rather than resist evil).

Assagioli contends that our will can be and needs to be trained. If we have grown up with other people deciding things for us, then we may have little experience of exercising the will. And as Shad Helmstetter (1992) points out, we are not able to use our will freely if we have received programs which conflict with it. Psychosynthesis offers techniques for strengthening our will for everyday purposes. Ferrucci's many suggestions include doing something we haven't done before, doing something very slowly, postponing doing something we'd like to do right away, and making a minor choice without hesitation.

Finally, many PD tutors make the point that knowing our **goals** (what we want) is not enough. We must be clear also what we are willing to do in order to achieve them. This tends to translate into questions such as, 'What sacrifices am I prepared to make?', 'What costs am I prepared to bear?' or 'What resources am I prepared to commit?'. If we don't address such questions, then we are *wishing* not willing, and as Muriel James says, 'Wish without will is merely daydream'.

Worry

We all know that worry is what we experience when we have nagging, harassing thoughts that rarely seem to lead us anywhere. Worry has also been defined as misdirected nervous energy and as negative goal-setting, for whenever we worry we create mental images that our subconscious seeks to bring into reality. Since our subconscious is apparently unable to recognize negatives, telling ourselves not to worry is no more effective. It is likely to program us to do the reverse.

Worry is generally regarded as a waste of time and energy, and so one of the least productive of all the states we get into. It tends to induce anxiety and to have biochemical effects which can be harmful. All the time we are worrying we are not doing the kinds of things that could enhance our happiness and growth.

Worry need not be construed as entirely negative, however. Worrying can be better than pretending that the source of the worry does not exist. It's probably better to worry about debt than to ignore it altogether. Some PD tutors encourage us to welcome a worry (eg, Edwards, 1991) on the assumption that it's part of a process of psychic elimination. Worry is the mind releasing some of its deeper doubts; once they surface they can be processed or disposed of. For example, if we worry about spending money, then the mind may be showing us that we have some beliefs we need to re-examine.

Worry has been a favourite topic with self-help writers for decades, and is at the heart of Norman Vincent Peale's many books on positive thinking. There is no shortage of suggestions about what to do if we are susceptible to worry. NLP techniques, since they work directly on our mind and neurological make-up, are probably the most effective ways to overcome worry. They include reviewing core beliefs, including those which link worry to guilt or its absence (eg, 'I worry because I care', 'I deserve to worry'), and interrupting the thought patterns which trigger worrying behaviours (see **Pattern Interrupt**). Another method that can be enhanced by NLP techniques is to place our worry in a different time frame, to look back on it from a point in the future, say, so that it appears (literally) distanced and diminutive.

We can also place our worry in a 'time lock'. That is, we can make a contract with ourselves that we won't worry about a certain thing until a particular time and date. For example, we may promise ourselves to give attention to the source of concern on Sunday evening at 9.00pm so as to have a worry-free weekend. Or we may agree not to worry at all until certain conditions are met. Since most worries turn out to be 'unjustified', this is a logical thing to do.

Some PD tutors suggest we keep logs of our worries, again so that we can look back at the many 'unnecessary' worries, and also see whether our worry actually *changed* anything. Since worry usually occupies the psychic space between a triggering thought linked to a concern and action (if any), the obvious step to take is to contract the timescale - ie, take action immediately, if any is needed (see **Negative Thinking**).

Other worry-busting techniques are setting aside 'worry time', considering the worst-case scenario and becoming either more or less self-orientated. Worry can be a sign that we don't like ourselves enough, particularly if our worries concern what others do or don't think of us. But we can worry also because we are insufficiently concerned for others. If we help others with their concerns then we are unlikely to be preoccupied with our own.

Many PD tutors today take the view that worry, like other mental behaviours and states, is a choice. We can choose to focus our minds in ways that will empower us and make us feel good, or we can choose to worry.

Writing (Personal)

Writing about ourselves, for ourselves and from our own points of view can play a significant part in our personal development. So also can writing in which we draw upon our own creative resources (eg, poetry), even though the content or viewpoint may not be personal. Many PD tutors acknowledge and advocate the value of writing for development purposes.

Writing that can benefit our development takes many forms. We can write *about* and often *for* ourselves in logs, diaries, journals, portfolios, autobiographies and the like. At one end of the writing continuum are the informal, even scrappy notes and jottings we might make and at the other are carefully crafted statements, and even 'literary' pieces, like memoirs. Between the two extremes come many other forms, including free writing, where expression takes priority over editorial control. We can write matter-of-fact lists on the one hand (eg, as part of a **skills audit**) and, on the other, long and in-depth pieces in which we interrogate our experiences.

Why might we choose to write? How can writing assist our development? The PD response is that writing serves a number of important functions, the most straightforward of which is simply to record anything that we might consider personally worthwhile. It might be a thought, a feeling, a quotation, a meditation or an insight. As Gill Edwards (1991) observes, anything like this 'can be a vital step in our personal growth'. Beyond recording, we can use our jottings as the material for self-reflection. Free writing, diary and journal entries and more extended autobiographical writing can be used for exploratory purposes. Writing can help us sort out confusing feelings or work out why we seem to be resisting personal **change**. It can help us to ascribe significance to personally meaningful events, gain an insight into what something means to us or understand why we made a particular response. For those of us who are 'seekers' rather than 'success hunters', 'autobiography provides a unique and vital way' for us to 'make a search for personal meaning' (Metcalfe, 1986). This might include getting a better understanding of how our present relates to our past and perhaps to our future (see **Time**). As JP Powell (1985) says, the aim of keeping a reflective journal is 'to reveal, describe and interpret the past experiences of the individual in order to illuminate the present and make manifest the potentialities of the future.'

Through writing we can sometimes distance ourselves from relevant experiences and feelings. The struggle to verbalize and give form to them can contribute to this. We can also identify patterns which may be blocking personal change – **negative thinking** and self-sabotaging patterns of behaviour, for example. We can also explore our strengths and weaknesses through writing, and then base development plans upon these self-evaluations.

When people are encouraged to write about themselves they often say that doing so served both to value and validate the feelings and experiences they might otherwise have thought too 'ordinary' to be of any consequence. Of relevance here is the observation of Bannister (1981) that 'one of the most marked features of our culture is that it does not demand (or even suggest) that we formally monitor our lives or that we record our personal history in the way in which a society records its history.' In the context of personal development, personal writing offers both a context and a pretext for doing just this. And as some PD tutors say, if our lives are worth living, then they are also worth recording.

Writing can also be a powerful tool in our **personal development planning** kit. It can help us to make clear and explicit our missions, **visions** and **goals**, and to commit clearly thought-out interactions to paper. This can be an indicator that we have taken these things seriously. It also leaves us with a permanent record of our plans and commitments which we can return to time and again. Merely thinking our goals or saying them out loud is like writing on water. The very act of writing goals and **affirmations** serves also to imprint them on our subconscious. It would seem that making marks on paper (or a screen) engraves new neural pathways in line with our intentions.

Significantly, journals and the like are part and parcel of many self-development programs. In the Pacific Institute's *Investment in Excellence* program, opportunities to reflect upon the material presented is built into the very structure of the course books. These 'reflective inputs' are there to help participants see that 'most barriers to personal growth and development are self-erected'.

Personal writing and personal development are mutually sympathetic. Some key presuppositions underpin both, including the belief that we are able to shape and direct our experience. We are to a significant degree the authors of our own life scripts, and as authors in the literal sense we give form and meaning to experience rather than simply express it. Another common assumption is that process – the process of writing, the process of living – is at least as important as the end products or outcomes – a finished piece of writing, goals accomplished etc. PD tutors often say that the journey is even more important than the destination. Anthony Robbins puts it neatly in one of his *Powertalk* tapes when he distinguishes between, on the one hand, setting out to achieve happiness and, on the other, happily achieving. A third point of sympathy is the idea of the mutability of the past. When we write about remembered experience we soon discover that this is not a fossilized 'given'. Similarly, from the perspective of **NLP** and other psychotechnologies, our pasts can be re-written. In particular, we can install resourceful 'experiences' to impact positively upon subsequent life events (see **Change Personal History**).

Bibliography

Abbott, John, *Learning Makes Sense*, Education 2000, Hertfordshire, 1994.

Adams, J, *Conceptual Block Busting*, Freeman, San Francisco, 1974.

Alder, Harry, *NLP: the new art and science of getting what you want*, Piatkus, London, 1995.

Alexander, Jane, *Supertherapies*, Bantam Books, London, 1996.

Alexander, Scott, *Rhinoceros Success*, The Rhino's Press, California, 1980.

Andreas, Connirae & Steve, *Heart of the Mind*, Real People Press, Moab, Utah, 1989.

Assagioli, Roberto, *The Act of Will*, Turnstone Press, Wellingborough, Northants, 1974.

Assagioli, Roberto, *Psychosynthesis: a manual of principles and techniques*, Turnstone Press, Wellingborough, Northants, 1990.

British Association for Counselling, *Counselling: definition of terms*, BAC, 1991.

Ball, Ben, *Careers Counselling in Practice*, The Falmer Press, London, 1984.

Bandler, Richard, *Using Your Brain for a Change*, Real People Press, Moab, Utah, 1985.

Bandler, Richard & Grinder, John, *The Structure of Magic*, Vol. 1, Science and Behavior Books, Palo Alto, California, 1975.

Bandler, Richard & Grinder, John, *Frogs into Princes*, Real People Press, Moab, Utah, 1979.

Bandura, A, 'Self-Efficacy: Towards a unifying theory of behavioural change' in *Psychological Review*, 84, pp 191–215, 1977.

Bannister, D, 'Knowledge of Self' in David Fontana (ed), *Psychology for Teachers*, Methuen, pp 252–64, London, 1981.

Bannister, D & Fransella, F, *Inquiring Man: the psychology of personal constructs* (3rd ed), Routledge, London, 1986.

Beaver, Diana, *Lazy Learning*, Element, Shaftesbury, 1995.

Beck, A T, *Cognitive Therapy and the Emotional Disorders*, New American Library, New York, 1979.

Beck, A T, *Love is Never Enough*, Harper & Row, New York, 1982.

Berne, Eric, Transactional Analysis: A new and effective method of group therapy. *American Journal of Psychotherapy*, 12, pp 735–43, 1958.

Berne, Eric, *Games People Play*, Penguin, Harmondsworth, 1968.

Black, Jack, *Mindstore*, Thorsons, London, 1994.

Bloomfield, Harold H; Cain, Michael Peter; Jaffe, Denis T & Korg, Robert B, *TM: Discovering Inner Energy and Overcoming Stress*, George Allen & Unwin, London, 1976.

Boak, George, *Developing Managerial Competences*, Pitman, London, 1991.

Borysenko, Joan & Miroslav, *The Power of the Mind to Heal*, Eden Grove, Middlesex, 1995.

Burgoyne, J, 'Doubts about Competences' in M. Divine (ed) *The Photofit Manager*, Unwin Hyman, London, 1990.

Buzan, Tony, *The Mind Map Book – Radiant Thinking*, BBC Books, London, 1993.

Caldwell, Margaret, 'How personal is personal development?' in *Management Training*, Aug/Sept, 1995.

Cameron-Bandler, Leslie, *Solutions: enhancing love, sex and relationships*, Real People Press, Moab, Utah, 1985.

Carnegie, Dale, *How to Win Friends and Influence People*, World's Work Ltd, Tadworth, 1938, 1953.

Casey, David, *Managing Learning in Organisations*, Open University, Milton Keynes, 1993.

Chave-Jones, Myra, *Listening To Your Feelings*, Lion Publishing, Oxford, 1989.

Chopra, Deepak, *Creating Health: how to wake up the body's intelligence*, Houghton Mifflin, Boston, 1987.

Chopra, Deepak, *Ageless Body, Timeless Mind*, Rider Books, London, 1993.

Claxton, Guy, *Live and Learn*, Harper & Row, London, 1984.

Clynes, Manfred, *Sentics, The Touch of Emotions*, Souvenir Press, London, 1977.

Considine, Mike (ed), *The Whole Person Catalogue*, Brainwave, London, 1992.

Cooper, Cassie, 'Psychodynamic Therapy: the Jungian approach' in Windy Dryden (ed) *Individual Therapy*, pp 39–68, 1991.

Corey, Gerald, *I Never Knew I Had A Choice* (3rd Ed.), Brooks/Cole, Pacific Grove, California, 1986.

Cousins, Norman, *Anatomy of an Illness*, Bantam Books, New York, 1979.

Covey, Stephen R, *The Seven Habits of Highly Effective People*, Simon & Schuster, London, 1992.

Cox, Richard H, *Sport Psychology* (3rd ed), Brown and Benchmark, Madison, Wisconsin, 1994.

Cudney, Milton R & Hardy, Robert E, *Self-Defeating Behaviours*, Harper, San Francisco, 1991.

Cunningham, Ian, 'Someone to Watch Over Me' in *Human Resources*, Winter, 1992/3.

Dattilo, Frank M & Padesky, Christine A, *Cognitive Therapy with Couples*, Professional Resource Exchange, Sarasota, Florida, 1990.

Davies, Philippa, *Total Confidence*, Piatkus, London, 1995.

Dawes, Martyn, 'Personalising Development' in *Training Management*, 26 Jan–9 Feb., 10, 1995.

de Bono, Edward, *Six Thinking Hats*, Penguin, London, 1990.

Dilts, Robert B & Epstein, Todd A, *Dynamic Learning*, Meta Publications, Capitola, California, 1995.

Dowrick, Stephanie, *Intimacy and Solitude*, The Women's Press, London, 1992.

Dryden, Gordon & Vos, Jeannette, *The Learning Revolution*, Accelerated Learning Systems, Aylesbury, 1994.

Dryden, Windy (ed), *Individual Therapy*, Open University Press, Milton Keynes, 1990.

Dryden, Windy & Feltham, Colin, *Developing Counsellor Training*, Sage, London, 1994.

Edwards, Gill, *Living Magically*, Piatkus, London, 1991.

Egan, Gerald, *The Skilled Helper*, (5th ed), Brooks/Cole, Monterey, CA, 1994.

Elbow, Peter, *Writing Without Teachers*, Oxford University Press, London, 1973.

Ellis, A, *Reason and Emotion in Psychotherapy*, Lyle Stuart, Secavers, NJ, 1962.

Ellis, A & Harper, RA, *A New Guide to Rational Living*, Prentice-Hall, Englewood Cliffs, NJ, 1975.

Ellis, A & Dryden, Windy, *The Practice of Rational-Emotive Therapy*, Springer, New York, 1987.

Esp, Derek, *Competences for School Managers*, Kogan Page, London, 1993.

Eysenck, Michael W (ed), *The Blackwell Dictionary of Cognitive Psychology*, Blackwell, Oxford, 1990.

Fallon, Val, 'Advice on Setting up a Self-help Group' in Considine, Mike (ed), *The Whole Person Catalogue*, 1992.

Fanning, Patrick, *Visualisation for Change* (2nd ed), New Harbinger, Oakland, California, 1994.

Faulkner, Charles and Robert McDonald, *Success Mastery in NLP* (audio program) NLP Comprehensive, Nightingale-Conant Corp., New York, 1994.

Ferrucci, Piero, *What We May Be*, Aquarian, London, 1990.

Fontana, David, *Psychology for Teachers*, Macmillan, London, 1981.

Fontana, David, *The Elements of Meditation*, Element, Shaftesbury, 1991.

Fontana, David, *The Meditator's Handbook*, Element, Shaftesbury, 1992.

Gardner, Howard, *The Unschooled Mind*, Basic Books, New York, 1991.

Gardner, Howard, 'Creativity: new views from psychology and

education' in *RSA Journal*, May, pp 33–42, 1995.

Gaudry, Eric & Spielberger, Charles D, *Personal Power*, HarperCollins, Victoria, Australia, 1995.

Gawain, Shakti, *Creative Visualisation* (revised ed), New World Library, San Rafael, California, 1995.

Gilbert, T F, *Human Competence: engineering worthwhile performance*, McGraw-Hill, New York, 1978.

Gillen, Terry, *Positive Influencing Skills*, Institute of Personnel and Development, London, 1995.

Glouberman, Dina, *Life Choices, Life Changes*, Thorsons, London, 1995.

Goulding, Robert L. and Mary M., *Changing Lives through Redecision Therapy*, New York, Brunner Mazel, 1979.

Hall, Jill, *The Reluctant Adult*, Prism Press, Dorset, 1993.

Hamilton, Reg, *Training Management*, 12–26 June, p 7, 1994.

Hanson, Karen, *The Self-Imagined*, Routledge and Kegan Paul, London, 1986.

Hardy, Jean, *A Psychology with a Soul: psychosynthesis in evolutionary context*, Routledge and Kegan Paul, London, 1987.

Hare, Beverley, *Be Assertive*, Optima, London, 1988.

Harris, Thomas A, *I'm OK, You're OK*, Pan, London, 1970.

Hay, Julie, *Transactional Analysis for Trainers*, McGraw-Hill, Maidenhead, 1992

Hay, Louise H, *You Can Heal Your Life*, Eden Grove, London, 1988.

Helmstetter, Shad, *Life Choices*, Harper Collins, London, 1992.

Henry, Jane (ed), *Creative Management*, Sage and Open University London, 1991.

Hill, Napoleon, *Think and Grow Rich*, Wilshire Book Co. Hollywood, California, 1966.

Hill, Napoleon & Stone, W Clement, *Success Through A Positive Mental Attitude*, Prentice-Hall, Englewood Cliffs, NJ, 1960.

Hodgkinson, Liz, *The Personal Growth Handbook*, Piatkus, London, 1993.

Holbeche, Linda, 'The Price of Flatter Structures' in *Developing People* (newsletter from Roffey Park), Spring, 1995.

Holland, Ron, *Talk And Grow Rich*, Thorsons, London, 1993.

Honey, Peter, *Improve Your People Skills*, Institute of Personnel Management, London, 1988.

Honey, Peter & Mumford, Alan, *The Manual of Learning Styles*, Peter Honey, Maidenhead, 1986.

Hopson, Barrie, 'Counselling and Helping' in Martin Herbert, *Psychology for Social Workers*, (2nd ed), Macmillan, London, pp 122–202, 1986.

Hopson, Barrie & Hough, Patricia, *Exercises in Personal and Career*

Development, CRAC, Hobson's Press, Cambridge, 1973.

Hopson, Barrie & Scally, Mike, *Lifeskills Teaching*, McGraw-Hill, Maidenhead, 1981.

Hopson, Barrie & Scally, Mike, *Build Your Own Rainbow*, Mercury, London, 1991.

Hopson, Barrie & Scally, Mike, *Investment in Excellence*, The Pacific Institute, Seattle.

Irving, Janis & Mann, Leon, *Decision-Making*, The Free Press, New York, 1977.

ITC, *Beyond The Personality: the Beginner's guide to enlightenment*, The Implicate Technology Centre, London, 1987.

James, Muriel, *Breaking Free: self-reparenting for a new life*, Addison-Wesley, Reading, Massachusetts, 1981.

Jampolsky, Gerald & Keeler, Jack O, *Love is Letting Go of Fear*, Celestial Arts, Millbrae, CA, 1979.

Jeffers, Susan, *Feel The Fear And Do It Anyway*, Arrow Books, London, 1991.

Johnson, David W, *Reaching Out: interpersonal effectiveness and self-actualisation* (2nd ed), Prentice-Hall, Englewood Cliffs, New Jersey, 1981.

Johnson, Rex & Swindley, David, *Awaken Your Inner Power*, Element, Shaftesbury, 1995.

Juniper, Dean Francis, *Successful Problem Solving*, Foulsham, London, 1989.

Kallench, John, *Being The Best You Can Be In MLM*, John Kallench/MIM Publications, (no place of pub. given), 1990.

Kaminer, W, *I'm Dysfunctional, You're Dysfunctional*, Addison-Wesley, Reading, MA, 1992.

Kampf, Harold, *The Speed Technique To Alpha Meditation and Visualisation*, Quantum, London, 1995.

Kapleau, Roshi Philip, *Zen: dawn in the west*, Rider, London, 1980.

Kassorla, I C, *Go For It!*, Dell, New York, 1984.

Knight, Sue, *NLP at Work*, Nicholas Brealey, London, 1995.

Korb, M; Garrel, J & Van de Riet, V, *Gestalt Therapy*, Pergamon, Oxford, 1989.

Land, George, *To Grow or Die*, Wiley, New York, 1986.

Latner, Joel, *The Gestalt Therapy Book*, The Gestalt Journal Press, Highland, New York, 1986.

Lemme, Barbara Hansen, *Development in Adulthood*, Allyn and Bacon, Boston, 1995.

Lessem, Ronnie, *Intrapreneurship*, Gower, Aldershot, 1987.

Levinson, David, *The Seasons of Man's Life*, Knopf, New York, 1978.

Lewis, Byron & Pucelik, Frank, *Magic of NLP Demystified*, Metamorphous Press, Portland, OR, 1990.

Liddell, Lucy, *The Sensual Body*, Simon and Schuster, New York, 1987.

Lisnek, Paul M, *Quality Mind, Quality Life*, Meta Publications, Capitola, California, 1995.

Loevinger, Jane, *Ego Development: Conceptions and Theories*, Jossey-Bass, San Francisco, 1976.

Mager, Robert F, 'No Self-Efficacy, No Performance' in *Training*, April, pp 32–36. 1992.

Maltz, Maxwell, *Psycho-Cybernetics*, Prentice-Hall, Englewood Cliffs, New Jersey, 1960.

Margulies, Nancy, *Mapping Inner Space*, Zephyr Press, Tuoson, Arizona, 1991.

Maslow, A H, *Toward a Psychology of Being*, Van Nostrand, New York, 1962.

Maslow, A H, *Motivation and Personality*, Harper and Row, New York, 1970.

May, Rollo, *Love and Will*, Souvenir Press, London, 1970.

McCrimmon, Mitch, 'Get Wise' in *Human Resources*, March/April, p 17, 1995.

McGovern, Jeanne, 'Consciousness in Motion' in *The Catalyst Magazine*, Issue 1, Jan/Feb, 1995.

McKay, Matthew; Fanning, Patrick & Paleg, Kim *Couple Skills*, New Harbinger, Oakland, California, 1994.

Metcalfe, Marion, 'An Enhanced Affirmation of Self' in *Autobiography and Education*, Trevor Pateman (ed), University of Sussex, 1986.

Milteer, Lee, *Coping With Change: life strategies for the '90s* (audio program), Lee Milteer Associates, Virgin Beach, Virginia, 1990.

Mumford, Alan, *How Managers Can Develop Managers*, Gower, Aldershot, 1993.

Murphy, Joseph, *The Power of Your Subconscious Mind*, Simon and Schuster, London, 1988.

Napoli, Vince; Kilbride, James M & Tebbs, Donald E, *Adjustment and Growth in a Changing World*, West Publishing, Saint Paul, Minnesota, 1982.

Nelson-Jones, Richard, *Effective Thinking Skills: Preventing and Managing Personal Problems*, Cassell, London, 1989.

Nelson-Jones, Richard, *The Theory and Practice of Counselling*, Cassell, London, 1995.

Neugarten, B & Neugarten, D, 'The Changing Meanings of Age' in *Psychology Today*, May, pp 29–33, 1987.

Nevis, Edwin C, *Organisational Consulting: A Gestalt Approach*, Gardner Press, New York, 1987.

Nideffer, Robert M, *Psyched to Win*, Leisure Press, Champaign, Illinois, 1992.

Nye, Robert D, *Three Psychologies: Perspectives from Freud, Skinner, and*

Rogers (4th ed), Brooks/Cole. Pacific Grove, California, 1992.

O'Connor, Joseph & Seymour, John, *Introducing Neuro-Linguistic Programming*, Aquarian/Thorsons, London, 1993.

O'Connor, Joseph & Prior, Robin, *Successful Selling With NLP*, Thorsons, London, 1995.

Oja, Sharon Nodie, 'Teachers: Ages and Stages of Adult Development' in *Perspectives on Teacher Professional Development*, Holly, Mary Louise & McLoughlin, Caven S (eds), The Falmer Press, London, 1989.

Ostrander, Sheila & Schroeder, Lyn, *Super-Learning*, Dell Publishing, New York, 1979.

Open University Course E530: *A Portfolio Approach to Personal And Career Development* (various materials), 1992.

Peck, M Scott, *The Road Less Travelled*, Arrow Books, London, 1990.

Peel, Malcolm, *Career Development and Planning*, McGraw-Hill, London, 1992.

Peiffer, Vera, *Positive Thinking*, Element, Shaftesbury, 1989.

Perkins, D N, *The Mind's Best Work*, Harvard University Press, Cambridge, MA, 1981.

Perls, F S, *Gestalt Therapy Verbatim*, Real People's Press, La Fayette, California, 1969.

Peterson, Cadey, 'Jim Rohn's 5 major pieces to the life puzzle' in *The Catalyst Magazine*, Issue 1, Jan/Feb, 1995.

Phillips, E L, 'The ubiquitous decay curve: service delivery similarities in psychotherapy, medicine and addiction' in *Professional Psychology: Research and Practice*, 18, pp 650–2, 1987.

Poissant, Charles-Albert, *How to Think Like a Millionaire*, Thorsons, London, 1989.

Porter, Patrick, *Awaken the Genius*, Pure Light Inc, Phoenix, Arizona, 1993.

Powell, J P, 'Autobiographical Learning' in *Reflection: turning experience into learning*, Boud, D, Keogh, R and Walker D, (eds), Kogan Page, pp 41–51, London, 1986.

Robbins, Anthony, *Unlimited Power*, Simon and Schuster, London, 1988.

Robbins, Anthony, *Awaken the Giant Within*, Simon and Schuster, London, 1992.

Robbins, Anthony, *Personal Power* (audio program), Robbins Research International, San Diego, California, 1993.

Robbins, Anthony, *Powertalk* (audio program), Robbins Research International, San Diego, California, 1993.

Rogers, C R, *On Becoming a Person*, Houghton Mifflin, Boston, 1961.

Rogers, C R, 'In Retrospect: Forty-six Years' in *American Psychologist*, 2, pp 115–23, 1974.

Roman, Sanaya, *Personal Power Through Awareness*, H J Kramer Inc, Tiburon, California, 1986.

Rose, Colin, *Accelerated Learning*, Accelerated Learning Systems, Aylesbury, Bucks, 1985.

Rushall, B S; Hall, M & Rushall, A, 'Effects of three types of thought content instructions on skiing performance' in *The Sport Psychologist*, 2, pp 283–92, 1988.

Rusk, Tom & Read, Randy, *I Want To Change But I Don't Know How*, Thorsons, London, 1986.

Schwartz, David J, *The Magic of Thinking Big*, Wilshire Book Company, Englewood Cliffs, New Jersey, 1959.

Scott, W A, 'Conceptions of Normality' in *Handbook of Personality Theory and Research*, (ed) Borgatta, EF & Lambert WW, Rand McNally, Chicago, 1968.

Sharpe, Robert & Lewis, David, *The Success Factor: how to be who you want to be*, Souvenir Press, London, 1976.

Shea, Gordon F, *Mentoring*, Kogan Page, London, 1992.

Sheehy, Gail, *Pathfinders*, Sidgwick and Jackson, London, 1982.

Siegel, Bernie, *Love, Medicine and Miracles*, Random House, New York, 1986.

Simonton, Carl & Stephanie, *Getting Well Again*, Bantam Books, New York, 1980.

Smith, Maggie, *Changing Course* (new ed), Mercury Books/Lifeskills Communications Ltd, London, 1992.

Storm, Rachel, *In Search of Heaven on Earth*, Aquarian/Thorsons, London, 1991.

Sutherland, Margot, *Draw On Your Emotions*, Winslow Press, Oxford, 1993.

Syer, John & Connolly, Christopher, *Think to Win*, Simon and Schuster, London, 1991.

Thoroughgood, B, *Training Management*, June, 18, 1994.

Tracy, Brian, *The Psychology of Achievement* (audio program) Nightingale-Conant AUDIOWORKS, Simon and Schuster, London, 1994.

Trungpa, Chogyam, *Shambhala: the sacred path of the warrior*, Shambhala, Bartan Books, New York, 1984.

Turner, Colin, *Born to Succeed*, Element, Shaftesbury, 1994.

Van Deurzen-Smith, Emmy, 'Existential Therapy' in *Individual Therapy*, Dryden, Windy (ed), 1990, pp 149–74, 1990.

Van Nagel, C; Reese, Edward J; Reese, Maryann and Siudzinski, Robert, *Mega Teaching And Learning*, Metamorphous Press, Portland, Oregon, 1985.

Wagner, Abe, *Say It Straight Or You'll Show It Crooked* (audio program), Abe Wagner and Associates Inc, Denver, Colorado, 1990.

Wallas, G., *The Art of Thought*, Franklin Watts, New York, 1926.

Watson, Donald, *A Dictionary of Mind and Spirit*, Andre Deutsch, London, 1991.

Watts, Tony, 'Individual action plans: for whom?' in *Education*, 2, August, 89, 1991.

White, John (ed), *What is Enlightenment?* The Aquarian Press, Wellingborough, Northants, 1984.

Wilson, Colin, *Religion and Rebel*, Victor Gollancz, London, 1957.

Wood, Sue (ed), *Continuous Development*, Institute of Personnel Management, London, 1988.

Woodruffe, Charles, *Assessment Centres* (2nd ed), Institute of Personnel Management, London, 1993.

Wright, Bridget, Career Management, in *Training and Development*, April, pp 24–8, 1991.

Michael Waters offers training and consultancy services in many areas of personal development. He can be contacted at the following address:

Colyer Hall, Colyer Road, Northfleet, Gravesend, Kent DA11 8BN
Tel: 01474 362733 Fax: 01474 536094